COLORS
and
BLOOD

COLORS

and

BLOOD

FLAG PASSIONS OF

THE CONFEDERATE SOUTH

Robert E. Bonner

PRINCETON UNIVERSITY PRESS
PRINCETON AND OXFORD

Library of Congress Cataloging-in-Publication Data

Bonner, Robert E., 1967–

Colors and blood : flag passions of the Confederate South / Robert E. Bonner.

p. cm.

Includes bibliographical references and index

ISBN 0-691-09158-7

1. Flags—Confederate States of America. 2. Symbolism in politics—Confederate States of America.
3. Symbolism in politics—Southern States. 4. Political culture—Southern States—History.
5. United States—History—Civil War, 1861–1865. I. Title.

CR113.5 .B66 2002

929.9′2′097509034—dc21   2002016918

This book has been composed in Berkeley Book

Printed on acid-free paper. ∞

www.pup.princeton.edu

Printed in the United States of America

10   9   8   7   6   5   4   3   2   1

Dedicated to
Lillian Ramsey Bonner
and to the memory of
Marie Wood Miller

THE WIND BLEW upon all the vanes of all the churches of the country, and turned them one way—towards war. It blew, and shook out, as if by magic, a flag whose device was unknown to soldier or sailor before, but whose flap and flutter made the blood bound in our veins.

Who could have resisted the fair anticipations which the new war-idea brought? It arrayed the sanctity of a righteous cause in the brilliant trappings of military display; pleasing, so the devout and the flippant which in various proportions are mixed elements in all men. It challenged the patriotism of the sober citizen; while it inflamed the dream of the statesman, ambitious for his country or for himself. It offered test to all allegiances and loyalties; of church, of state; of private loves, of public devotion; of personal consanguinity; of social ties. To obscurity it held out eminence; to poverty, wealth; to greed, a gorged maw; to speculation, legalized gambling; to virtue, purity; and to love, what all love most desires—a field wherein to assert itself by action.

—Sidney Lanier, *Tiger Lilies*, 1867

WITHOUT SYMBOLS . . . social feelings could have only an unstable existence. . . . While emblematizing is necessary if society is to become conscious of itself, so it is no less indispensable in perpetuating that consciousness.

—Emile Durkheim, *The Elementary Forms of Religious Life*, 1912

CONTENTS

List of Illustrations and Tables, xi

Acknowledgments, xiii

Introduction: Waving Colors and Boiling Blood, 1

1   The Stars and Stripes of Senator Davis. A Prologue, 8

2   The Standards of State Resistance, 19

3   Selecting and Singing a New Constellation, 39

4   Blood Sacrifice and the Colors of War, 67

5   The Southern Cross and Confederate Consolidation, 96

6   Treason's Banner and the Colors of Loyalty, 125

7   Conquered Banners, Furled and Unfurled, 153

Notes, 179

Index, 213

ILLUSTRATIONS AND TABLES

Figures

1.	Martyrdom at the Battle of Buena Vista, 1847	12
2.	"The Traitor's Dream," 1860	16
3.	"Jefferson Davis on His Stand," 1861	17
4.	Selection from the *Charleston Courier*	23
5.	Sergeant William Jasper at Fort Moultrie	27
6.	Occupation of Castle Pickney by the Charleston Militia	29
7.	Harry McCarthy, "Our Flag"	32
8.	Inside the Montgomery Congress	44
9.	Flag Design Sent to the Montgomery Congress	50
10.	Confederate Patriotic Envelopes	57
11.	Flags in New York City	58
12.	Score for "The Flag of the South"	63
13.	Ellsworth and Jackson	71
14.	Presentation Flag of Sixth Alabama Infantry	76
15.	"Women Hounding Their Men to Rebellion"	78
16.	New Orleans Ladies Presenting Colors	87
17.	A Gallant Flag-Bearer	89
18.	A Charleston Harbor Exploit of 1863	91
19.	Cross Designs Sent to Montgomery	99
20.	Proposed Seal Designs, Great Seal of the Confederacy	110–111
21.	"The Star-Spangled Cross and the Pure Field of White"	116
22.	Anti-Confederate Patriotic Envelopes	129
23.	Baltimore Confederate Wearing Her Colors	134
24.	Adelbart Volck, "The Search for Arms"	136

25.   A Slave's Advice to His Master   140

26.   Celebrating Emancipation in Virginia   142

27.   Ceremony at Port Royal, January 1, 1863   144

28.   "Freedom to the Slave"   146

29.   A Conquered Stars and Stripes   155

30.   Inscribed North Carolina Battle Flag   157

31.   Father Ryan, "The Conquered Banner"   161

32.   Welcoming Banner on Patriotic Envelopes   166

33.   General Custer Presents Trophy Flags to the War Department   169

34.   Confederate Banners Returned to the South   173

Tables

3.1   Identifiable Flag and Seal Petitioners to the   47
       Montgomery Congress, February–March 1861

3.2   Designs for National Emblems Submitted to the   52
       Montgomery Congress, February–March 1861

5.1   Flag and Seal Petitions to Congress and Actions Taken,   104
       1861–1863

ACKNOWLEDGMENTS

A GREAT MANY TEACHERS, friends, and colleagues have influenced what I have to say in the following pages. While I was in college, Reid Mitchell introduced me to the Civil War's big questions, and when I became a graduate student, he encouraged me to keep asking them. My dissertation on slaveholders and American nationalism benefited from the superb guidance of the late John Blassingame, Jon Butler, Nancy Cott, Robert Forbes, David Montgomery, Harry Stout, and, especially, David Brion Davis. Benedict Anderson and Alan Trachtenberg allowed me to audit graduate seminars that introduced me to several of the ideas about nationalism and about antebellum culture that emerge in this book.

The impetus for a separate study of Confederate flag culture came only when I began teaching at the University of Southern Maine, where Gary Johnson, Wim Klooster, and Christine Holden encouraged my efforts. It was completed at Michigan State University, where David Bailey, Lewis Siegelbaum, and Bill Hixson, among many others, have lent their support. John Boles and readers at the *Journal of Southern History* pushed me forward with good suggestions about a much briefer survey of flag culture, as did T. Michael Parrish. Audiences at several public forums asked important questions about the implications of this project, and David Waldstreicher, Kathleen Clark, and Patrick Rael made specific suggestions. Charles Dew and three anonymous readers provided very helpful comments on the entire manuscript, while Thomas LeBien of Princeton University Press helped me to shape my arguments and bring out the study's primary themes. John Coski of the Museum of the Confederacy shared his unparalleled knowledge of Civil War–era flags with truly remarkable generosity.

Financial support is important for any scholarly project; this one has received particularly generous assistance. The Huntington Library awarded me both a Keck Fellowship and James C. Caillouette Research Fellowship to use their Confederate materials, and the American Antiquarian Society granted me a Joyce Fellowship that allowed me access to their unrivaled newspaper collection. Roy Ritchie, John Hench, and the staffs at these two fine research centers helped me to make the most of these wonderful experiences in San Marino and Worcester. I had the benefit of a remarkably supportive set of colleagues at both these libraries, with Tim Breen, Dorri Beam, Alice Fahs, Mark Neely, Rip Lhamon, and Lou Masur heading the list. A Mellon fellowship from the Virginia Historical Society came at a crucial stage of this book, and allowed me the privilege of sharpening my perspective just a short distance from Richmond's Monument Avenue. Conversations with Nelson Lankford and Charles Bryan at the Historical Society and with Rebecca Rose at the Museum of the Confederacy helped me to see issues in Confederate symbolism that were not so obvious from the perspective of mid-Michigan. An Intramural Research Grant from Michigan State University assured a full set of images, as did Erin Konarske, who worked as my research assistant. Georgia Barnhill and Terri Tremblay of the American Antiquarian Society and Peter Berg at Michigan State were especially helpful in the process of obtaining illustrations.

Research on the postbellum segments of this book has helped me to realize what I already sensed—that southern men surrendered their Confederate allegiances more easily than did their women. I dedicate the work to my two grandmothers, who saw into the future while keeping the past alive for later generations. Having been raised in that "twilight generation" that still had a living connection to the Civil War, they each shaped my initial interest in the South's special historical burdens. The rest of my extended family of Bonners, Bigbees, Butlers, and Phillipses have fostered my education and career and supported it at every stage. Patricia Bigbee listened while this topic evolved and then gave the manuscript a thorough reading. Leslie Butler has stretched my imagination and offered encouragement, advice, and so much more. The ever-exuberant Will Bonner made his own contributions, not least by putting scholarship in perspective. All three of these special people have shown me again and again the advantages of substance over symbolism.

COLORS
and
BLOOD

INTRODUCTION

Waving Colors and Boiling Blood

IN THE 1990s, rebel flags became front-page news. Across the American South, Civil Rights groups worked to discredit a symbol they associated with slavery and racism. Self-proclaimed heritage organizations mounted a fierce counteroffensive, defending the Confederate battle flag as a proud relic handed down from heroic ancestors. Though neither side retreated from its stance, legislative compromises in South Carolina and Georgia produced a momentary truce. Then, early in 2001, Mississippians voted by a lopsided margin to retain the diagonal rebel cross in their state's flag. As the twenty-first century opened, a design created 140 years earlier remained the most visible symbol of America's unfinished Civil War.[1]

Recent Confederate flag controversies say something important about the times in which we live. They remind us that the stubborn legacies of race and region still matter in the contemporary South, even as they have moved into the realm of cultural memory. This interest in how the past is remembered is a tribute to the success of the Civil Rights movement in discrediting overt racism in the present. Conflict that now swirls around the Confederate colors is shaped by an ascendant conservatism distrustful of government and hostile toward "political correctness." Flags have become flashpoints in the contemporary South because of current tensions that make two sharply opposed visions of a regional heritage more relevant than ever. At stake in these struggles is the ability to set the regional agenda and determine how the nation's most self-conscious region will remember itself.

Disputes say something too about how easily pieces of waving banners work their way under Americans' skins. Participants in flag debates go beyond explaining what the symbol means; they testify passionately about how it makes them feel. African Americans describe the chill the flag sends up their spines and the sickness it brings to their stomachs, comparing their reaction to the experience of Jews before the Nazi swastika or of army veterans witnessing an American flag in flames. Pro-flag groups also invoke the visceral aspects of these colors, staging tributes intended to quicken the pulse, moisten the eye, and bring a lump to the throat. Such emotional appeals recall the similarly contentious disputes over the desecration of the United States flag. These two flag controversies—over Confederate symbols and over official protection of the Star Spangled Banner—have more in common with each other than is usually recognized. Both show Americans' preference for passion over reason when it comes to symbols that have been imaginatively soaked in blood.[2]

Colors and Blood explores how these waving swathes of cloth acquired their enormous power to inspire and to repel. It introduces a wartime flag culture that set the emotional tone of the Civil War in the Union as well as in the Confederacy and brought together powerful themes of defiance, sovereignty, and bloodshed. The flags that generated such passions in the 1860s provided in durable form a range of messages about a common undertaking. In doing so, these symbols extended popular understandings of sacrifice, defense of community, and treason, while they served also to shape relationships between men and women, masters and slaves, and soldiers and civilians. Northerners and southerners alike devoted enormous energy to flag-related activity during the Civil War, which was at once a watershed moment for the Stars and Stripes and a generative period for the cult of Confederate flags. Confederates faced two unique challenges, however, that make an extended story of their symbols particularly worthwhile. First, they recast elements from an inherited American flag culture to forge their own symbolic system, doing so with no little controversy among themselves. Then, defeated Confederates confronted an even more difficult task in making the prime symbol of their nationalism into a relic of a Lost Cause. In this, former rebels against government created an afterglow of wartime passions by extending earlier themes of soldierly devotion with an emphasis on the nonpolitical nature of their most cherished icon, the diagonal Southern Cross.

By focusing on flag culture in the wartime South, this study contributes to a debate over Confederate nationalism, a topic every bit as old, and nearly as contentious, as rebel flags themselves. Confederates were quite self-conscious about their nationhood during the Civil War, claiming that they and the Yankees were part of "two distinct nations" differing from each other "in blood, in race, in social institutions, in systems of popular instruction, in political education and theories, in ideas, in manners." Choosing a set of flags for their new republic was a concerted effort to furnish a distinct people with distinct symbols of their own. Whether or not there was an objective basis for Confederate claims of distinctiveness has stirred considerable disagreement ever since. Many scholars have concluded that the entire notion of a distinct southern nationality was fraudulent and that few Confederates fully supported political independence. The supposed deficiency of southern nationalism has become a familiar theme in historical scholarship, as has the notion that the Confederate enterprise was quixotic and artificial. Some have even suggested that internal weaknesses associated with the insufficient nationalism of the South had more to do with the outcome of the Civil War than the strength of the Union armies.[3]

Southern historians have only recently begun to approach Confederate nationalism as a process worthy of study in its own right and not just one of many deficiencies that helped the Yankees win the war. Drew Gilpin Faust set a new agenda by incisively comparing the Confederacy to other new nations, noting how its citizens actively fashioned a sense of nationhood that had not existed prior to secession. Confederates did so, Faust explained in 1988, by engaging in an ongoing set of cultural practices that intersected with ideological, religious, and military developments in a society mobilized for combat. Her approach, which coincided with a blossoming scholarly interest in modern nationalism's paradoxical mixture of transparent artificiality and its pretenses to ancient lineage, provided one of the most effective American case studies of how rituals and symbols legitimated power. Historians who have since written on this topic have been indebted to Faust's insights, even while they do not always share her conclusions. Gary Gallagher has made a particularly important contribution, following Faust in treating Confederate nationalism seriously, though placing much more attention on the martial themes in Confederate purpose.[4]

Despite the increasingly sophisticated approaches to Confederate nationalism, there remains an important gap in the literature, which an examination of the emotional dimensions of the South's popular flag culture can help to fill. Current work has yielded considerable insight into ideology—whether expressed in the language of theology, constitutionalism, political economy, or nineteenth-century ethnology. We also have a great deal more understanding than we once had of how the clergy and military leaders worked to inspire popular allegiance to the common cause. Yet in trying to explain such fundamentally emotional issues of loyalty and sacrifice, neither ideology nor the leadership of a few can satisfactorily explain that gut-wrenching patriotism that was felt, rather than thought, by the many.[5] The Union effort was clearly bolstered by "an emotional attachment to vague but numinous symbols of national solidarity," as the historian Charles Royster has put it. Yet because the Confederacy did not win this flag-draped war, it has been harder to see how patriotic symbols were powerful sources of cohesion within the wartime South as well.[6]

Confederate flags helped to focus patriotic emotions from the early days of the secession crisis in 1860 past the moment of military defeat in 1865. A series of banners generated a multimedia flag culture characterized by the breadth of its cultural practices. Poetry, songs, and orations that paid tributes to specific flags appeared constantly in print, providing a set of common understandings about collective aims. Inherited conventions about the meaning of certain flags elements, such as stars, stripes, and crosses, became a topic of common discussion and wide understanding. Just as important, a series of impromptu rituals drew attention to flags, which were endlessly raised, blessed, presented, and, in a similarly dramatic fashion, protected through bodily sacrifice. Cloth, words, and public performances together conveyed to millions of participants what their country stood for and what their suffering during war was meant to accomplish.[7]

The popular patriotism that placed flags at its center has largely eluded the attention of cultural historians of either the Confederacy or of the Union. The conventional, syrupy aesthetic that informed wartime flag culture has been all too easily dismissed as the "Patriotic Gore" that Edmund Wilson derided in his classic study of Civil War literature. Confederate flags that already drew forth sentimentalism during wartime were further softened by their association with a nostalgic Lost Cause and with the mass-marketing of regionalism of the twentieth century. Until controversy over these flags flared in recent years, the diagonal rebel flag had been reduced to a quaint marker of a Dixieland that had passed into the mists of history. As this vestige of the 1860s became part of later cultures of memory and heritage, the sharper wartime edge of banners, poems, and activities became hard to take seriously. Even while the Civil War remained America's "felt history," it was difficult for many to see anything other than nostalgia in the sort of patriotic reverence for flags and for the cause that was expressed while the conflict was still underway.[8]

The Civil War generation accorded their flags more importance than subsequent scholars have allowed. They recognized the powerful ways that these emblems expressed political commitments and elicited military courage in battle. Living in an age of popular nationalism, Confederates were as attuned as their northern counterparts were to the sort of public display in which flags worked best to churn emotions. To a far greater degree than patriots of the American Revolution, Victorian men and women who rallied the faithful during the Civil War immersed themselves in dramatic mythmaking, taking their symbols with tremendous seriousness. Seeing how Confederates chose their symbols and celebrated them seems straightforward, since this process was done in public, especially through the burgeoning world of print journalism. Yet since patriotism rested then, as now, on how things ought to be rather than how they how they were, professions about what these flags meant must be placed in the context of larger objectives to be fully understood.

The scholarly respect accorded to nationalism in the past twenty years has recently been extended to the contours of emotional life. Particular efforts have been made by American historians to understand Victorian sensibilities and the value placed during the mid-nineteenth century upon both emotional intensity and the restraint of dangerous passions. Men as well as women, we have learned, were committed to a culture of sentiment that saw immense positive value in what later generations would consider excessive weepiness and needlessly inflamed ardor. The most intense displays of emotion have usually been associated with private settings, especially the domestic sphere. But as an emotive wartime flag culture made clear, feelings were an important part of public life as well. In normal times, society might hold together with sober self-interest and a modicum of sympathy for one's fellow citizens. But when it faced war on the scale witnessed in the 1860s, a stronger set of emotions was needed. Under these conditions, Victorianism distinguished itself as a culture "impatient of limitations and hospitable to luxuriant sensations," as the historian Anne Rose has put it.[9]

Taking the wartime passions of the 1860s seriously requires reconsidering many cultural figures and forms that have been long dismissed. Sidney Lanier provides a good example, since he was singled out in Wilson's *Patriotic Gore* for his tendency to be "at once insipid and florid" and apt to be "sometimes a little stupid" in his rhetorical excess. Yet Lanier not only produced the sort of purple prose featured in this book's epigraph, from *Tiger Lilies*. He also worked out a larger philosophical stance based on the belief that "a man must always *feel* rightly (that is his *emotion* must operate rightly) before he can *think* rightly (that is before his *intellect* can operate rightly)." Given this understanding, Lanier believed that "the initial step of every plan and every action is an emotion." Though he developed his insights by immersing himself in German Romanticism, Lanier's outlook fit the circumstances when he made these observations late in 1860. Just a few weeks after his philosophical speculations, he noted how a flag presentation at his small Georgia college had called forth "sparkling eyes and flushing cheeks" of all assembled. His explanation of how "woman's sanctity" would instill in the soldiers a "still but thrilling war-cry in the hearts" as they moved from feeling to action echoed a series of similar formulations made in literally thousands of American communities.[10]

As the following chapters make clear, that flag culture which Lanier both observed and later joined as a Confederate soldier operated at distinct stages and through a variety of distinct emblems. Resistance banners, which were the first cloth symbols to challenge the Stars and Stripes, hastened disunion while representing new commonwealths to the world. The Stars and Bars flag, chosen soon thereafter as the first national flag, provided a new and untested government a powerful means of eliciting popular support through a burgeoning body of patriotic poetry, song, and ritual. Military banners drew even wider attention, especially at the local level, where communal ceremonies engaged a range of martial themes that would intensify after blood had been shed and regimental colors had become a central part of how both soliders and civilians imagined combat. The Southern Cross, the same rebel flag that still generates controversy, emerged in this martial context, becoming the leading Confederate symbol at least by 1863, when it was incorporated on a new national flag known as the Stainless Banner. Midway through the war, a coordinated martial iconography had been created that allowed both soldiers in the field and civilians in occupied areas to show their true colors. At each of these stages, wartime flag culture helped to push forward Confederate efforts to found a new republic and injected questions of national purpose into the vibrant realm of popular culture.

Every distinct stage of wartime flag culture was marked by shared sensibilities. The symbolic grammar in which Confederates worked out their flag designs continued to owe much to the American flag practices that had been established decades earlier. The range of Confederates' flag-related productions also drew from a national "melodramatic mode" that, as Alice Fahs has recently shown, pervaded American life during the Civil War.[11] Melodramatic features of flag culture included a characteristic concern for highly charged language and actions and for an underlying emotional extravagance. In this, flag patriotism was part of a larger configuration, as several studies of mid-Victorian public life on both sides of the Atlantic have suggested. The basic conventions of melodrama—its exaggerated moral, its tendency to feature an unexpected turn of events and to focus on the lives of average people, and its explicit rendering of sharply etched emotions—provided all citizens with the same overt message, making this genre a quintessentially democratic form. Such aspects of melodrama were easily translated from the stage to other forms of public discourse. The flag-draped patriotic performances of the 1860s echoed conventions of the stage in the stock roles played by vulnerable females and vigilant males and by the overriding sense that a lurking evil foe would be vanquished, to name just two examples.[12]

If this theatrical, highly stylized flag culture could inspire passion, it also channeled strong emotions, thus restraining popular patriotism from potential excess. This result was important, since Victorians' appreciation for emotional intensity in the mid-nineteenth century was accompanied by profound anxieties about unregulated appetites and drives. In the case of civilian flags, insurgent energies that mobilized Confederates were soon channeled into a commitment to sovereign authority and collective national order. The even more perilous passions drawn forth by battle flags were also tamed. Combat in the Civil War, as has been true of large-scale war in all human societies, threatened to reduce soldiers to barbarism. In their military uses, flags gave structure to the most extreme and violent elements of war—killing one's enemies and putting one's own life at risk. These banners legitimated bloodshed by lending transcendent meaning to the horrific business of combat. The larger system of values evoked by flags first highlighted national independence, but by the end of the war they also stood for a warrior's code of honor. Understanding the development of a martial flag culture can help to explain how Confederate soldiers surrendered their flags in 1865 and how they prided themselves on honorable acceptance of their loss even as they placed their nationalist cause, and all the carnage that had come with it, firmly in the past.[13]

The efforts made by ordinary white southerners to create and consecrate their flags had certain unintended results. Even before surrender, the national Stars and Bars and the army's diagonal Southern Cross provided the North with strongly negative symbols to rally against. These motivated Unionists to fight on, just as today's rebel flag has stirred anger and helped mobilize Civil Rights forces during the 1990s. In the case of African Americans, their fight for the Stars and Stripes and against a "banner of treason" linked the cause of their own freedom to a broader struggle for national existence. At the same time that the American flag expanded its associations beyond the battlefield to herald freedom for slaves, Confederate emblems became ever more oriented toward themes of combat and conflict through war. Martial themes that ran through mature Confederate flag culture may have sustained popular support for armies in the field. But the attention that it directed toward regular combat troops would discourage civilian resistance after these same armies surrendered. The centrality of battle flags would, in the postwar period, help to divorce martial honor from a dead nationalist cause. In retrospect, a flag culture that during wartime nurtured a far richer Confederate patriotism than most have appreciated proved incapable of sustaining southern separatism after 1865.

An analysis of Civil War flag culture can provide new insights into America's most divisive conflict. It might also lend some perspective to controversies of our own day, showing the wartime roots of arguments both for and against rebel colors and providing a greater understanding of the appeal of cloth symbols in American culture. Readers looking primarily for answers to today's struggles, however, should be forewarned. As a contribution to Civil War history, the following pages focus far more attention on how Confederate emblems came into being than on what they would eventually become. The story it tells starts not with current passions or even with flags of the Confederacy. The curtain rises instead in 1860, as a war hero from Mississippi considers the American Stars and Stripes for which he had once risked his life.

CHAPTER ONE

The Stars and Stripes of
Senator Davis. A Prologue

IN THE WANING DAYS OF 1860, Jefferson Davis selected the last book he
would ever borrow from the Library of Congress. The senator had developed
a taste for biography over the previous year; political leaders, musical composers, and authors clearly intrigued him, though Davis was also pulled toward
masters of the theater such as Richard Sheridan and George Matthews. Study-
ing these life stories would prove useful in Davis's immediate future. But none
was as urgent as his final choice, whose hero just happened to be, at least in
the most technical sense, an inanimate object.[1]

Schuyler Hamilton's *History of the National Flag* sketched a more complicated narrative than Senator Davis might have expected. It also presented him
with a set of specific facts that he would soon put to use in one of the most
memorable speeches of his career, when he took to the Senate floor to express
a final tribute to the Star Spangled Banner. Though Davis had already subjected
the American flag to the nineteenth-century equivalent of literary deconstruction, Hamilton's book, especially its detailing of the various flags that had preceded the Stars and Stripes, provided other subversive strategies. This information gave Davis a means of deflating the American flag's mythic status by
revealing its relative novelty and allowing him to identify the wide range of
local symbols that predominated during the American Revolution. However
clever such arguments might have been, however logical their presentation,
Davis's reading would not accomplish as much as he might have hoped for.
His excursion into the history of this symbol would convince few Unionists to
accept peaceful separation. And he failed in what was perhaps an even greater
objective. It soon became clear that the senator had not freed even himself
from the emotional tug of an emblem that he would soon relinquish.[2]

The winter of 1860 was a fitting time for Davis to turn to the history of the United States flag. With the ultimate test of loyalties at hand, the Stars and Stripes suddenly seemed more useful than one more treatise on the Constitution, slavery, or the law of nations. Americans evaluated disunion not merely as a question of right or of law, but as a more personal matter involving the emotional investments that individuals had made in their country's rising glory. Accordingly, a set of abstract, though highly emotive, symbols would be among the most important guides to action. And with these considerations, Schuyler Hamilton's cloth hero presented Davis and other secessionists with their greatest challenge; the red, white, and blue flag hit the gut in a way that the closely reasoned passages of Hamilton's much more famous grandfather, who had written as "Publius" nearly two generations earlier, simply did not. Confronting the power of the country's flag acknowledged its potency to frame future commitments. In considering its meaning, Davis undertook a quixotic attempt to neutralize what would soon prove to be one of the most powerful weapons in the Union's arsenal.

The American flag would not have been nearly so important a generation earlier. Though the United States would eventually establish a distinctive flag culture unrivaled by any other country, this phenomenon was developed later than one might assume. The mania for the Stars and Stripes that developed during secession had been a relatively minor theme at the time of Davis's own birth, in 1808. The flag's central position within American patriotism would not, in fact, be assured until the war for the Union of the 1860s consecrated this emblem as the embodiment of both a popular government and a citizenry willing to die on its behalf. In the half century before this war, several elements of a later cult developed, making the Stars and Stripes enough of an anthropomorphic presence to draw a handful of official biographers. Most important in breathing life into a piece of fabric was the stirring anthem by Francis Scott Key, written to commemorate its survival in Baltimore Harbor during the War of 1812. Endowed with a name taken from this song, the Star Spangled Banner achieved even more prestige in leading victorious armies across Mexico in the mid-1840s. As the banner extended its metaphorical sway across an entire continent, it intimidated external enemies and promised protection to Americans traveling beyond their country's borders. And during the 1850s, the flag even became a protection against internal threats, as members of the secret Order of the Star-Spangled Banner made the national flag a central component of the nativist American Party, which they helped guide into existence.[3]

If antebellum reverence for the flag was underdeveloped by today's standards, other symbols and icons now taken for granted were even more stunted. The Capital building where Davis worked was yet again under renovation, while down the hill, the Washington Monument was little more than an unfinished stump near a swamp. The Statue of Liberty in New York Harbor would not appear for more than a quarter of a century, and such revolutionary memorials as the Bunker Hill obelisk, and even George Washington's Mount Vernon estate, had been badly tarnished in the sectional sparring over slavery. With a patriotic landscape still under construction, Americans relied more on the example of the Founders for inspiration. The ethereal influence of the revolutionary generation—and especially of George Washington—was codified in key texts these men had written and in a series of legends that grew up around them. These were as likely to elicit the patriotic feeling as any living, breathing presence.[4]

Yearnings for something beyond Washington's rather stiff model of self-control were satisfied by a range of patriotic celebrations that dated from the period of the Revolution. With the help of a rapidly developing print network, a festive culture of contestation and mobilization had spread across the country and become a crucial means of elaborating early American nationalism, especially on such national holidays as the Fourth of July. These gatherings were more effective at saying something about the present and the past than about the future, however. By contrast, a waving banner had an uncanny ability, especially when accompanied by music, to achieve immortality and to function as a beacon for all time. As it marked a permanent presence on the physical landscape, the American flag, no less than its counterparts in Europe, united past and present with a national destiny to be transmitted to posterity. In both its elements and its associations, it compounded a powerful set of messages about what it meant to live as an American citizen.[5]

Waving flags also put the blood in American nationalism by evoking distinctly martial associations. While these banners have nearly always invoked soldiers' sacrifice, such messages were even more acute in the period before the Civil War. This was partly due to the actual display of national flags, which prior to the war flew primarily over military installations or at militia gatherings, and almost never atop churches, businesses, and private homes or in schools. The Stars and Stripes had become part of political rallies, but leaders made none of the fuss over them that would later be the case, instead using them to rally the faithful to "march to the polls" as if preparing them for battle, albeit an electoral one. Efforts to codify proper flag etiquette for civilians lay at least a generation in the future. As a consequence, veterans who had pledged their lives to the flag were far and away its most enthusiastic defenders.[6]

The martial connotations of the Stars and Stripes made this flag naturally important to southwestern imperialists like Jefferson Davis. The quest for American dominion on the country's far borders had generated a distinctively southern set of heroes, ranging from Andrew Jackson, the victor at the battle of New Orleans, to the more recent generals of America's war with Mexico. These military conflicts bred a patriotism among white southerners that was no less intense for often being accompanied by growing tension with the free-labor North. John Quitman, a Mississippi neighbor of Davis, made it clear that slaveholders should leave the Union if its government ever passed decisively into Yankee hands. Yet even while Quitman counseled resistance to the point of disunion, he gloried in the distinction of having raised the first American flag above Mexico City, a feat he performed during his army's occupation of that capital in 1847. Clearly, he did not agree that "the devices adopted . . . for the National ensign of our country were intended to intimate the perpetuity of that country's union," as Schuyler Hamilton had written. Like other slave-holders, Quitman believed that pride in American dominance need not require a pledge of absolute loyalty to the United States government.[7]

Davis's combined commitment to protecting "southern rights" and to his flag was felt perhaps even more deeply than Quitman's. As Davis explained in 1858, he had grown to love that flag "with even more than a filial affection" ever since he was "bound to her military service" as a youth. For what he considered "many of the best years of my life," Davis had "followed the flag and upheld it on fields where if I had fallen it might have been claimed as my winding sheet." As a Mexican War general, he had witnessed at first hand patriotic martyrdom for the flag at Buena Vista in 1847, during the battle that assured Davis's reputation as an American war hero. Others recognized the glory that his actions had shed on the Star Spangled Banner. One southerner would soon plead to the Confederate Congress to "retain the stars and stripes," maintaining that it was "not an abolition flag" because "Col. Jefferson Davis won glory under it in Mexico."[8]

Well into 1860, Davis hoped that national glory and regional security could both be maintained. His own experience as war hero, senator, and Secretary of War showed that strengthening the country's military was an important means of assuring southern slavery's continued vitality. Yet Davis knew as well as anyone that Abraham Lincoln's election as president would upset this symbi-otic relationship between nationalism and the power of southern slaveholders. Awareness of a coming crisis would not have made his efforts to disenthrall himself from his country and its flag any easier. If he had been from Virginia, he might well have followed the path of Robert E. Lee, opting to defend the ancient heritage of the Old Dominion against an upstart Union. This was harder to do for a Mississippian, and an adopted one at that. The state he had called home as a boy and an adult had few of the historical memories or cultur-ally defining emblems of its older Atlantic neighbors. Davis was thus ill equipped to relinquish his national orientation in favor of a local one, even during the moment of secession.

The senator worked his way out of his conundrum by turning to the national flag itself, wringing from its design a symbolic rationale for peaceful disunion. He had previewed this rhetorical strategy before the Mississippi legislature in 1858, focusing attention on his state's own star in the national flag's wider blue field. After conjuring up this image of a single point of light, he pledged that rather than have this star's "luster dimmed," he would "tear it from the flag and make it a sign to rally Mississippi's best and bravest to the harvest-home

1. The Battle of Buena Vista made Jefferson Davis an American hero and strength-
    ened his emotional ties to the Stars and Stripes. Patriotic martyrdoms in this
    and other Mexican War battles endowed the Stars and Stripes with new
    power, as this depiction of Henry Clay, Jr.'s death, suggested. Courtesy,
    American Antiquarian Society.

of death." The primacy of the states, which was expressed in the very stars of
the American flag, was the true genius of republican government, he maintained, as he accused "consolidationists" of betraying this core commitment by
attempting to establish a single large planet in place of a diffuse constellation.
In short, he projected his dilemma onto cloth, honoring the flag's true principles at the same moment he admitted that the Union it represented was not
worth the betrayal of the country's underlying principles.[9]

On January 10, 1861, Davis put a secessionist gloss on the Stars and Stripes
once more, this time before a more skeptical Senate audience. He again charged
Republicans with ignoring the flag's central lesson—that the Union depended
on allowing "each planet to revolve in an orbit of its own." Obliterating the
rights of the states would only "destroy the constellation which, in its power
and its glory, had been gathering one after another, until, from thirteen, it had
risen to thirty-three stars." Davis used this constellation metaphor, and the
symbolic grammar of a distinct star for each of the states, to place the onus for
disunion on his opponents. This allowed him, along with other southerners,

to sing the praises of a constellation that had "served to bless our people" and to act as a "regenerative power" across the globe. Whatever the accomplishments of the American flag in the past, Davis considered it far better to let each of the states spin out from its path rather than to let them all merge into a common mass that would obliterate their singularity.[10]

The Senate speech Davis gave that afternoon was one of the most anticipated addresses of the session. Neither Mississippi nor the flag was its central concern. Like most congressmen during this short session, Davis focused on South Carolina and the tense stand-off in Charleston Harbor that had begun around Christmas, when a small party of federal officers suddenly evacuated Fort Moultrie. After ordering the destruction of the flagpole there (to assure no other standard might be raised in place of the Stars and Stripes), commander Robert Anderson moved to an island fortification known as Fort Sumter and raised his flag on a pole ten stories high. As James Buchanan contemplated the crisis, Davis joined a chorus of southerners who urged the lame-duck president to order these federal troops to withdraw along with their oversized banner. Whatever one thought about South Carolina's recent decision to secede, war was still unpopular, and a direct provocation in Charleston Harbor was thought to be unlikely. Increasingly, however, it became clear that Fort Sumter was a fuse waiting to be lit.[11]

Davis was frustrated about the impasse and angry that it could not be settled quickly. His speech lamented that the North's primary objection to transferring the fort to South Carolina was simply a stubborn "unwillingness to lower the flag." This seemed to him grossly unfair, since it overlooked the fact that South Carolinians were "brethren" who had "shed as much glory upon that flag as any equal number of men in the Union." He reminded senators that Carolina patriots had been among the first to raise the Union banner, having done so in 1775. He could not resist adding that this flag had not been that of the "thirteen stripes and thirty-three stars." Having read Schuyler Hamilton's book closely, Davis briefly digressed to mention some details about the actual flag that had waved during the Revolution, concluding simply that, in tribute to South Carolina, "her ancient history compares proudly with the present."[12]

This excursion into those details he had recently gleaned from Hamilton's book could have been far more polemical. Other Confederates would expend far greater efforts to deflate the power of the Stars and Stripes by reminding southerners that this banner had not been used widely during the battles of the Revolution. But what distinguished Davis's speech, and made it memorable, was its emotional texture, which featured an effective mixture of peevishness, defiance, and melancholy. This emotional range was punctuated by a series of rhetorical invocations of the flag that centered his appeal and gave his words their unity. While his flag references were often figures of speech, they nonetheless provided him with an unlikely prop for a secessionist, setting a melodramatic tone and allowing him to pose as a mourner rather than a revolutionary. His performance in this regard showed how much Davis had learned since the start of his career, when he had been judged a clear speaker but not a particularly effective one.[13]

At a crucial moment of his speech, Davis asked his fellow Senators to experience some of the dilemma that he now faced, knowing that his state had voted to leave the Union just one day earlier. "It may be pardoned to me" to ask for sympathy, he explained, as someone "who, in my boyhood, was given to the military service, and who have followed under tropical suns, and over northern snows, the flag of the Union." Though knowing "it does not become me to speak it," Davis still was compelled to express in public: "the deep sorrow which always overwhelms me when I think of taking a last leave of that object of early affection and proud association, feeling that henceforth it is not to be the banner which, by day and by night, I am ready to follow, to hail with the rising and bless with the setting of the sun."

Establishing his own emotional distress allowed Davis to suggest what most of his northern listeners must have considered a naive plea for humility and understanding. Denouncing exclusive use of the flag as vainglorious, he explained a humbler understanding reflected in his hope "that that flag shall not be set up between contending brothers." Instead, the future Confederate president urged, "When it shall no longer be the flag of the common country, it shall be folded up and laid away like a vesture no longer used." Imagining a peaceful future, he foresaw the day that the once-beloved Stars and Stripes would be "kept as a sacred memento of the past, to which each of us can make a pilgrimage and remember the glorious days in which we were born." Needless to say, his northern colleagues in the Senate had no intention of doing anything of the sort.

In the years to come, Davis only partly lived out his prediction that "men may become indifferent even to the object of early attachments." His Senate speech of January 10, 1861, represented his last public reflections on the Stars and Stripes, which Confederates would soon contemptuously regard as a "gridiron" emblem ruined by Republican infamy. Selected to lead a new Confederate government, Davis traveled to Montgomery, Alabama, before delegates were able to agree on a proper national flag of their own. En route, he encountered an array of patriotic symbols, even briefly marching behind the "old and tattered flag" of his Mexican War regiment. When he arrived at his final destination, he saluted the new state flag of Alabama.[14]

As president, Davis received several designs for the American flag's replacement, but he routinely forwarded them to the proper authorities with no comment or additional reflection. When the capital moved to Virginia, he promised that Confederates would realize "another Buena Vista" there that they would "drench with blood more precious" than any that had been shed in Mexico. In July of 1861, he also took time to present a silk rendering of the new Confederate flag, which was known as the Stars and Bars, to soldiers from Maryland and South Carolina. In his public speech that day, he explained that this shift of flag allegiances honored the spirit of country's Revolutionary forebears, who had cast off the Union Jack of Great Britain for the American red, white, and blue. Here, Davis relied on a known myth, which his reading of Hamilton would have shown to be untrue, that there had ever been a single Revolutionary ensign that guided the colonists against England. A simple story was useful, however, in dramatizing how adopting new symbols furthered past commitments and provided the basis for an even deeper emotional ties to country in the future. Changing flags, whether in 1776 or in 1861, was one of the costs entailed in creating the "purest, freest, happiest" as well as the "most enduring Government the world has ever known."[15]

The new president's main association with the Confederate national flag would be in the pairing of his portrait with it in a variety of prints. Those sympathetic to the Confederacy gloried in the familiarity of a well-known leader and a flag that was consciously modeled on its predecessor. Images of Davis by northern illustrators, on the other hand, portrayed both the Confederate president and the new country's flag in starkly negative terms. The fact that he had served the Stars and Stripes honorably earlier in his career made his rejection of it all the worse. Likened to Benedict Arnold, or even Lucifer, Davis was shown to have succumbed to the temptation of higher glory only after reaching the top levels of service to his original cause. He and his country's Stars and Bars deserved nothing less than execution for their treason.[16]

Though visually associated with the flag of the new republic, Davis would not take a prominent role either in selecting or in celebrating new southern banners, remaining largely aloof from the flag developments that would simmer throughout the life of the Confederacy. A handful of Confederate congressmen, including the South Carolinian William Porcher Miles, did try to guide public opinion on the matter, as did at least one general, P.G.T. Beauregard of Louisiana. But the real impetus in flag concerns came from outside the government and the halls of power. The newspaper and periodical press drove many aspects of flag culture, reporting the appearance of flags, guiding the debate over designs, and printing a torrent of flag-related verse. A variety of civilian patriots and poets produced a wide array of artifacts and staged a regular series of impromptu flag rituals. But more than anything else, it would be ordinary deaths on the battlefield that shaped how flags would be understood.

These activities involved not just a few individuals, but an entire political community. A wide range of figures with notable energy, and no little creativity, sought to work through themes of common purpose and sacrifice in confronting the need to forge new symbols. Despite postwar efforts to produce a single heroic story of the sequential rebel flags, these Confederate banners were adopted and understood by the larger southern public in a series of fits and starts. Disagreements among white southerners probably did as much to de-

2. This 1860 lithography, entitled "The Traitor's Dream," condemned Jefferson Davis for surrendering to diabolical temptations, though it also captured some of the anguish he expressed before the Senate in relinquishing his flag. Courtesy, Library of Congress.

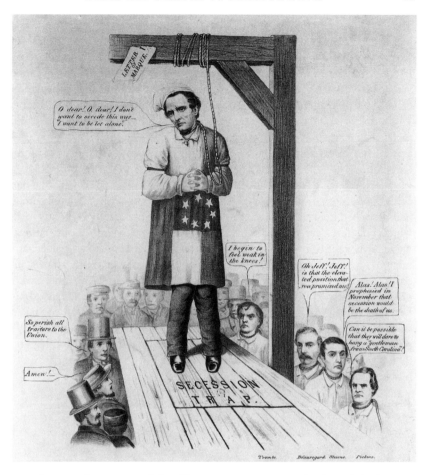

3.   This print from 1861, titled "Jefferson Davis on His Stand," showed the fate
     that Unionists imagined for the treasonous new Confederate president and
     the country's new flag. Courtesy, Library of Congress.

velop notions of collective purpose as the final products themselves did. Accounting for the discord reveals as much as identifying the underlying consensus that informed mature Confederate flag culture.

   If there was a single figure that loomed over these developments, it was no
one man or woman, but the American flag itself. Secessionists worked within
a set of flag conventions developed within the United States, just as they
worked within recognizably American traditions of popular government, evangelical religion, and a patriotism that presented soldiers and women as the
chief supports of national virtue. Self-styled Confederate patriots chose new
constellations from the symbolic grammar of antebellum American flag culture.

They sang of martial glory, glorified feminine sacrifice, and imbued each new flag with a transcendent, spiritual aura. In each of these activities, they never ceased to be in dialogue with their own past, and with the contemporary initiatives of their Yankee enemies. Just as the Stars and Stripes had presented Senator Davis with a personal dilemma and a public opportunity in the winter of 1861, it thereafter furnished Confederates with an important touchstone. This emblem would soon be recognized as an enemy standard to displace and to defeat in battle. But it never quite lost what it had been from the beginning— a prototype for bolstering loyalties and for making patriotism an issue of popular emotion.

Jefferson Davis's family retained the actual Stars and Stripes flag that he had carried into Mexico, perhaps as a reminder of the time when a young general had described himself "as an American, whose heart promptly responds to all which illustrates our national character, and adds new glory to our national name." This relic from the 1840s was later deposited in the Mississippi Department of Archives, where it still remains alongside an array of Confederate standards. Strangely, at some point in its history, the stars in its blue field were physically removed from the cloth, though the rest of the red, white, and blue flag remains. Legend had it that his wife, Varina, was responsible, having taken custody of her husband's flag after the war. As the story goes, the Confederacy's only first lady cut each of the stars out of her husband's American flag and then awarded them individually to those few men who had remained true to him and his cause.[17]

CHAPTER TWO

The Standards of State Resistance

SYMBOLS AND SYMBOLIC ACTIONS have mattered most during periods of sweeping political change. This fact was clear in the early days of the American Revolution, when patriots produced both tears and giddy laughter by staging mock funerals for King George III and pulling down statues that had been built in his honor. More than two centuries later, the sledgehammering of the Berlin Wall brought an even wider sense of exhilaration, as millions watched CNN's live coverage of its demolition. Blue cockades sparked riots in Revolutionary France, while red books moved crowds in Mao's China. Destroying vestiges of the old order and circulating signs of the new have repeatedly electrified participants and informed outside witnesses that revolution was underway. By giving new political arrangements a visible form, symbols have proved uniquely effective in generating strong emotions.[1]

Late in 1860, flags were Americans' favorite symbolic medium, as large swathes of colored cloth set the tone for a conflict that would last for the next four-and-a-half years. In the early days and weeks of secession winter, white southerners took the initiative by executing, hoisting, and insistently waving a wide array of banners in cities and towns across the region. American flags were in evidence across the upper South, as well as in the United States Senate, where Jefferson Davis bid an emotional farewell to his colleagues. But these signs of Union patriotism were drowned out by the scores of resistance banners that proliferated farther south. Secession emblems that waved above streets, in massed gatherings, and in crowded theaters led forward a chaotic, dizzying process of political mobilization. News of these banners, and of the crowds that cheered them, alerted readers across the country of the grave crisis that was at hand. As such, resistance flags became not just a means of conveying a message, but were the main message itself. The palmetto standards, Lone Star flags, and other banners that the seceding states adopted early in 1861 provided compelling evidence that seven separate states had chosen to desert the Union. The unveiling of new state flags showed to the world what an avalanche of words could only begin to suggest—that political communities had broken old ties and were charting new destinies.

Those who wielded the secession banners and subsequent state flags rarely sat down to record their thoughts, choosing instead to let their symbolic actions speak for themselves. These early banners sometimes featured detailed verbal messages explaining the familiar icons they accompanied. Rituals performed for various banners and songs written in their honor injected traditional themes of local pride with new significance. In a range of media, these flags were first and foremost about politics. In the few short months between the election of Abraham Lincoln and the start of war, banners that had not yet been unfurled on the battlefield offered a set of powerful messages. They defied those who would infringe on slaveholders' rights, while they gave citizens at home a means of affirming devotion to sovereign power and order. In the process, a vibrant southern flag culture began to take form. Even before soldiers' blood became a primary part of this flag culture, banners proved their effectiveness, moving citizens to action and rallying them to a united effort.

Barely two weeks after the 1860 presidential election, the *Charleston Courier* announced to its readers: "We can scarcely pass through a street without finding additions to the banners, flags, and ensigns that are given to the breeze." A New Orleans paper described Charleston as "emphatically a city of banners," noting that they "flutter from windows, housetops, and liberty poles, and over streets" in numbers too high to count. In the interior of South Carolina, Columbia was every bit as decked out in cloth. The president of South Carolina College argued that "flags in hands, flags across the streets, flags at printing offices, stores, shops, booths, on omnibuses, in every direction" proved that secession was popular in the state's capital city. His own college proudly boasted one of the city's first secession banners, while a variety of signals flew over the statehouse that would, early in 1861, fly a palmetto flag that represented the newly independent republic of South Carolina. This flurry of resistance flags helped Carolina's two largest cities to become dual epicenters of disunion.[2]

The first manifestations of a distinct southern flag culture served specific and immediate needs. Radicals hung banners above the streets to sustain the momentum that had developed during the recent presidential campaign. Fire-eaters had come to recognize over the preceding thirty years that delay was the "canker of great enterprises," to use a phrase from Robert Barnwell Rhett. Ever since the nullification episode of the early 1830s, caution had led in every instance to Union-saving compromises. Hoping to avoid a similar paralysis in 1860, radicals filled the air with colors, sensing that the emotional tenor of crisis might easily be lost. As Rhett himself warned, the greatest danger faced by disunionists was hesitancy, since this would "cool the ardor of our people, who incensed now would resist promptly." For those most committed to disunion, the clock was ticking. The four months that stretched between Abraham Lincoln's election and his inauguration was barely enough time to have a new government up and running before the United States administration passed into new hands.[3]

Calls for immediate and decisive action were an explicit message of many of these early flags. "Strike Now or Never," one banner urged, depicting, as did several others, the famous image of a coiled rattlesnake that dated from the American Revolution. Another proclaimed, with a bit more wordiness, "The time for deliberation has passed—the time for action has come." The words "South Carolina, Going, Going, Gone" were featured on a flag that, appropriately enough, waved above one of Charleston's main auction houses. A short time later, a secession banner in Mobile, Alabama, announced, "The Time Has Come." A widespread insistence on quick resolve lent Deep South cityscapes a distinctively revolutionary quality. This spirit was intensified by repeated renditions of the "Marseillaise" and the sudden vogue of resistance cockades for men and of secession bonnets for women. Echoes of the French Revolution were often intentional. The president of the South Carolina convention offered an exemplary motto from none other than the Jacobin Georges Jacques Danton. "To dare! and again to dare! and without end to dare!" was his charge to delegates assembled to make history.[4]

Banners announced the radicals' desire for speed and became in fact a direct means of hastening the process of separate state secession; "the time for argument has passed" was an argument itself. But argument, dispute, and perhaps delay were eliminated if the object conveying this resolve was a flag bearing these same words. A message on a flag was something more than mere communication—it was action that marked the crossing of a crucial boundary. Earlier in American history, the erection of a Bear Flag in Alta California and the hoisting of a Lone Star in Texas had announced that negotiations were at an end and that preparation for conflict had begun. By 1860, flags had become, both within and beyond the United States, one of the most potent means of communicating serious intent and of offering a statement of defiance that would last even after the loudest words could no longer be heard. The banner that flew above the office of the *Charleston Courier* in this way carried its own explanation. Though not a single vote had been cast for disunion when it appeared, the lone star on one side of the banner made good what the other side proclaimed to the world: "South Carolina leads the way, other States will follow."[5]

Telegraph dispatches sent from South Carolina to the rest of the country reinforced the notion that flying a flag was an event worthy of reporting far and wide. While local papers tended to describe each particular resistance banner in great detail, most of the national press ignored the immense variety of these cities' visual landscapes. A centralized wire service that spread word of secession emblems generally filtered out the extraneous information, merely alerting readers that new flags were waving in places once reserved for the Stars and Stripes. The presence of these symbols in the columns of newsprint was as important as their actual embodiment in cloth, since popular journalism was constitutive of the country's "imagined community"—the place where Americans turned to understand matters of national concern. The newspaper press was a central part of Americans' national public life in the early years of the republic, becoming as important as physical localities in providing citizens with a shared space to debate and resolve issues of common concern.[6]

By the time of the Civil War, such community-forming media had evolved in ways that helped accentuate the urgency of flag-related news. Detailed information had long been transmitted across great distances, in large part because of a dynamic federal postal system. But in the 1850s, the magnetic telegraph and a corresponding centralized wire service had restructured the news, making it virtually instantaneous and remarkably superficial. Dispatches concerning what one editor called "cockades and bloody strips of bunting with savage mottoes" typified what he condemned as a growing journalistic interest in covering "the rage of the day, the sensation, the excitement, the panic, or whatever else is generally uppermost in the public mind on the streets, in the shops, in the hotels, on the cars, or wherever men are to be found."[7] Operating at the very speed that secessionists desired, the national press system tracked the process of revolution by circulating standardized snippets of news on a daily basis. The raising of resistance banners was reported by telegraph first from the cities of South Carolina, and then from one city in the Deep South after another. This reporting provided readers from Michigan to Massachusetts with the latest and seemingly most authentic sentiment that existed in the slave states.[8]

American newspaper readers hungered for this information, since the future depended largely on how those in the Deep South would respond to the election of a president who had drawn virtually no support in their region. Readers far from the streets of Charleston learned through a continual hail of flag-related news in their daily papers that those secessionists they had suspected of mere bluster were taking concrete steps to make good on a plan of action. Worse yet, the proliferation of symbols suggested that swift resolve had mass support. There were plenty of complaints from sober observers about the telegraphic dispatches and their part in shaping perceptions about the South. Some even placed the war's ultimate responsibility on a blundering press corps. A New Jersey paper predicted that future historians explaining the war would "give a prominent place to the contradictory, exaggerated and inflammatory telegraphic dispatches which filled the columns of our more influential papers with startling capitals and display lines." The visual images of a city waving

A glorious occasion is anticipated in the inaugu-
ration of the Liberty Pole of the merchants of
Charleston, which will take place this day at 11 A.
M., near the Charleston Hotel.

Action! Action! Action!—The general sentiment
of Charleston is now in favor of that which De-
mosthenes considered the great essential of oratory
—action.

In proof of this, we need only refer to the banners which are exhibited over our streets.

The Pavilion Hotel has unfurled a well executed
banner, showing a portrait of Calhoun, with a Palmetto tree, a star, and other devices, with the
initials S. C., meaning either "South Carolina," or
"Southern Confederacy," as the case may require·
The motto is the memorable sentence of the great
Georgian, Troup—'The time for argument has
passed; let us stand to our arms."

The design was suggested by the patriotic and
popular host, Butterfield, of the Pavilion, and
was executed by L. L. Cohen, at the Art Gallery of
Osborne & Durbec, 223 King-street.

The Carolina Clothing Depot, 261 King-street, on
the West side, two doors above Wentworth, unfurled on Friday evening the banner to which we
referred in our last issue.

This banner shows on the South, a full portrait
of Hon. A. G. Magrath, late Judge of the United

☞ *Union* (Nashville, Tenn.) please copy.

SECESSION BADGES.

HARPER & CALVO,

JOB PRINTERS,

59 BROAD-STREET,

HAVE PREPARED FOR THE CONVENIENCE OF
the citizens generally, a neat BLUE BADGE, with
PALMETTO TREE and LONE STAR, printed in gold,
which can be had on application to Messrs. WELCH,
HARRIS & CO., and at F. PATTERSON'S DEPOT, 201
King-street.

PRICE 10 CENTS.

November 16

PALMETTO BANNERS,

PAINTED WITH DESPATCH

AT THE

PALMETTO PAINT STORE,

400 KING-ST., NEAR JOHN-ST.

November 16   6   **BROWER.**

4.   Southern newspapers provided news about symbols during the secession crisis, while they also helped foster participation by advertising cockades,
badges, and flags for purchase. This image is from the *Charleston Courier* of
November 16, 1860. Courtesy, Michigan State University Libraries.

with banners were as important as any headlines; the formulaic descriptions
of cheering, defiant crowds gave dramatic evidence that the people themselves
were leading the revolt against federal authority.[9]

During the secession crisis, southern newspapers assumed a crucial role in
Civil War flag culture that would continue in the future. Beginning immediately after Lincoln's election, secessionist editors competed with one another
to be the first to raise banners above their offices, and they then broadcast
such displays as news to readers across the country. They would do the same
with state flags and those symbols chosen to represent the Confederacy. Wire
reports sent by press offices shaped calculations about the future, as Americans in both sections took account of the seemingly inevitable result even
before the first votes for disunion were cast. The penchant of journalists for
banners would continue after the secession crisis, as editors became even more
important than politicians in debating the proper design for a Confederate
flag. Detailed descriptions of flags in the papers were accompanied by a flood
of flag-related poetry, which quickly became, through the medium of the daily
press, one of the most important subgenres in patriotic verse. As such, new
technology interacted with a very old method of conveying the news with

colored flags. Hearkening to an earlier era, papers began to live up quite literally to such titles as the *Herald*, the *Banner*, the *Telegraph*, or even the *Flag*.[10]

In circulating the news of these banners, the press helped to spread the
practice of defiant flag-waving across most of the Deep South. While the week
following Lincoln's election saw a flurry of secession banners primarily in
South Carolina's two chief cities, it was not long before other urban locales,
especially along the Gulf Coast, took on a similarly festive appearance. By early
December of 1860, more and more flags were appearing in small towns and
byways all down the Atlantic and across to the Texas plains. In her Civil War
novel *Macaria*, Augusta Jane Evans remembered back to this period when the
"convulsed throbbing heart of a great revolution" began with a "thundering
tramp of events." The fictional town she portrayed in her 1864 novel was no
metropolis, but the craze for colors that had begun in cities could be seen there
as well. "Flag-staffs were erected from public buildings, private residences, and
at the most frequent corners," she wrote. From these new perches "floated
banners of all sizes, tossing proudly to the balmy breeze."[11]

The resistance banners that spread from the cities of South Carolina across the
Deep South often conveyed more than the simple desire to move quickly. A
series of messages and images bolstered their urgency by depicting the prosper-
ity, peace, and stability that were endangered by the incoming Republican
administration. The banner prepared by five employees of the South Carolina
Rail Road, for instance, displayed black slaves picking cotton on one side of
its eighteen-foot length and slaves rolling cotton bales on the other. In addition
to the ubiquitous palmetto tree and rattlesnake in the center of its design, there
were also church spires on the horizon and mountains in the background.
Across the flag ran two separate trains, one of which carried a single-starred
flag and a line of platform cars carrying cotton to market. All of these images
conveyed that immediate independence—and a new single-starred flag—was
needed to preserve the South's slave-based economy.[12]

This banner was noteworthy less in its detail than its variety, packing as it
did most of the common themes into one typically busy design. There were
other evocations of cotton and slaves on flags of this period, as there would be
once the new Confederacy turned to its own flag. Yet the reference to religion
made by the banner's church spire was even more common. At first, there was
a wide variety of religious motifs. The Bible appeared on some flags, such as
the first banner raised over the Carolina capitol, which placed an open book
below a palmetto tree, explaining both with the prolix inscription:

> God is our refuge and our strength, a very present help in time of
> trouble; therefore we will not fear, though the earth be removed,
> and though the mountains be carried into the sea. The Lord of
> Hosts is with us, the God of JACOB is our refuge.

Other banners were affixed with the motto "Resistance to tyranny is obedience to God," while a poetic tribute to the palmetto on another flag made even this tree into a religious symbol, explaining how "in His name / We fling its folding free." An "all-seeing eye" peered out from several designs, acknowledging the omniscience of God as it had in earlier Masonic symbolism. The Christian cross soon established itself as the most common religious emblem, a development that would finally result in the adoption of a Southern Cross battle flag late in 1861. Such public displays of faith through symbols invoked both the legend of Constantine and the tradition of the ancient Hebrews, who had both made a similar public covenant with God. It was little wonder that several South Carolina ministers chose in this period to focus on the refrain of Psalm 36: "In the Name of God, we have set up our banners."[13]

The palmetto tree was perhaps the most common image of the secession crisis. This tree's place in Carolina iconography had been established in the battle for Charleston Harbor in 1776, which had been one of the signal patriot victories of the American Revolution. Though the Carolina flag flown in this battle did not feature a palmetto, but a simple crescent, the fort itself that had been built from the trees, since this was the only material available. The patriots' unusual choice of wood proved decisive. The "spongy, though strong" palmetto logs did not splinter when assaulted by the British navy, instead absorbing enemy shots that otherwise would have ricocheted and reduced the fort completely. In the colonists' first and most decisive victory over their enemies, Carolina material had proven its worth, gaining the palmetto a special status in local legend. Though the tree was not placed upon an official state flag until January of 1861, it had already become a martial emblem for local militias and for the state's Mexican War regiment. Images of the palmetto kept a heroic past in mind, even as it kept company with contemporary secessionist symbols that clearly pointed toward the near future.[14]

The revolutionary-era story of the Palmetto Fort become inextricably linked to a central flag-related act of heroism performed there. In the years after the battle, General William Moultrie, Parson Weems, and other patriotic chroniclers helped to make Sergeant William Jasper into one the most celebrated southern heroes of the American Revolution. Jasper's two best known exploits each involved military banners flying over entrenched positions. In the first, during the famous repulse of the British navy at the Palmetto Fort, he attached the crescent flag to a cannon halbert, raising it after its staff had been shot in half. Later in the war, he attempted to rescue a similarly endangered flag on the outskirts of Savannah, though this time his gesture resulted in death. In his final act, victorious hero became fallen patriot, and the sergeant became a natural candidate for martyrdom. Besides being celebrated in popular histories for his flag valor, Jasper became the subject of a variety of plays, poems, paintings, and public celebrations. Several immigrant militias cherished his memory with particular enthusiasm, considering him (though probably inaccurately) as the quintessential hero for the urban, Irish-born working classes of Charleston and Savannah.[15]

In a series of tributes to Jasper's heroism, the sergeant's defense of the Palmetto Fort flag became a key element of South Carolina's civic culture. The palmetto tree, associated both with the fort and with Jasper's valor, invoked a geography both more and less expansive than the other icons of the slaveholding South. Unlike the cotton flower, which became a popular item on several Alabama banners, or the magnolia, soon to be adopted on Mississippi's official flag, the palmetto's native habitat did not encompass much actual territory. This was made clear by the concerted effort required to transplant the first actual specimen of the coastal tree to Columbia, South Carolina, in December of 1860. Such limited scope did not undermine the authenticity of the symbol, however, since its appeal rested less on shared flora than on a shared history of commitment and sacrifice. It could be adopted by those sympathetic to secession as far away as Memphis, New Orleans, and Baltimore, or even in Philadelphia and New Haven with no apparent incongruity. Its more particular associations were with Charleston Harbor, where one poet hoped that "if our enemies invade us again" they would find once more a "Jasper to keep it from stain." As the waving of flags over Charleston Harbor once more captivated the nation's attention, James B. D. DeBow argued that one could "erase 1776 from the record and substitute 1860, and history need not be written anew."[16]

Jasper's cult emerged during the early nineteenth century as part of a steadily intensifying flag-related patriotism. While his heroics of 1776 would have been recognized and lauded by his contemporaries, they would not have conveyed to the generation of the American Revolution the same confluence of bravery, popular mobilization, and transcendent national ideas that latter-day enthusiasts would associate with a defense of the colors. Flags were simply not as important in the 1770s as they would be a century later, a fact demonstrated by the late-nineteenth-century patriotic fabrication—out of whole cloth, one might say—of an elaborate Betsy Ross legend. The crescent flag Jasper saved at the Palmetto Fort had not been designed to inspire patriotism or elicit widespread popular pride, the explicit concerns of later generations. Its function was simply to signal the approach of warships and hold the attention of soldiers at their post, a practicality that marked most military insignia of the Revolution. The founding revolutionaries adopted a range of symbols during their own resistance movement, though they did not yearn, as the Confederates would, for a single standard that might unify and inspire an extended political community.[17]

The growing association of revolutionary resistance with a popular flag emerged during the French Revolution, which followed American independence. The adoption of the red, white, and blue tricolor was one of the most significant innovations of popular political culture to result from this upheaval;

5. Sergeant William Jasper became one of the leading southern heroes of the American Revolution by saving his flag at Fort Moultrie, a scene depicted by this nineteenth-century lithograph. Courtesy, Gibbes Museum of Art / Carolina Art Association.

banners that had once symbolized monarchical authority became a powerful means to challenge the standing order. Cockades and liberty poles were a more decisive expression of individual defiance of authority, but flags would also become a crucial part of revolutionary insignia during the national liberation struggles that swept Latin America, eastern Europe, and Ireland during the first half of the nineteenth century. The use of flags by Chartists in England and other radical groups on the Continent extended their association with popular insurgency. By 1860, flag cults similar to that inspired by Jasper had spread across the Atlantic world. This was a relatively new development, however, which would be decisively altered during a civil war in which "rallying to the flag" would be established as the supreme duty in expressing one's love for country.[18]

Even as Jasper and the palmetto assumed some of this era's revolutionary appeal, they remained insurgent emblems in a quite limited sense. In the antebellum period, the multiple representations of Sergeant Jasper depicted his patriotism as more vigilant against outside interference than challenging to leadership at home. In a scene endlessly repeated by eulogists, the hero showed himself to be a "modest fellow" rather than a revolutionary, refusing a promotion from the same Charleston notable that presented him with a ceremonial sword. Illiteracy was his reason for refusing the honor, since, as William Gilmore Simms explained in his popular history, Jasper "had been uneducated, and a commission implied the necessity for some degree of education." The palmetto made famous by a humble patriot roused rebellion again in 1860: the Carolina Convention adopted it in January, not as a sign of more sweeping social change, but as the emblem of the state's sovereignty. With the overthrow of illegitimate power, this symbol and flag would turn from inciting resistance to directing new loyalties to a new government.[19]

The mixture of defiance and respect for state authority was even more evident in the only secession symbol to rival the palmetto's popularity—the single star that was taken up, at one time or another, by each of the seceding states. Several writers have traced the history of this icon to the West Florida rebellion of 1810 and then to the famous "Lone Star" of the Texas Republic, a banner that had already acquired a set of lasting popular legends by 1845. What has been generally overlooked is how the single star symbols worked within conventions set by the American Stars and Stripes. In their first uses, these star symbols echoed the grammar of the American flag, offering the United States an implicit invitation to add a province detached from another government to their own constellation. The adoption of these single star flags during the secession crisis ran this process in reverse, as states "plucked" their stars, to use the language of Jefferson Davis, rather than face future consolidation into a single mass. Behind these symbolic gestures were the concrete commitments that underlay them, which in 1860 meant fending off any threat to slavery that might result from a shift in the country's political direction. What was to be overthrown, secessionists agreed, was the relationship of one political community with its coequal partners. The primary reason for doing so was to preserve the social status quo, not to introduce basic change.[20]

Single star flags made claims for sovereignty in their imagery and in their practical use during the secession crisis. As slave republics left the Union one by one, they temporarily took on all the attributes of separate nationhood and thus quickly needed distinctive flags to symbolically convey sovereign authority. This was an especially urgent matter in the successful attempts to capture federal installations, a trend that began well before the formation of the Confederacy, and, in a few notable cases, even before states that occupied these forts had finalized secession. On each occasion, the American Stars and Stripes needed to be replaced by an emblem of state jurisdiction, which typically was either a single star flag or one that took an icon from the state seal. South Carolinians used the palmetto device, Louisianans flew the popular Pelican Flag over forts outside New Orleans, while Texas relied on the five-pointed Lone Star that had been transposed from the banner to its state seal in 1845. States like Georgia that had a less popularly recognized seal (and no tradition of state colors) were placed in a more awkward position. It was left to a committee of three to decide what new flag would replace the Stars and Stripes over

6.   Single-starred banners symbolized state possession of federal forts like
     Castle Pickney, which the Charleston militia occupied in the scene shown
     here from *Harper's Weekly*, January 12, 1861. Courtesy, Michigan State Uni-
     versity Libraries.

the Savannah arsenal, though such a formal process was rare during such moments of crisis. Citizens in Milledgeville merely hoisted what the press described as a "colonial flag"; those in Augusta raised a simple red star on a white
field. Above the U.S. Custom House in Savannah, a former Federal officer
displayed a banner featuring the "all-seeing eye," which had more to do with
Masonic tradition than with Georgia's own history.[21]

These improvised state flags might have been rendered obsolete with the
adoption of a new national banner for the Confederacy. As most expected, a
new Confederate administration operating in Montgomery quickly adopted a
flag and took responsibility for all the military and diplomatic functions that
the United States had earlier exercised. As such, the curious vacuum that separate secessions had created was soon filled. Yet, significantly, most of the states
held on to the flags that had been endowed with a special status by their
secession conventions. Some argued that their retention would heighten awareness of shared responsibilities between state and Confederate authority. On
the eve of the Confederate convention, the *Charleston Courier* explained how

a system of state flags might prevent "the violation or neglect of the federative principle," which it considered, as had Jefferson Davis, the "fatal error in the old Union." Flying both state and national colors simultaneously, the paper suggested, would be "one mode of asserting distinctly and conspicuously this principle and educating all officers and citizens into its perpetual recognition." What would eventually become routine—the flying of state and national flags at the same time—was conceptually new in 1861. One of the first trials for such a display was Fort Sumter, where both the palmetto banner and the Confederate Stars and Bars replaced the American flag in mid-April. In the months that followed, every one of the seceding states adopted its own distinctive flag, bringing the number of southern state banners created during the 1860s to a total of thirteen.[22]

The choice of a design for a particular flag was only the first step in realizing a banner's emotional potential. These emblems were occasionally subjected to ritual action, such as the practice of "moistening" a resistance banner with spirits, as if christening a ship. Banners were also sanctified by grandly unfolding and presenting them at official gatherings, such as state secession conventions. More typical than either of these were those communal actions in which patriotic crowds cheered the elevation of flags, sang songs in their honor, and made toasts and pledges on their behalf. Cumulatively, activities directed toward symbols of state resistance generated much of the emotional significance that these colors would take on through a coordinated flag culture.[23]

Music set the tempo for the secession winter, providing flag wavers a beat to accompany the forward march of events. The hoisting of the most important flags—those monumental pieces of bunting that were raised in the major squares and parks of the urban South—featured music as well as booming cannon, firing rifles, and rounds of cheers from the assembled audience. Brass horn ensembles and drums, often associated with a local military company, kept the passions of the crowd at a fever pitch, choosing recognized tunes such as the French "Marseillaise" and the popular minstrel song "Dixie" in order to extend the frenzy of the moment. The latter song's vogue at these flag ceremonies of secession winter extended an important connection between southern banners and musical scores that would intensify once lyrics were written explicitly to address the various emblems of the Confederate cause.[24]

The most notable musical creation of the secession period was Harry Macarthy's "Bonnie Blue Flag," which would become one of the most famous flag-related songs in all of American culture. The song was a Confederate sensation by the summer of 1861, becoming famous enough to inspire a steady series of replies and parodies from Unionists in the North. Macarthy later traced the inspiration for his effort to the presentation of single star flag on blue cloth at the Mississippi Secession Convention in Jackson. He recognized in this early January scene the perfect metaphor for the steady progress of secession. When "our rights were threatened," he sang to the tune of a traditional Irish melody, "the cry rose near and far, / Hurrah for the Bonnie Blue Flag, that bears the Single Star!" The song continued by listing more and more southern states that resolved to adopt single-star flags to protect the "property we gain'd by honest toil." By the end of the process, and by the end of his song, he was left with a flag on which the number of these separate state stars "had grown to be eleven."[25]

As the origins of the "Bonnie Blue Flag" demonstrate, flag presentation ceremonies could provide performers with new cloth props to use in their own acts. Macarthy was not the only professional actor to bring the secession-era craze for banners indoors to the stage, though he arguably did so with the greatest effect. In the years to come, he made the "Bonnie Blue Flag"—both the song and the accompanying banner—the true star of his "personation concerts." Building upon this phenomenal success, Macarthy soon added other flag-related songs to skits he and his wife, Lottie Estelle, presented across the South until 1864, when Macarthy fled North to elude the Confederate draft. His songs were clearly written with dramatic performance in mind, and their scripts drew several imitators. One Florida soldier had vivid memories of watching a performance of the "Bonnie Blue Flag"; the actor-singer slowly unrolled a blue banner until, at the completion of the last chorus, he grandly flipped the single-starred flag to reveal the reverse image of eleven stars, representing a new southern constellation. This gesture caused those present to "at once lose their reason," and for ten full minutes the entire audience "sprang to their feet, rushed forward frantically waving their caps and wildly gesticulating, some out of joy beating comrades with fists, others embracing and kissing, still others shouting and yelling like mad men." This "scene of bedlam" resulted, the soldier later recalled, not merely from the defiant words of the song, but from the occasion of being with other volunteers at an army training camp, and from the "highly dramatic rendition of the whole recitation."[26]

Other secession-era performances also used flags to enhance the emotional appeal of their acts. In the week before Alabamians voted for secession delegates, the English actress Maggie Mitchell rounded out a Montgomery performance with a burst of flag gestures. Receiving a "lone star" Alabama flag from the theater manager at the end of her play, she then performed a new "southern" version of the "Marseillaise" as a flurry of various resistance flags appeared behind her. She ended the rousing song by pulling down an actual Stars and Stripes banner that hung from a theater box and stomping it to the wild cheers of the appreciative audience. In Charleston, meanwhile, Christy's Minstrels, a northern troupe of blackface entertainers, made the palmetto flag the highlight of their acts, in part to alleviate suspicion about their loyalties. Similar scenes marked the New Orleans theater, which had already recast the minstrel tune "Dixie" into a song of southern rights. John H. Hewitt, who would become the single most important figure in Confederate theater, seized upon the dramatic

7.   Best known for "The Bonnie Blue Flag" of the secession period, the actor Harry Macarthy toured the Confederacy for most of the Civil War. He is shown here with his wife, Lottie Estelle, who accompanied Macarthy's patriotic performances. Courtesy, American Antiquarian Society.

possibility of flags in a series of tributes to the South's various banners, first performing them on the Richmond stage and then circulating their lyrics through newspapers and broadsides and their original musical scores through sheet music.[27]

The use of flags in southern theater was not just a simple case of art imitating life. Public ceremonies such as the one that inspired the "Bonnie Blue Flag" were themselves careful pieces of stagecraft. The scene at the Mississippi convention that so inspired Macarthy seemed to have been planned for weeks by a group of female patriots who coordinated their efforts to design and construct an oversized banner and then choreograph the proper moment to present it to elected officials. The Mississippi women unfurled their flag immediately after disunion had been officially enacted, as was the case with similar female presentations that took place at state conventions meeting in Montgomery, Austin, Tallahassee, and Baton Rouge. The Alabama flag, whose story is better documented than any other, was a particularly elaborate production and was accompanied by appropriate fanfare. After planning for this flag's creation since early November, women presented this twenty-foot banner to delegates on January 14. The gesture was understood by one delegate as an effort by passionate women to "import to our veins the burning currents of their own enthusiasm!" Having witnessed those "graceful devices of female ingenuity" featured on the banner, he hoped that the emblem would continue to "lift us up to the height of their own hallowed inspiration!"[28]

The joyful tears that were reportedly shed at such decisive moments were induced in part by relief, as the unsettling uncertainty of political crisis gave way to the reality of disunion. Yet the way in which sovereignty was made visible by previously hidden cloth designs, unfolded by enthusiastic young women at just the right moment, was a highly charged gesture that could capitalize on the moment even more successfully than professional drama could. The new state flags signaled that local women stood by their men in striking out in a new direction, just as flag presentations to military companies would signal solidarity between the sexes in months to come. But during secession winter, flags were the clearest representation of a new central power, which in itself imbued such symbols with a mystical aura. Observers of these state flags were seeing before their eyes the emergence of a new member of the international community. Unlike later military flag ceremonies in local communities, which were overshadowed with the prospect of imminent death and sacrifice, the key metaphor in these earlier scenes was birth, providing the women who staged them a clear maternal role, or at least that of midwife.[29]

Birth of new communities meant the death of the old Union, a fact that caused sadness to be mixed with exhilaration when secession emblems were first sighted. Writing decades after the war, John Sergeant Wise still found it "impossible to describe the feelings with which I saw the stars and stripes hauled down from the custom house, and the Virginia state flag run up in their place." He explained that "never until then had I fully realized that this step involved in making the old flag" that he had loved into "the flag of an enemy." He seems not to have exaggerated, since other reflections made at the time similarly register how freely tears flowed when the American flag came down and how even "those most anxious for action" reacted to the news with a "pang."[30]

In an ode popularly known as "Ethnogenesis," Henry Timrod captured what these new sovereign flags conveyed. Though addressed to the Confederate Congress, his poem evoked the decisive moment that disunion was enacted by each of the states. "Hath not the morning dawned with added Light?" he asked: "Will not evening call another star / Out of the infinite regions of the night. / To work this day in Heaven?" To such questions, the clear answer was that:

At last, we are
A nation among nations and the world
Shall soon behold in many a distant port
Another flag unfurled!

In this rendition nationhood was not the culmination of slow organic growth, but the sudden determination to present new symbols for all the world to see.[31]

Timrod's lines made clear that the aura of a new flag depended on garnering respect from the larger international community. His selection of a naval scene was an appropriate metaphor in this regard, since the sovereign authority of banners had strong historical links with the rules of the open sea. Flags that had long been the tools of military units and dynastic authority had become associated with nation-states primarily through the necessities of early modern sea-borne trade, when elaborate naval signals were codified. The several contemporary accounts of secession flags hoisted above outbound boats continued this long international history of the use of national colors, as secessionists imagined the ambitious scope of the new sort of politics they had undertaken.[32] Particularly revealing in this regard was the story of the *James Gray*, which raised the palmetto flag in Charleston Harbor the day after Lincoln's election. The ship captain caught popular attention by announcing that he would carry a cargo of cotton under this new banner to England, thereby forcing the British to recognize South Carolina's entry into the community of nations. When informed of these plans, British officials recognized that allowing a ship carrying the palmetto ensign into their port would "encourage the Southerners to further acts of a secessional character." The Law Offices of the Crown decided to avoid any precipitate action, resolving to treat the *James Gray* as a United States vessel, as long as its papers were in order. Their decision would have frustrated the captain's plans even as it also meant to deprive Unionists of what would have been an enormously satisfying humiliation of the new Carolina colors.[33]

In the end, neither the *James Gray* nor any other ship carrying state flags would cross the Atlantic. Confederate naval ensigns, which would be seen abroad regularly during the next four years, were a different matter. When the British and other Europeans granted Confederates belligerent status, and thus the ability to wage regular war as a de facto government, southern naval regalia received a special status on the sea. This leveled the playing field with the more powerful Union fleet, providing a range of rights that rebel ships acquired as legitimate vessels. Yet perhaps just as important, the image of a new Confederate flag being carried to the far reaches of the ocean from the top of masts swelled pride in the grandeur of the southern initiative. Not only were these incidents widely reported in the press; they inspired several poetic images of new colors striking out "where the eternal billows roam," as one verse put it. On these trips, southern symbols showed the rest of the world that something special had happened in North America.[34]

State flags carried to the loyal states during the winter of 1861 conveyed a different message altogether. Rather than seeking respect, the display of rebel colors to enemies was clearly meant to spark disturbance. Unionists saw little difference between the most incendiary resistance flags and the least objectionable state banners; both explicitly insulted the authority of the Stars and Stripes, and for this reason alone were considered emblems of treason. State flags did not even have to be southern to be considered dangerous. In California, the reemergence of the Bear Flag, after a hibernation of more than a decade, stirred the concerns of the U.S. army and sparked a huge rally in San Francisco for the Union cause and the Stars and Stripes. In eastern cities like Philadelphia, Boston, New Haven, and the port of Baltimore, the display of palmetto banners caused several small riots. Those who were spoiling for a fight soon learned that flags had the ability to bring forth curses from enemies that were every bit as heart-felt as the adulation offered to them by friends. While Confederate flags would soon become the primary symbols of treason, this pattern was set by state colors in the first stages of disunion.[35]

With a few minor exceptions, states that remained loyal to the Union did not adopt official state flags until the early twentieth century. In this, the secession period left a divided legacy between the flag cultures of the North and the South. As late as 1891, the former president Rutherford B. Hayes still remembered with disgust the "rabble of flags" chosen by each of those states that had attempted to leave the Union. Speaking before the Loyal Legion of New York, he ridiculed the idea that these wayward states had ever needed their own symbols. One of the achievements of Union victory, he believed, was the vindication of a Stars and Stripes that was good enough for all Americans. If secessionists had gotten their way, he darkly warned, there would be no fewer than forty-four sets of colors waving between Canada and Mexico. Worse still, "each would represent a separate government, a separate army, and a separate navy, and all of them would wave helplessly and miserably over 'States discordant, dissevered, belligerent!' "[36]

Frank DeBow worried in mid-November of 1860 that there were "too many flags hung out" in Charleston, a development that he considered "unnecessary show" and mere "excitement," rather than "real solid substance." Other southern conservatives shared his anxiety about faceless urban crowds waving banners, wearing cockades, and singing songs of rebellion. The history of Europe over the preceding seventy years provided ample evidence that popular revolutions were more easily begun than controlled, and that such upheavals had an unnerving tendency to take on a momentum of their own. The possibility that forces driving secession might spin out of control caused Senator James Henry Hammond to despair at the "scenes of the French Revolution" that were reported in his own state of South Carolina. Trying to quiet his own long-standing fears of disorder, Hammond made the case, perhaps only half believing it himself, that the days to come were likely to witness "a great change, but not a revolution according to the political definition of that word usually recognized."[37]

The secession conventions selected to govern during this crisis were intent on quieting such fears. Once the urgent calls for disunion had yielded their proper results, many considered it time to place an emphasis on legitimacy rather than on fervor. The Reverend James Henley Thornwell, a staunch Unionist before Lincoln's election, marked this transition by contrasting "the stirring scenes with which the streets of Charleston were alive" late in 1860 with the "calm and quiet sanctuary" where the South Carolina convention solemnly dissolved the Union. Ignoring the Jacobin language that cropped up occasionally within this chamber, Thornwell focused on how a "body of sober, grave, and venerable men . . . deliberated without passions" as they "sat with closed doors" so that "the tumult of the populace might not invade the sobriety of their minds." Both the mobs in the street and the statesmen at the convention involved themselves with selecting the right flags for their cause. But the spirit of the provocative, defiant banners that flew outside was brought under the control by restrained, reasonable authority that selected emblems worthy of conveying dignity and quiet resolve.[38]

Discomfort with popular radicalism seemed to have the greatest immediate effect in Louisiana, where the selection of a new state flag became a means of distancing the convention from earlier crowd actions. The pelican banner, which featured the state seal of a female bird feeding her young, had been taken up during mass demonstrations in New Orleans and Baton Rouge as a popular rebuke to Lincoln's election. As this flag became more prominent, one patriot was even inspired to plead in verse:

Fling to the Southern wind
The banner with its type of motherhood;
Home, hearth, and friends within its folds we bind
In one strong, mighty cord of brotherhood.

When the state secession convention assembled, however, there developed a consensus among the delegates that while the "flags on the street" had roused considerable enthusiasm, something more noble than a bird "filthy in habit, cowardly in nature, and unsightly in form" was needed to replace it. Sensing the latent Union sentiment among Louisiana's leading citizens, the convention decided to retain stripes that had not been spoiled by the "discord, dissension, and frenzied hate" sweeping the country. Rather than merely copy the red and white from the American flag, the convention adopted blue stripes, to represent the state's French heritage, and explicitly linked the red stripes with the period of Spanish dominion rather than with republicanism. This tribute to empire did feature the single star of separate statehood, but the design was less attuned to generating popular enthusiasm than with rivaling the majesty of the American flag.[39]

Other radical symbols that might have taken the secession movement in new, dangerous directions were tamed in more modest ways. The several versions of the "Southern Marseillaise," for instance, replaced the conspiratorial kings of the original French lyrics with a denunciation of outside disturbers of order. Though the rousing revolutionary tune remained the same, Maggie Mitchell called out to the "white men" in her audience to beware of "vile, insatiate robbers." With the same decidedly proslavery slant that appeared in other Confederate versions of the French anthem, she sang:

> Now, now, the abolition storm is rolling,
> Which treacherous States, fanatic, raise;
> Their dogs of war, let loose, are howling,
> And Texian cities burn and blaze!

Other secessionists even tried to strip the cockade of its Jacobin associations. A Mobile editor reassured his readers in the week following Lincoln's election that there was nothing "secret, illegal, or improper" about these pieces of ribbon, which merely expressed "loyalty to the [state] government and laws thereof." Such decorations might stir the patriotic blood, this writer admitted, but nothing about them should deny them "the respect of conscientious, conservative and patriotic citizens."[40]

DeBow, Thornwell, Hammond, and other southern conservatives might have eased their own anxieties by denying the radical content of secession winter. But their desire to wish away the frenzy of the moment was ultimately futile. Once flag passions had been aroused, there was little that such sober leaders could do about the hoisting of rebellious banners or the singing of defiant songs. The revolutionary tone of southern symbols would become less threatening in the years to come. But these were subdued largely through the exigencies of governing and of fighting a war with the same sort of cloth symbols that had earlier helped to accomplish a political revolution. As banners helped southerners break their patriotic ties with the United States, they also set the standards of a multimedia flag culture that would nurture Confederate nationalism. A popular patriotism that spread across the South in these few weeks thus became one of the most important legacies of a crisis of disunion marked by both symbolic creativity and emotional intensity.

CHAPTER THREE

Selecting and Singing a
New Constellation

EVEN BEFORE THE PROCESS of secession had fully run its course, a new symbolic challenge emerged within the South. Confederates early in 1861 began to consider how they might not just overcome the cultural power of the American Stars and Stripes, but match it with a national flag of their own. The founders of a new southern republic needed something more than the quick and impulsive frenzy that secession banners had called forth. Soon after meeting to form a government, they sought a defining emblem capable of nurturing deep attachments and inspiring steadfast devotion to face the difficulties that lay ahead. The necessity of replacing the Star Spangled Banner raised difficult questions about the new country's immediate future. The initial outcome of this process, the adoption of a Stars and Bars flag strikingly reminiscent of the Stars and Stripes, would not be a long-term success. But this first national banner began a series of important conversations about how new symbols for the Confederacy would be chosen and how love for a new and untested government could be cultivated through a cloth embodiment of collective honor and dignity.

Adopting and celebrating a new national flag was not a trivial concern, as southerners who were drawn into the process appreciated. Those who stood apart from the proceedings and looked upon them without passion could see how this activity mattered. William Howard Russell of the *London Times* offered such a perspective when, in the aftermath of the North's own rush to the colors in April of 1861, he ventured a stunning prediction. "If ever there is a real *sentiment du drapeau* got up in the South," he wrote the week after hostilities had begun, "it will be difficult indeed for the North to restore the Union."

Confederates might still level the symbolic playing field, Russell realized, by developing its own flag cult as powerful as to the craze for "Old Glory" that swept the North after the bombardment of Fort Sumter. Seeing how symbols touched a popular chord among Americans, Russell appreciated how outward displays could be internalized and made an important means of bolstering core convictions. "These pieces of coloured bunting seem to twine themselves through heart and brain," he explained, memorably expressing how national flags touched Americans when they faced moments of crisis.[1]

At the time that Russell offered these reflections, ordinary white men and women across the South had already involved themselves in the creation of a *sentiment du drapeau* by submitting a range of flag designs to the Provisional Congress meeting in Montgomery. Their participation in the unofficial contest came at a good time for the founders of the Confederacy, who were hindered from the outset by questions concerning their own legitimacy and the direction that they would take the new southern union. Yet over the course of the next two years, those politicians responsible for the choice of symbols would yield the initiative to citizens and to writers for the major southern newspapers. A popular flag culture sustained the link between the people and their banners, especially as the national flag became a primary theme in patriotic verse and music. As a new banner quickly situated itself at the emotional heart of Confederate nationalism, the passion for colors that Russell had contemplated became a reality. What was still unclear was whether the Stars and Bars—or any other Confederate flag—could match the emotional resonance of the American Stars and Stripes.

The excitement that swirled through Montgomery in early February of 1861 was accompanied by the sober recognition of the enormous challenges that lay ahead. Delegates who gathered in the Alabama capital were charged with adopting a new federal constitution, a task that had not been undertaken since 1787, and with laying the cultural basis for a new nation that faced almost certain war. This ambitious agenda was compromised from the beginning by a series of complicating factors. Delegates lacked a popular mandate, since none had been elected to their positions and each of them, save the South Carolinians, represented states that had been badly split on the basic question of disunion. The near future was even more divisive than the immediate past, since there was no consensus over what policies the new government should undertake. Across a range of issues, the most pressing decisions involved either continuing earlier norms or departing from them. To heighten the tensions, this basic choice was closely bound up with a struggle between those who wanted to replicate the government of the United States and those who wanted to articulate proslavery ideas in the new republic more explicitly than ever before.[2]

The Provisional Congress faced its job by carefully cultivating a public tone of calm deliberation and broaching nearly all the controversial issues behind the closed doors of secret sessions. This attempt to cloak differences in secrecy was disrupted, if only momentarily, during the convention's second week, when the question of a new national flag generated the first open display of tempers. Representative Walker Brooke of Mississippi, himself a former Unionist, precipitated the sharp, short debate on February 13 when he took up a matter of "much importance" that should be "acted upon immediately." Having witnessed the presentation by colleagues of flag designs over the previous four sessions, Brooke wanted to do his part to shape the debate. Eliciting only faint applause from the staunchly radical audience, Brooke passionately urged members to adopt a banner "as similar as possible to the flag of the United States," changing it only enough to "distinguish one easily from the other." William Porcher Miles, a fire-eating radical from South Carolina, drew a far more enthusiastic round of cheers by immediately denouncing Brooke and condemning what he sensed was "the undertone of a desire to reconstruct with the U.S. government."[3]

Brooke's call to emulate the Stars and Stripes provoked this rebuke precisely because his plea had been heard before. The moderate New Orleans press had already argued that southerners should keep the American flag even if they left the United States. The "sacred associations" of a symbol that had helped incorporate the Mississippi Valley into a continental empire should be preserved, one of the city's dailies wrote, since they "cluster around every patriot's heart and are all intertwined with its best affections." Another paper focused on the anthem to the "Star Spangled Banner," noting that not only had it been written by a Marylander, but had "burst upon the world when the whole country was slaveholding." Contrasting the military service of southerners with that of the supposedly less patriotic Yankees, one Atlanta paper echoed such arguments, urging, "Let not its prestige and glory be claimed by those who have fought against every step of our national progress." By keeping the flag, it continued, the Confederacy could hold on to "the glorious emblem of a white nationality." Another paper acknowledged that even if some minor changes were necessary, Congress should "make as little alteration in the starry banner as the circumstances will permit—not enough to destroy its American character, or the thousand recollections of patriotic devotion, pride, and enthusiasm that are inseparably bound up with, and must ever remain a part of it."[4]

In Montgomery, Brooke echoed these nostalgic pleas for the American flag almost verbatim, grandly explaining how "time [could] never efface or grow dim" those memories that the Stars and Stripes brought forth for most white southerners. He offered several more general points to his fellow congressmen, urging, as earlier conservatives had, that "in revolutionary times it is desirable to make as little change as possible in those things to which the people have long been accustomed." A body selected to serve the people should "respect even their prejudices," he counseled, since such feelings were "not those merely of custom or habit," but those "of association" over two generations of history. He took the same cautious line in matters of policy, consistently opposing secret sessions, radical efforts to reopen the Atlantic slave trade, and the restriction of free states from membership in the Confederacy. It was his plea for continuity in symbols, however, that gained him the most publicity. His argument that southerners should stake a claim in the "emblem of the former glory, strength and power of our nation" registered a response far beyond the halls of Congress. He made a compelling case by a straightforward claim that "we . . . as well as the Northern Confederacy, have an interest in its past history" and that "there is no reason why the North should appropriate that flag to itself."[5]

Brooke's resolution exemplified the paradox that North and South had by 1860 become "separated by a common nationalism," to use the historian David Potter's classic formulation. Americans on both sides of the Mason-Dixon line paid homage to the same set of revolutionary heroes and legends, while they also basked in the common glory of an American flag that had increased its stars from thirteen to thirty-three in the years since independence. Shared traditions of American patriotism were a powerful antidote to sectional particularism, which was often condemned as narrow selfishness. Contesting regional claims to national ideas was thus a potent strategy, especially since local interests and national traditions could nearly always be made to coincide, at least at the rhetorical level. Repeatedly, the key challenge involved claiming the American heritage as the preserve of one's own state or section while blocking rivals from doing the same. To frame the political debates of the 1850s and the subsequent civil war as a contest over the true owner of American nationalism does not imply a bland consensus. Indeed, the struggle between different interpretations of shared American ideas made this a high-stakes conflict, whose outcome seemed to involve the destiny of the entire hemisphere, if not the world.[6]

The latent feelings that existed in the South for traditional American symbols perturbed William Porcher Miles, who would use his chairmanship of the Congressional Committee on Flag and Seal over the next year to lobby incessantly for a wholly different flag from that of the United States. In his response to Brooke, he lamented the "over-estimate" that his fellow southerners placed on "the glories of the flag of the United States," especially since he had learned during his own fire-eating childhood that this was "not a friendly flag" but the "flag of a hostile Government." He preferred the palmetto banner, whose Revolutionary antecedents he did not have to read about, as Jefferson Davis had done a few weeks earlier. If Confederates wished to emulate the Founding Fathers, they should appreciate the "great reluctance and pain" they experienced in relinquishing their British inheritance. In living up to a revolutionary tradition, southerners needed to see that the only way to be true to the spirit of the past was to break those "many ties hard to sunder" and to forget those "many memories difficult to erase."[7]

Miles recognized that his tough-minded advice could not be forced upon average citizens. His sharp attack on the American flag made clear that it was up to southerners themselves, not their leaders, to make the final disavowal of previous emotional commitments. As if recognizing the limits of his own input, he faulted Brooke's resolution for its premature attempt to usurp the work of his own committee, which was "to receive suggestions from all quarters." As models and designs continued to pour in, Miles made sure to thank those "patriotic citizens who have been so industriously employed" and assured them that even if each could not be discussed on the floor of Congress, his committee would give serious consideration to them all. Petitioners themselves claimed that "in these stirring times" it was the "privilege" and perhaps the "duty" for "each citizen to cast his mite in all matters of public interest." While delegates might have conducted most of their business among themselves, they gave special consideration to the public when it came to choosing symbols for the new collective cause.[8]

The charged public exchange between Brooke and Miles came in the middle of a week when flags had become the "engrossing topic of discussion" in Montgomery. The upturn of interest in symbols coincided with a lull in other activity. Representatives had already framed a constitution, taken their oaths, and now awaited the arrival of Jefferson Davis from his Mississippi plantation. During this interim, delegates realized that presenting flags on the floor of the Congress might provide the satisfying patriotic oratory that spectators desired and that secret sessions had prevented. A round of daily flag speeches, performed with the requisite patriotic flourishes, continued for several weeks, after which the public balconies were cleared and representatives debated policy among themselves. These speeches, and the practice of hanging the most popular models in the galleries, elicited interest from well beyond those who attended the ongoing drama in Montgomery. As the newspaper press covered the steady stream of designs, dozens of patriots entered an informal contest to choose a new flag, often making quite striking claims about the nature of their new government. The patriotic oratory of Confederate congressmen focused less on the content presented to them than on the spirit of inspiration that came from average citizens. Although the Congress itself was as a body with questionable claims to popular legitimacy, these glowing flag speeches allowed delegates to show that the people themselves were taking control and defining the most visible evidence of having a new country.[9]

Popular participation in this theatrical process of flag selection required that some on the committee settle for a design nearer to the Stars and Stripes than they would have preferred. In making his committee's report, Miles ventured well beyond his earlier critique of the Star Spangled Banner, paying particular attention to the practical difficulties of adopting a design that was likely to be

8. Speeches about flag designs sent to the Montgomery Congress were open to the public, unlike most matters taken up by Congress. The print, from *Frank Leslie's* of March 2, 1861, shows one of the several flag designs featuring a cross. Courtesy, Michigan State University Libraries.

confused with that of a potential enemy. Yet he admitted that "something was conceded" to the "strong and earnest desire to retain at least a suggestion of the old 'Stars and Stripes.'" The design finally chosen in early March of 1861 contained the same blue field and the same white stars to represent the number of states that had joined the new Confederacy. The major departure was the reduced number of stripes, from thirteen to three, which the Montgomery papers quickly dubbed "Bars" to distinguish them from the Yankee "Stripes." Brooke, who had been silenced by Miles's rebuke a scant two weeks earlier, provided the last major flag speech in Congress. "The tears may glisten in the eyes of many who witness the diminished number of the stars and stripes" he explained, with an echo of his earlier speech. "Yet, sir," he added, "they are tears of memories past, to be succeeded by the smiles of a brighter and better future."[10]

The gesture toward continuity in the choice of the Stars and Bars followed the choice of a constitution similar to that framed in 1787 and the selection as president of Jefferson Davis, that American hero of the Mexican War. Radical efforts to devise a more overtly proslavery republic were blunted by adoption of a governing framework similar to that of the United States. Many in the more moderate southern press applauded this result. One Georgia paper that had counseled such continuity congratulated the Confederate Congress on choosing a flag that bore "a sufficient resemblance to the old one to keep in everlasting remembrance the glorious deeds achieved beneath its fold." Another joined a chorus of papers who were "rejoicing to know the old emblems float over us." The retention of the same basic elements and colors was appropriate, since it was "under them that *our* commerce has sought the seas, and *our* soldiers and sailors have encountered victoriously all dangers." Those who had earlier condemned flag models based on the Stars and Stripes as "distasteful, not to say disagreeable" were silent, at least for the time being. Soon enough, however, charges would again be leveled against this first flag and the spirit of imitation it conveyed.[11]

The same day that the Provisional Congress opened its business in Montgomery, Robert Gilchrist sat down in Charleston to write a letter. While other correspondents were flooding the Confederate Congress with requests for patronage or with unsolicited policy suggestions, Gilchrist had a loftier goal in mind. He proclaimed in the short note that accompanied a model banner that he was "ambitious of being the author of the new flag, which will float over every sea, protect the citizens of the proudest nation on the earth." Over the next month, more than 120 other individuals would send designs for a new national flag to Montgomery, entering what became an informal competition to select the Confederacy's first national symbol. Over half of these submissions, which are now housed in the National Archives, contained lengthy descriptions of why flags were sent and of what effect their designers hoped the banners would evoke as a national symbol. Though this sample may be incomplete, these comments and the models that accompanied them provide the best available evidence of southerners' sentiments about national flags at the outset of the Confederacy.[12]

Gilchrist was one of the very first to send in his idea, which may account for his unusually ambitious tone. His emphasis on his own fame would be matched only by the self-serving campaign of Jacob Platt of Augusta, Georgia, who lobbied friends to support his design and who then put Congress on notice that he would contest "any surreptitious adoption of my really original idea to the injury of my just claims." Far more typical, however, was the note struck by Ed Emerick Sell, who admitted, "To be the author of the standard for that glorious Confederacy is about more than a humble citizen like myself would hope for." A spirit of supplication ran through most of these flag offerings, which usually presented themselves as free of all self-interest or self-aggrandizement. One anonymous writer registered a typical "unwillingness to thrust myself before the eyes of the great" before inviting President Davis to burn the offering if it proved unworthy. Joseph Shellman likewise identified himself as "a plain, unpretending man, who has now, for the first time, ventured to obtrude his views on any public." He realized that his sketch—a simple transposition of colors from the American flag—might not be acceptable, in which case he urged Congress, "Please suppress it."[13]

Southern women who offered flag designs were particularly self-effacing in their letters. "I need not speak of the extreme gratification it would afford me was [my design] adopted" Julia Boutheneau confessed to delegate Laurence Keitt of South Carolina. But while she predicted her son's pride if her flag were chosen, she wanted to "assure you I am far from expecting or even hoping such a result." Barred by her sex from "leaping to the guns," she considered her design as merely a way for her to "contribute even a mite in aid of the glorious Cause" and to supply evidence that her heart was "overflowing with patriotism." A "Lady of Georgia," similarly thought her "bright gay and cheerful" magnolia design deserved every consideration. Yet she too was even more concerned about proving to the world that "our Beloved South" held "a dear place in the hearts and minds of her children." Mrs. C. Ladd of South Carolina conveyed her idea for a flag along with a statement of willingness to offer up her two sons to the army. In both instances, she recognized that a "mother's jewels" should be "freely given when needed." Along with her family and her artistic inspiration, Ladd sent her "prayers and sympathies" and the confidence that all true southern women would be willing to do likewise.[14]

Expressions of sacrificial female duty were well suited to the uplifting oratory of the Confederacy's early days. As a result, female participation in this informal flag contest became a significant theme, even though most of these

TABLE 3.1
Identifiable Flag and Seal Petitioners to the Montgomery Congress,
February–March 1861

Gender	Number	Percentage of Total (N = 100)
Men	70	70
Women	13	13
Gender-neutral pseudonym	17	17

Residence	Number	Percentage of Total (N = 84)
South Carolina	38	45
Charleston	27	32
Alabama	12	14
Georgia	12	14
Louisiana	7	8
Mississippi	4	5
Washington, D.C.	3	4
Virginia	2	2
Tennessee	2	2
Other (KY, PA, NY, UK)	4	5

SOURCE: Confederate Flag Designs, Record Group 109, National Archives.

designs were sent by men (see table 3.1). Delegates themselves paid considerably more attention to female contributions in their speeches on the floor of Congress, often merely forwarding the efforts of male designers to Miles's committee without public comment. In presenting Ladd's design, W. W. Boyce was especially effusive, claiming that her gesture was "worthy of Rome in her best days." He predicted that "as long as our women are impelled by these sublime sentiments," then "the lustrous stars of our unyielding Confederacy will never pale their glorious fires." The press also gave greater attention to women's efforts in the flag speeches they chose to publish and the designs they chose to describe. As a result, women became linked to flag designing, whereas previous patriotic conventions had emphasized female responsibilities in sewing and presenting banners that had been first designed by men.[15]

South Carolinians contributed a surprisingly large number of designs, accounting collectively for more letters than from the rest of the seceded states put together. In this, they continued the symbolic leadership they had displayed during the secession crisis, a fact graphically conveyed by the half-dozen letters sent to Congress on palmetto flag stationery. Boutheneau, who was one of twenty-seven designers from Charleston alone, reported that her relatively late start put her at a disadvantage, since local flagmakers who could have helped put her idea onto cloth were backlogged for weeks. A major effort to produce cloth symbols continued in the city, with palmetto banners and national prototypes competing with a bevy of regimental colors that would soon be presented to local troops. Boutheneau was forced to make up a pattern into silk herself, which she forwarded to the Congress by express after first sending two lengthy written descriptions of what she had in mind. Besides heralding her own design, her letters criticized the "Southern Cross" motif that Gilchrist and several other Charlestonians had suggested. In doing so, she joined a contentious local debate about this cross symbol, which would eventually be featured on the best known of all Confederate flags.[16]

Those who demanded the sharpest break from the past introduced the question of slavery into this initial consideration of national symbols. Here again, the lead was taken by Carolinians, who had recently ventured an important attempt to depict slaves as the source of their state's wealth and power. Several months before secession, the commission for a new South Carolina statehouse had been awarded to Henry Kirke Brown, a New Englander with well-documented antislavery convictions. This strange collaboration between the Yankee artist and the Carolina political elite rested on a common commitment to "exposing slavery," as the art historian Kirk Savage has recently explained. The pediment that Brown designed featured seven African American slaves, making it an extremely rare depiction of black southerners in visual culture. Though the Civil War interrupted the work, and caused a different design to be adopted during Reconstruction, this incident showed how a sculptor like Brown might draw negative attention to southern bondage through his public art. Those who commissioned the work apparently were undaunted by the possibility of a hostile outside reaction. As sectional relations worsened, they were confident that they could withstand the dangers associated with trumpeting their institution and the central place it occupied in their culture.[17]

F. Gaston of Columbia, South Carolina, was ready to undertake a similarly audacious display of proslavery principles through one of the most striking designs for a new Confederate flag. In a sketch and accompanying letter, Gaston described to "fellow patriots" how the incorporation of red, white, and black bands on a new flag would be "emblematic of these three races of our people." With a potential alliance with Native Americans in sight, red was closest to the staff, with white stars over this field. Then, on the fly of the proposed flag, a white bar in the top half conveyed the "superiority of the Anglo-Saxon," while a black bar beneath signaled the "determination to direct the negro to the gaining of our Southern Independence." This arrangement, accompanied by white stars for both the states and the master race, would "express the relative positions of distinct portions of the population in a political aspect" and make clear that Confederates were establishing a proudly proslavery republic. This design was not taken up publicly by any Confederate congressmen, probably because most knew that focusing attention on it would have set off a flurry of negative comments in the North. Not until the entire set of flag petitions was seized by Union officials at war's end would Gaston's effort be held up, by the Unionist Francis Lieber, as visual evidence of the rebellion's "absurdity, coarseness, and ignorance."[18]

The silence of Congress and the press about all four of the proslavery flags sent to Montgomery in the spring of 1861 is one example of how Confederates selectively disassociated their new government from slavery. As the historian Charles Dew has recently showed, slaveholders were most candid about their proslavery convictions when speaking directly to one another. Placing black on a flag that would represent the cause to the entire world was more risky. Such an attempt to broadcast their slave society openly and proudly would have helped their most avowed enemies to link the new nation to a controversial institution. An emblem of the Deep South slaveocracy would surely have alienated Europe, where slavery was widely discredited, and might also have had an effect on border states like Virginia and Tennessee, where commitment to the plantation economy was less pronounced than it was among the original members of the Confederacy. Henry Kirke Browne had been aware that proslavery iconography would stir negative feelings against the South as he designed the new capital in Columbia. Lieber's response to a proslavery flag sent by Gaston in 1865 proved this diagnosis correct.[19]

Even before the Civil War began, Confederate symbols served as a way of deflecting attention from the crucial issues of slavery and race that defined the sectional crisis between North and South. Designs like Gaston's that featured black slavery too openly were largely ignored by the Montgomery Congress, just as proslavery flags suggested over the succeeding two years would be. Chairman Miles wanted even to eliminate the "black" associations of the Stars and Stripes, explaining in his flag report of March 1861 that the American flag had been "pilfered and appropriated by a free Negro community and a race of savages," in providing Liberia and Samoa with models for their own national standards. The whitewashing of Confederate symbols would be pursued most aggressively during the postwar period, when a focus on battlefield sacrifice would cleanse battle symbols of their associations with the politics of a proslavery rebellion. These efforts would continue, as the organized efforts of today's pro–Confederate flag heritage groups make clear. This persistent quest to avoid racial themes in Confederate symbols was an attempt to obscure the important role that slavery played in precipitating the Civil War and in shaping nearly every aspect of Confederate politics and culture. Attempts to distance the southern rebellion from the South's most controversial institution were a tactical success. From the beginning, Confederates avoided anything that would link their rebellion to slavery too openly.[20]

Some designs were eliminated not for the controversy they might spark, but because they contained what Miles called "elaborate, complicated or fantastical" elements. Busy arrangements of snakes, palmettos, pelicans, crescents, sickles, phoenixes, globes, crowns, and chain links ran through a great many

9.   Among the approximately 120 designs sent to the Montgomery Congress, and
     are now held at the National Archives, was that of Mary Carpenter, shown
     here. Courtesy, National Archives.

of those designs sent to Congress. While several of these were quite interesting,
they were impossible to mass-produce and thus impractical. Some suggestions
seemed determined to combine as many symbols as possible on a single piece
of fabric. Mary Carpenter contributed one such flag, noting that her design
had originally been meant for the regimental colors of a local Georgia militia
company. In addition to stars and stripes, it portrayed a dove, an olive branch,
a heart, a sword, a cross, and that "all-seeing eye" that had been seen during
the secession crisis. All of these were arranged in a pattern that representative
Augustus Wright considered "the prettiest yet offered."[21]

A majority of contributions conveyed a sounder understanding of what
went into making banners and of how simplicity was preferable to clutter. It
became clear that originality was less important than the ability to compact
diffuse sentiments about collective purpose into easily recognizable form.
Whether employing the rules of heraldry, figural elements, or the example
of prior American practices, most designers knew that the main purpose of
the flag would be, in the words of one designer, to "express an idea" capable
of capturing for Confederate citizens what their new country was all about.
The need for careful consideration was urged again and again. "The destinies of our newborn Government are immeasurably great," one contributor
wrote, concluding that this required adopting "such majestic and gorgeous

symbols as are not only fit and beautiful emblems of the present, but grandly typify the power and beneficence, strength, triumph and expansion of its glorious future."[22]

Those designs taken most seriously by Congress employed a recognizable symbolic grammar that had been established by earlier American flag practices. These showed that a new departure did not necessarily need to leave all remnants of the past behind. Instead, designers realized if they rearranged familiar elements, the flag would change its syntax and thus send a new message. Similarities in arrangement outweighed differences, and the final selection of the Stars and Bars conveyed much of what was popularly assumed was worth keeping in a new flag. During the postwar period, a hotly contested dispute arose between two rival claimants for the honor of having designed the Stars and Bars. This was rather odd, given the fact that the Confederate public would soon roundly condemn this first national flag for its derivative character. Yet such postwar claims also misrepresented one of the most important aspects of this process as it unfolded in the spring of 1861. The Stars and Bars resulted not from a single act of genius, but from a collaborative and cumulative plea from constituents to retain some elements of their former flag while disregarding others. In this, change and continuity were held in tension. The new flag offered itself as an appropriate symbol to the newborn Confederacy, resolving the lingering uncertainties of what this new venture was all about by transposing the country's dilemma onto bunting.[23]

Tabulating these designs by their elements reveals a general consensus about what was most important to include in any new flag (See table 3.2). There was near unanimity that stars should represent each of the Confederacy's member states. J.B.D. DeBow was practically alone in his fierce opposition to these stars, making a clever argument that these "belong to the night," while "it is morning with us." Representing a new federal Union with a cluster of stars continued the motif of an earlier dissolving constellation that had assumed such significance in secession symbolism. While many writers explicitly associated the presence of a star for each state with federalism and a state's right to chart its own destiny, some also used a constellation to welcome future growth. The metaphor of a growing number of stars had long signaled the ability of the United States to expand membership in its Union, as star after star was added to a common field. Such flexibility was particularly attractive to Confederates in 1861, since it was unclear how many states the new country would encompass. Restricting membership to the original group of seven cotton states was sometimes urged, though pleas to include all fifteen slaves states, including faraway Delaware, were far more common. Anne Wightt, a southern sympathizer in Philadelphia, sent Jefferson Davis a flag that could contain even a greater number of stars, since she could not "help clinging to the hope that we might all be one again." From Brooklyn, a Louisiana native envisioned a flag with perhaps an even bigger constellation than that of the United States, hoping

TABLE 3.2
Designs for National Emblems Submitted to the Montgomery Congress,
February–March 1861

Design Element	Number	Percentage of Total (113)
Stars for states	107	95
Red, white, and blue	106	94
Stripes for states	49	43
Central star or sun	24	21
Cross feature	22	19
Objections to cross	9	8
Crescent	8	7
Birds	8	7
Circle or sphere	5	4
Plants or trees	5	4
Slavery emblem	4	4
"All-seeing eye"	4	4
Globe	3	3
Crown	3	3
Snakes	2	2
Links	1	1

SOURCE: Confederate Flag Designs, Record Group 109, National Archives.

as he did that it would float "over the grandest, richest republic of the world— the South, Cuba, and Mexico."[24]

Desire to retain red, white, and blue as the new flag's primary colors was nearly as popular as keeping the stars. One writer associated this color scheme with "republican forms of government," while another merely noted that these provided the best chromatic contrast to one another and were the most "showy" in their display. Most designers were less self-conscious, apparently assuming that these three were the only colors worthy to wave over southern Americans. The reallocation of the colors—making the stripes blue and the field red, for instance—was one of the most common ways of using identical elements to distinguish the new country's emblem from that of the old Union. A few designers wanted something bolder; at least two suggested that the seven stripes of the flag take on the colors of the rainbow. Those who wanted a reference to slavery in the flag, as we have seen, included at least some black. There were scattered references to purple and yellow as well, though there were not endowed with the same sort of symbolic importance as the other colors.[25]

Stripes were more controversial than either stars or the "republican tricolor," though they still appeared as an element in nearly half the designs. They were featured most often by those hoping to evoke the American flag. As one designer implored, "Change it, improve it, alter it as you will, but for Heaven's sake keep the stars *and* stripes." The public rebuke of Brooke apparently caused some designers to distance themselves from any lingering sympathy with the Union. A pair of young female students in Alabama apologetically asked delegates to "appreciate the difficulty" confronting them, as, "amidst all their efforts at originality," they were unable to escape the influence of "the star jemmed flag, with its parti-colored stripes, that floated so proudly over the late United States." Another designer explained that the beauty of the old flag, rather than its associations, was his primary motivation in copying it, urging Congress to adopt a banner "approximating, yet differing essentially from the flag of the United States." There was a plea for one model that "comes as near without resembling" the popular American banner, which would thus be "welcomed by those who feel warm-heartedness" toward their old country. Mary Brown hoped that her invocation of the Stars and Stripes would "still cause a throb of patriotism" as long as we "bear the name of Americans." In the actual design process, the apparent divergence between departure and continuity often became a matter of degree and interpretation, as such careful attempts to parse meanings made clear.[26]

Working with the same colors and elements allowed a great deal of room for those who wished to convey particular messages that might capture the new Confederacy's relationship to the United States. Several did so by honoring the leadership of South Carolina through the inclusion of a palmetto or a crescent. Others paid homage to the six original member states either by featuring six-sided stars or by including six "permanent" stripes, just as the American flag had retained a tribute to the thirteen colonies in its design. One Alabama designer proposed that the Congress "secede from the Union to the center" by placing the blue field of stars as a circle in the middle of the flag, rather than in the upper-left-hand corner. Stripes were turned diagonally or rotated ninety degrees. Somewhat surprisingly, a fair number of designers represented the central confederacy itself by a star larger than those individual representations of each of the member states. This modification of traditional flag conventions implied that at least some Confederates recognized central power as something to strive toward rather than instantly reject.[27]

Some scholars have taken the derivative nature of Confederate flag design as evidence of the "thin and fragile" nature of southern nationalism, arguing that rebels depended on American themes mainly because they had none of their own to offer. Such a judgment seems overly severe, especially given how other movements have succeeded while making similarly minor adjustments to shades of meaning in their symbolic practices. David Waldstreicher's recent study of early American nationalism details how heavily the Revolutionary generation depended on their colonial heritage, concluding that if the patriots had "not been so British" in their rituals, "they could not have celebrated themselves into an American future." The case of the red flag of revolution is perhaps the most striking example of a subversive attempt to appropriate and transform a recognized symbol. This signal, which had originally been used by urban police to warn of riots, became over the course of the nineteenth century the internationally recognized emblem of a workers' call for armed revolt. Such a modification of original meanings created an emblem that was at least as powerful as could have resulted from more fundamental innovation. In the case of Confederate symbolism, reassembling the elements of the American flag was clearly an attempt to capture popular energies that reached into the past. But, as these letters to Congress make clear, selecting a tricolor flag with stars and wider-than-usual stripes was meant to redirect positive feelings toward a new political future, not to lead Confederates back to the Union.[28]

The choosing and unveiling of the Stars and Bars drew as much attention as its derivative design. Many Northerners were at first hesitant to take the flag designs of the Confederates very seriously. The same Union papers that had reacted gloomily to secession banners interpreted the flag speeches underway in Montgomery as "foolish pother," more worthy of ridicule than trepidation. The editors of Harper's Weekly were typical in noting that "the discussion of new flags and new national emblems are all very easy and very pleasant work," but that these patriotic flourishes were frivolous compared to the real work of governing and establishing foreign relations. A writer for the New York Tribune made a similar point, remarking that after a month of meetings, the "sole and sublime amusements" of Confederates had been "the construction of paper constitutions, the begetting of body politics, the evocation of cash out of chaos, and the general transmogrification of a small slice of the Old Union into a Confederacy." Amidst such flimsy efforts, it was "the millinery department" that had made "the weightiest drafts upon the Southern Congressional intellect." Flags shipped by the bushel to the convention were a farce, this correspondent wrote, worthy to be displayed with little more dignity than peddlers exercised in showing their "rainbow-merchandise to the old ladies."[29]

Confederate delegates hoped their final choice of a flag would transmit something more impressive to their former associates in the Union. The first presentation of the Stars and Bars, amidst booming cannon and stirring music, strove for the right mixture of dignity and defiance. Congressmen who staged this ceremony decided to unfurl their new banner at the exact moment that Abraham Lincoln took the oath of office in Washington, making the most dramatic statement possible that the Union dissolved for all time when it passed to Republican leadership. As with earlier secessionist demonstrations, there was a strong female presence at this ceremony, as seven teenage women were selected to represent each of the Confederate states in carrying the flag to the top of the Alabama capitol building. The honor of unfurling the flag was reserved for Letitia Tyler, a Virginian whose grandfather, John Tyler, had served as president of the United States. One reporter hoped that the selection of this "lady of extraordinary beauty, intelligence, and patriotism" would "force its significancy upon the Union sentiments" in her native state, which still remained in the Union. Another press correspondent sensed a holier presence, interpreting the pattern of vapor that rose around the flag from saluting cannon as a "providential omen" representing nothing less than a "divine augury of hope and national durability."[30]

Despite careful preparation and the enthusiastic description offered by a handful of southern newspapers, the ceremonial presentation of the first Stars and Bars failed to generate the attention that Confederates had hoped for. Over the next few days, most public commentary focused on Abraham Lincoln's inaugural address, his first statement of policy since his election four months earlier. The scene in Montgomery, by contrast, was described primarily in very short dispatches, and no sketches were made that might have captured the spirit of the day. There were even fears that what news did circulate by word of mouth would undermine the significance of the event. Mary Chesnut worried that the perception of a "lifeless crowd" on this occasion might give the wrong impression that "we have no pride and joy in this thing." She set her mind partly at ease in defensively remarking that "our mobs are gentlemen" and that "those who make the row in the northern cities" whether in voting, celebrating, or making trouble, "are here hoeing cotton." Having a mudsill class not only helped make slave society more stable, she suggested, but excused the South for falling short of the North in the tenor of their public celebrations.[31]

Chesnut need not have worried too much about the flag, however, since the appearance of the Stars and Bars across the South generated a cumulative effect far more potent than the unveiling of a single banner. The publicity generated by the informal design contest heightened anticipation for the ultimate selection, and Confederate partisans moved quickly after the announcement of the final choice to become the first to raise the national colors in their local neighborhoods. Urban flag makers who had been overworked for the past four months promised new Stars and Bars at the earliest possible date. Citizens who lived outside of cities, or who simply could not wait, made their own flags, regardless of whether their own states had yet seceded. Even more elaborate ceremonies and speeches greeted this national flag than had welcomed the secession banners hung out a few months earlier. In Jackson, Tennessee, a group of the "Southern Rights Guards" strung the flag on a cord stretching from the courthouse down Main Street to begin a day of electioneering for disunion. At universities from Virginia to Louisiana, students planted the new flag from the tops of classroom buildings to make their allegiances clear. On her Mississippi River plantation, Eliza Ripley did the best she could in combining pieces of red flannel, thin white cotton, and stiff blue denim to fashion a banner that she thereafter secured to a piece of driftwood only with the help of "cords, nails, and other devices."[32]

Newspapers played a crucial role in spreading awareness of the new Stars and Bars, just as they had taken the lead in reporting secession banners and publicizing the congressional competition. Press offices made good on their earlier pledges to become the first buildings to display the new design on the urban landscape. They also provided readers beyond their neighborhoods with Congressional specifications of how to make the flag and placed images of the new Stars and Bars on newspaper mastheads and in their columns. Many southerners would have first glimpsed the new national symbol in newsprint or on patriotic envelopes rather than in actual cloth. Local printers produced letter-paper and envelopes that presented the new flag accompanied by an array of arrangements and messages. The demand for such stationery became so intense during the spring of 1861 that vendors confessed that they were "scarcely able to supply it."[33]

The appearance of the Stars and Bars was particularly significant in those border states that remained in the Union. The *Richmond Daily Dispatch* spread news about this new national flag in Virginia, reporting Richmond's first version of this banner on March 9, a full month and a half before the state seceded. In all but one of the next twenty-three issues, the paper reported the appearance of this same Confederate flag in a number of new locations, often describing how Virginians would add an eighth star to the flag's field to represent their own state. Across Richmond, along railroad lines and depot stations, on boats plying Virginia rivers, and in an increasing number of towns and county courthouses, colors waved in numbers that rivaled the Deep South's flag fury of the preceding winter. As with those earlier emblems, Confederate banners in the border states became news items worthy of comment. After three weeks of reporting the flurry of flag activity, the *Dispatch* concluded that the crowds who hoisted Confederate colors across the state provided evidence of a "popular revolution" that was willing to push for disunion even while the Virginia convention attempted compromise. "County after county of the Old Dominion is gravitating to the true centre of its sympathies and interests in the *Southern Union*," it wrote. Two weeks later, the paper followed reports of even more flags with the observation that "secession is making rapid progress in localities heretofore strongly attached to the Union."[34]

The Stars and Bars became an even more important part of the patriotic landscape after Confederate cannon fired upon Fort Sumter in mid-April. In the aftermath of that electrifying event, William Howard Russell made his trip through the Carolinas, where he witnessed "dust, noise, and patriotism" swirling around the new Confederate colors that hung from pine trees and in courthouse squares. Going northward along the same tracks a week later, a reporter for the *Charleston Mercury* also noted the prominent display of the Stars and Bars. "Every station along the railroad, however humble in appearance, was bedecked with the Southern flag," he wrote. "Even the village maidens came out to the roadside in their sunbonnets and waved us a Godspeed with their

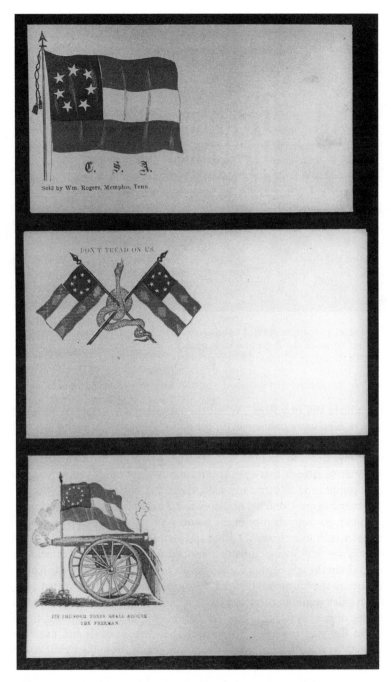

10. The Stars and Bars adopted by the Montgomery Congress appeared as regularly in print as in cloth, as this sample of flag-designed patriotic envelopes suggests. Courtesy, American Antiquarian Society.

11. The Stars and Stripes seemed to be everywhere in the North after war began, as this scene of the departure of a regiment from New York City demonstrated. Courtesy, Chicago Historical Society, ICHi-22210.

handkerchiefs and tiny flags." When the reporter finally reached Richmond, there were even more banners, with the national colors sharing honors with a new Virginia state flag, which featured the motto "Sic Semper Tyrannis," or "Thus always death to traitors." The feverish activity in Richmond prompted the reporter to remark that even those famously hot-blooded Charlestonians were by comparison a "singularly staid, quiet and undemonstrative people."[35]

However intense Confederate flag waving was after the bombardment of Fort Sumter, patriotic display in the South was overshadowed by the North's ever greater rush to embrace the Stars and Stripes. At a "monster rally" in New York City, the Star Spangled Banner seemed to be everywhere, appearing in "all sizes, from the tiny toy flags, stuck in the horses' headstalls or the hatbands of the men, to the full grown bunting, requiring a strong man to carry it." Other northern cities would become similarly covered with previously unimaginable quantities of red, white, and blue. In Boston, Edward Everett noted that the American flag was not just placed above the usual arsenals and mastheads, but floated "as never before" from "tower and steeple, from the public edifices, the temples of science, the private dwelling." This profusion of banners was matched by a simultaneous deepening of emotion. A flag that was "always honored, always beloved" was suddenly "worshipped" with the "passionate

homage of this whole people," Everett noted. He also explained that the recent "fratricidal" assault on the Stars and Stripes in Charleston harbor spurred
"one deep, unanimous, spontaneous feeling." A resolve moved "through the
breasts of twenty millions of freemen" that this flag's "outraged honor must be
vindicated."[36]

William Howard Russell was bemused at how a single "outrage on the flag"
had "produced all these banners" and "filled all these streets with soldiers"
across northern cities. No comparable furor had resulted as the Stars and
Stripes had been taken down from federal arsenals earlier, the Englishman
noted, concluding that only American irrationality could explain the sudden
sensitivity about the honor of their national flag. This diagnosis missed the
central point. Public attention had turned Fort Sumter and the national flag
that waved above it into an "emotional magnet" for the entire country. The
attack upon it by Confederate forces released energies that had long been sim-
mering just below the surface and offered an insult to national honor that was
so fundamental that only a "fight for the flag" could restore it. This sort of
symbolic escalation was not limited to democracies. Great Britain itself had
recently fought a four-year war in China to avenge an insult to the Union Jack.
And, late in 1861, England came perilously close to war with the United States
after its flag was treated with disrespect during the famous *Trent* affair, when
a Yankee officer forcibly boarded a British steamer and seized Confederate
diplomats. In the case of the Fort Sumter bombardment, the extended public
focus on Charleston harbor made the attack on the flag even more likely to
provoke outrage than had the unexpected assaults made upon the Alamo in
1836, on the *U.S.S. Maine* in 1898, or on the American fleet in Pearl Harbor
in 1941.[37]

The intensifying public interest in protecting the American flag's honor
changed the tone of Unionist consideration of symbols. *Harper's Weekly* tacitly
conceded that flags were more than the frivolous diversions that it had earlier
dismissed, condemning any individual unwilling to avenge the American flag
as a "moral monster" and a "lump of human selfishness." For someone to be
"incapable of that glowing emotion of patriotism which fuses all his thoughts
and hopes into one burning passion of loyalty to his native land" was evidence
of utter perversity, it concluded. Responding to the "flagmania" sweeping the
North, the *New Orleans Picayune* reminded Unionists that they were not alone
in battling for a national emblem. "We too have a flag," it wrote. Such banners
were "not only symbols to us of political rights, but bulwarks for the security
of everything which is worth preserving, without which we feel that all which
makes a country worth having would be irretrievably lost."[38]

Some Confederates witnessed this development with a bit of discomfort,
wondering whether southerners should emulate Yankee flag waving. The aftermath of the Union's rally to the Stars and Stripes brought forth considerable
cynicism from some rebels, who began to echo the barbs that had been aimed

at the flag obsessions of their own Confederacy a few short weeks before. Edward Pollard scorned Yankees for "employing the sentiments and symbols of patriotism as mere dramatic elements, with no feeling higher or worthier in their use." Ministers sensed the sin of idolatry, accusing Unionists of "submitting a gospel of the stars and stripes for the gospel of Jesus Christ." When a Richmond crowd offered a "thousand voices" to raise a Stars and Bars above the capitol after Fort Sumter's surrender, the press could not decide whether to emphasize the deafening noise and general enthusiasm of the assembled or their orderliness and the absence of "violence or rowdyness." Some continued to wonder how an emphasis on collective emotional unity might compromise more important principles of states' rights and local control. The question remained of how political independence might be gained without tapping into the most powerful sources of patriotic emotions, the idea of undying allegiance to widely shared national ideals and symbols.[39]

Despite misgivings on the part of a few, popular nationalism, with flags flying, would be a part of the Confederate experience no less than that of the Union. For both sides, the spring of 1861 was a watershed in showing how flags might both stir patriotic passions and help to crystallize an understanding of collective purpose and political conviction. At stake was a shared determination to support legitimate governments backed by popular will, whether that was defined by the majority of a united country, as Unionists would have it, or by the white majority within a defensive minority section, as Confederates would have understood. More than ever before, national flags came in these months to represent embattled governments that millions of mobilized citizens would pledge their all to support. Pieces of bunting provided tangible evidence of a set of institutions that would have been otherwise all but invisible. It provided a republic with the "majestic" part of government that allowed the less glamorous parts of administration to focus on efficiency. Alexander Stephens had noted late in 1860 that "the influence of the Government on us is like that of the atmosphere around us," since "its benefits are so silent and unseen that they are seldom thought of or appreciated." At the outset of war, the atmosphere of two imperiled governments would be filled by more red, white, and blue than had ever been seen before. And these colors took flight not just in physical form but in the tunes and words of music.[40]

It would have been peculiar indeed if Confederate flags had not inspired musical accompaniment, given the interconnections between banners and song in nineteenth-century American culture. Some white southerners seemed during secession nearly as reluctant to part with Francis Scott Key's "Star Spangled Banner" as with the American flag. "I sincerely believe I never could learn to get entirely over a certain moisture of the eyelids that always comes to me when listening to the sweet and stately melody," one Louisianan wrote late in 1860. Such sentiments were common at the time, as events suggested that the national banner and the music it inspired would soon disappear from the southernmost part of "the land of the free and the home of the brave." Hoping to fill a void, Confederates recast familiar musical themes for their own purposes, just as they retained the colors and stars of Old Glory. They paid particular attention to Key's effort, realizing that even though this song had not been established as an official national anthem, its tune and words had been part of what was special about the American flag. Without the same sort of stirring anthem of their own, Confederates knew there would be something incomplete about the pride they experienced while contemplating the new Stars and Bars.[41]

The upsurge in patriotic music and verse during the Civil War went far beyond the matter of flags. Efforts like "John Brown's Body," "The Battle Hymn of the Republic," and "Dixie" showed how thoroughly music could capture the popular imagination and shape attitudes and emotions throughout four years of war. Alongside such lasting contributions to American culture was a vibrant world of less familiar verse, which at the time was an important means for citizens to give popular expression to widely shared themes. For Americans of the 1860s, this range of lyrical productions proved that their patriotism welled up from below. While musical struggles in Europe were often managed from above, there were few official attempts to guide the production of patriotic music during the Civil War. Instead, it was up to average citizens to produce the flurry of patriotic music, though newspapers and printers of broadsides and music sheets played a crucial role in giving this verse a public airing. Seemingly endless tributes to country and to the cause came from both newly enthusiastic amateurs and those veteran composers who redoubled their efforts to give musical expression to widely shared values. As recent scholars have shown, such popular activity became a particularly important part of Confederate nationalism. The aural nature of song helped white southerners to sustain a national culture even after their region's printing industry was disrupted by military invasion and occupation.[42]

Popular poetic expression in the Confederacy provided the single most important forum for celebrating the new Stars and Bars, for disparaging the old Stars and Stripes, and for reflecting on why banners were such a powerful source of popular identification in the first place. Throughout 1861, Key's anthem provided a basic template, as his "Star Spangled Banner" was endlessly mimicked, parodied, or rejected. Many writers retained both his tune and his tone, emulating the majesty of the original in showing how, in the display of the Stars and Bars, "Freedom's proud Flag in the sunlight is gleaming." Others burlesqued the American anthem, asking, "Oh! Say has the Star-spangled Banner become / The flag of the Tory and the vile Northern scum?" In another nod toward Key, one poet presented a single defining moment for the new Confederate flag, substituting the events in Charleston Harbor for the more famous musical sketch of Fort McHenry in 1814.[43]

In these wide-ranging efforts, innovation and improvisation helped to convey an array of sentiments. Music and poetry became an important field for flag-related matters precisely because of their ability to modulate a variety of emotional tones. Banners themselves conveyed messages not only by the distinctive elements of their design, but by the sort of associations that could not be distilled into mere communications. Depending on their use, flags spoke to different audiences and with different ultimate effects. The musical component of flag culture did much the same. Whether inspiring action, explaining sacrifice, or counseling acceptance, the emotive vocabulary of verse became the lingua franca of the wartime cult of Confederate flags.

Confederate poets exemplified the emotional range of their verse in parsing the meaning of the American flag with the same dexterity that designers had shown in their suggestions to Congress. Songs gave a wide airing of such themes, while also providing clear cues to why a "new red, white, and blue" was something to be proud of. While some kept attention on what had been taken from the past, others magnified small differences from the U.S. flag through rhyme and imagery. One bit of doggerel typically focused on the difference between stripes and bars, explaining:

> The flag which they bear
> Is a snare:
> Its stripes writhe as snakes upon the air;
> And its Stars, no longer bright,
> Tell of chaos and of night,
> As of how they yet will set in despair.[44]

Those songs that bid "Farewell to the Star-Spangled Banner" went for the heart as much as the head, mixing melancholy with angry defiance toward those accused of spoiling the once glorious flag of the United States. "The one to which we clung . . . hath lost the charm it bore," one poet explained, but only after it had been "long trampled in the dust" by evil Yankees. A Mobile writer placed responsibility on "fell abolition," by dramatizing how antislavery "blots the stars and rends in twain the flag." Still another composer depicted how "the Star Spangled Banner dishonored is streaming O'er bands of fanatics / their swords are now gleaming." New Englanders were singled out for special scorn, appearing as "hucksters," "bigots," and "braggarts" in one poem and as a collective "Puritan demon" in another. A Baltimore paper repeatedly presented these original Yankees with a pointed challenge, printing in three sequential editions a poem to "The Flag" that not only gloried in earlier southern accomplishments, but threatened New England: "the makers can unmake, if you the heritage forget."[45]

Sentiments of betrayal were registered with particular effectiveness by those with earlier ties to the Stars and Stripes. Beside a poem he had written to the American flag in 1833, John McCabe placed an updated version that explained

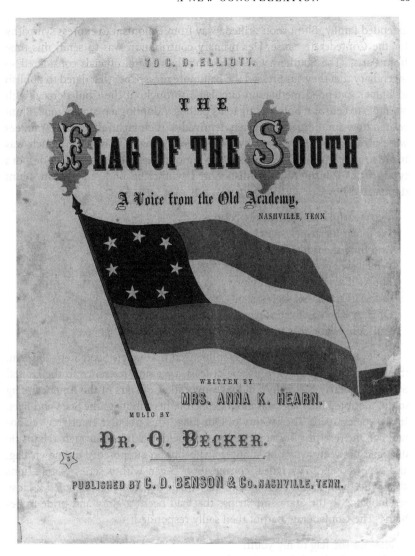

TO C. D. ELLIOTT.

THE
FLAG OF THE SOUTH

A Voice from the Old Academy,
NASHVILLE, TENN.

WRITTEN BY
MRS. ANNA K. HEARN.

MUSIC BY
DR. O. BECKER.

PUBLISHED BY C. D. BENSON & Co. NASHVILLE, TENN.

12. "The Flag of the South," by Anna K. Hearn, was one of the dozens of songs that made the Stars and Bars a pervasive theme in patriotic Confederate music. Courtesy, Duke University Special Collections.

how "here in the presence of God and man / I recant each word of that song!" An even more dramatic gesture was made by Francis Scott Key's own daughter. Though born in Maryland, Ellen Key Blunt was living in England during the secession crisis, where she wrote a Unionist plea for the country to "count Thou her stars" and to "keep every one" on the national flag. Like many of her extended family, Blunt soon drifted away from Unionism to express sympathy for the Confederate cause. Her primary contribution was to send, this time from Paris, "The Southern Cross," a song that federal officials considered so incendiary that they suppressed the Baltimore newspaper that dared to publish it. Blunt's extended meditation circulated throughout the Confederacy, with attempts to censor it only adding to its pathos. Adopting a plaintive tone, Blunt related how southerners felt when deprived of their rightful heritage. Yankees were proving their depravity by "singing our song of triumph / Which was made to make us free" while also "waving our flag above us, with a despot's tyrant will." Considering this dishonored symbol beyond redemption, Blunt dramatized how

> With tearful eyes, but steady hand,
> We'll tear its stripes apart,
> And fling them like broken fetters
> Which will not bind the heart.
> But we'll save our stars of glory
> In the might of his sacred sign
> Of Him who has fixed forever
> Our Southern Cross to shine.[46]

Not every flag-related song was influenced by Francis Scott Key's anthem, though few were unable to escape at least a passing reference to the United States flag. Harry Macarthy's indirect invocation of stars of the American flag in the "Bonnie Blue Flag" was more explicit in his tribute to the Stars and Bars. In a piece entitled "The History of Our Flag," this popular entertainer elaborated on the resetting of state stars in a new field. He did so through a dramatic dialogue between a patriot stranger, who bore a supposedly unknown flag, and a newcomer. The lyrical conversation began with a series of questions about the flag's origin and name, after which the interrogator noted a close resemblance to the Stars and Stripes that had been "a glory and pride to behold." The Confederate patriot then sadly responded:

> alas, for the flag of my youth
> I have sighed and dropped my last tear
> For the North has forgotten her truth
> And would tread on the rights we hold dear.

Confronted by northern jealousy, this character then explained that a new symbol, with the same colors, would now be "bless'd by the smiles of the fair" in the future.[47]

A final group of flag songs concerned neither the banner's history nor its meaning, but its overpowering physical presence. A Virginia poet demonstrated the awe it should rightly elicit from Confederates, asking:

Who can behold it, who that has feeling,
Can gaze on the charms that that banner is showing—
And not feel his bosom a transport revealing
His heart all so wildly with liberty glowing?

In one of the most widely circulated of all flag poems, Susan Elder of New Orleans acted out such homage directly, addressing the flag:

Bright banner of freedom! with pride I unfold thee,
Fair flag of my country, with love I behold thee,
Gleaming above us in freshness and youth
Emblem of liberty, symbol of truth.

Elder's verse, which was widely copied and quoted in patriotic oratory, emphasized how this new personification of the Confederacy was accessible through the full range of sensory experiences. Nearly all songs celebrated the visual impact of the flag, noting the "brightness" and the "gleaming" of the stars, just as Key's song invited listeners to see the colors "through the dawn's early light." Tributes to American flags had a long history of making the gaze itself into an act of patriotism. Music added another dimension in giving sound to allegiance, while some poetic efforts gave voice to the flag itself as it flapped in the breeze. Elder and others added the tactile sensation of unfolding the flag, as did other writers who conjured up how it felt to caress, kiss, or wrap one's body in the colors. She was more unusual in also associating the flag with smells, conjuring up the "fragrance and bloom" of the South in one of the lines from her tribute to the "bright banner."[48]

As the flag's design became familiar, and its message communicated, songs were increasingly apt to join Elder in metaphorically taking these banner's down and placing them in the patriot's arms. In a song he proposed as a new national anthem, John H. Hewitt even depicted how "the stalwart and brave round it rally / They press to their lips every fold." With such gestures, musicians reminded Confederates that their new banner was an object of intimacy as well as of collective power. Attaching one's self to it, and establishing a meaningful relationship between flag and citizen, seemed to require more than just a gaze. Touching the folds of silk, cotton, or bunting might help, these poets suggested, in taking it into one's heart. As William Henry Russell had suggested at the outset of hostilities, internalized devotion to cloth was the ultimate end of the Civil War's multimedia flag culture. Songs written to evoke the physicality of flags reminded Confederates that every patriot might possess one's own banner. Their yearnings could be turned into physical form with the most rudimentary cutting and sewing.[49]

Music played an important role in helping flags to embody the nation. Events would also be important in changing the meaning of flags and in altering the lyrics that endowed them with meaning. In the aftermath of the first battle, an anonymous Virginia poet conveyed what would be increasingly common in a call to "the soldiers of Virginia" to "wave aloft your flag, its graceful folds!" The verse attested to the fact that the flag's most important service would be on the battlefield and that to establish a country required more than a new flag and new songs. This emblem had to be put to new uses as well. Providing a poetic cue, the verse instructed an audience of fighters in a message they would continue to hear:

Grasp tight its staff and bear it on high
Mid roar of cannon and clash of steel.
Dismantled or broken it never shall lie
Forever its might the foe shall feel.[50]

CHAPTER FOUR

Blood Sacrifice and the Colors of War

A FLAG CULTURE that does not evoke bloodshed is like a *Hamlet* staged without the prince. The most vital part of the story is left out. This is not to say that banners were unimportant during the bloodless periods of disunion and reconfederation, when cloth mobilized energies and unified white southerners beneath a single defining emblem. But these symbols did not reach their full emotional potential until they called forth wartime sacrifices on their behalf. An upturn in the Stars and Bars' primal power was immediately evident with the Confederacy's first martyrdom, when a single act of devotion to this symbol extended earlier patriotic vows into a new sacred realm. Designing, waving, and singing about flags might have generated a sense of communal involvement; gazing upon banners waving in the wind or shedding tears of joy in their presence might also have profoundly intensified a patriot's devotion; the more intimate act of dying for a flag placed these objects in a new, quasi-religious category of symbols. As blood was not just quickened in the veins by these banners but spilled for them in conflict, Civil War flags became totems of a collective cause. Once transformed in this way, they proved to be immensely effective in inspiring devotion and bringing forth even more sacrifice. Flags helped to continue the carnage that made the Civil War the bloodiest period in American history, while they imbued hundreds of thousands of deaths with transcendent meaning.[1]

For soldiers, the battle flags of the 1860s unleashed the same sort of passions that had hovered around the tools of war for centuries. The numinous power of battle flags, like that of swords, shields, and other military implements, rested in their connection with the violent act of killing and the vulnerable act of exposing one's body to harm. Defending a flag was a duty for Victorian fighting men across the Atlantic world, a fact that caused Thomas Carlyle to marvel at soldiers' willingness to be "sabred into crow's meat" for "a piece of glazed cotton." Placing the safety of a banner above concern for one's own life demonstrated courage under fire to those who had been initiated into the martial code of honor. During the American Civil War, military colors would continue to inspire death-defying heroism in the ranks of the enlisted. The general populace also experienced pride and purpose in learning of defenses of their country's flag, as such acts eclipsed all other combat achievements in the popular imagination. Flags that had been "baptized in blood" moved soldiers to heroism, while they also reminded civilians that the quest for nationhood had come at an extreme cost and that falling short of victory would betray those who had already paid the supreme price for the common good.[2]

A variety of cultural practices helped to focus attention on the connections between battle flags, patriotic deaths, and the human price of victory. In the innumerable ceremonies staged within southern communities, elaborate presentations of regimental flags functioned as rituals of solidarity, with local women initiating young men into their prospects of future danger. The showy use of battle flags in later spectacles planned by southern generals continued these themes, while they also introduced the now-famous Southern Cross into Confederate iconography. A range of poems and stories built upon these activities, as battle flags were quickly elevated in the popular imagination above the Stars and Bars that had initially been chosen to represent the new nation. These cultural forms interacted with a continuing series of dramatic combat moments to help further the idea that all soldiers who fell in combat had "died for the colors." Fallen soldiers who bled for their banners turned the notion of passion back to its original religious meaning, as sacrifices were willingly undertaken and flag deaths became parables of collective salvation.

The Civil War began with the firing upon the Stars and Stripes that flew above Fort Sumter. Six weeks later, the war's first deadly struggle was sparked by a Stars and Bars banner raised from a Virginia hotel. The so-called Marshall House Affair that took place on May 24, 1861, was the sort of startling incident that "will sometimes flash like lightning, to show that the warring elements have begun their work," as one contemporary put it. As public attention shifted from South Carolina to Alexandria, Virginia, the Union commander Elmer Ellsworth was shot and killed while removing an oversized Confederate flag that could be seen from the White House itself. James William Jackson, the innkeeper who killed Ellsworth, became the first Confederate martyr when he also died in the affair. A witness to these events only slightly exaggerated when he later claimed: "under these apparently minor and insignificant operations, a spark was kindled into a flame which raged on both sides for four years."[3]

Though these two deaths would become less consequential after hundreds of thousands of others were killed, they were enormously important at first. Jackson's death showed those who had recently adopted and celebrated a new national banner what patriotic devotion might entail in actual practice. The Stars and Bars that he defended with his life acquired a totemic power from his death that would persist as it and other banners continued to mark patriotic deaths over the course of the war. Initially at least, Jackson was near the center of this transforming blood sacrifice. He drew extravagant accolades—one paper even claimed that his was "a deed of heroism without a parallel in modern history." Several months later, an observer could even judge that Jackson was "as widely celebrated throughout the Confederate and United States as that of any other man, either living or dead." These remarks overstated the case, though it was quite clear that the dead Jackson had been "anathematized, vilified, and detested" in the North, while in the South he had been "lauded as a hero, loved for his devotion to the flag of his country, and the terrible determination with which he defended it." Strangely enough, however, by the end of the war this first martyr had been all but forgotten. The fading of Jackson from the scene was as revealing as his earlier bright burst of fame, demonstrating as it did how enlisted soldiers displaced civilian patriots as exemplars of flag-related bloodshed.[4]

James Jackson, the man most clearly responsible for this deadly confrontation, was not an ordinary southern innkeeper. For two years prior to his death, he had broadcast his "strong southern sympathies" through a growing collection of "Black Republican Trophies." Among the prizes that he displayed to hotel patrons was a pike that John Brown had carried on his 1859 raid into Virginia, a Lincoln campaign flag raised the following year in Prince William County (which Jackson himself had cut down), and, perhaps most cherished of all, "a piece of flesh" that he claimed was the ear of John Brown's own son. Jackson had already earned a violent reputation by chasing a suspected abolitionist across the Potomac and by pummeling a priest who had refused to perform his wedding years earlier. Even his appearance conveyed a dangerous and impulsive streak. A later sympathizer described the forty year old as nearly six feet tall, and noted that a "grim, stern, obstinate determination was stamped emphatically on every feature."[5]

Jackson's impetuous hatred of Yankee Republicanism seemed to increase after Lincoln's election. At about the same time that the Confederates were choosing a new flag in Montgomery, Jackson leased the Marshall House hotel, presumably because of its location directly across from the federal capital. There he erected a flag pole tall enough to be seen from Washington City and, soon after Lincoln's inauguration, completed and displayed a Stars and Bars banner that measured forty feet in length. Northern correspondents quickly noted this flag and the message of scorn it conveyed. When Virginia seceded in April, Jackson himself added an eighth star to the center of the flag with "wildness of delight" and prepared himself to defend the border. He told all who would listen that he would surrender the flag only after first dying himself. For this, he would not have long to wait. Barely a month later, he actions drew forth a blow that would "peal, like the lightning of heaven over the vast forest, through the millions of burning hearts of the South."[6]

There was a steady stream of calls in the northern press to remove Jackson's taunt to federal authority. None expressed greater resolve than Colonel Elmer Ellsworth, who reportedly promised Mary Todd Lincoln, "Down shall come that starry banner, for it poisons nature's air!" There was little doubt that Ellsworth would perform this feat himself, since his well-known flair for the dramatic had already made him a minor celebrity. Drawn to the fanfare of military routine, he had worked hard to acquire a "dexterous precision" with rifles that a later eulogist admitted was "something akin to the slight of a juggler." In the late 1850s, he had toured the country with his "Zouave" troupe from Chicago, who had taken their name and their brightly colored outfits from French troops who had recently served in the Crimean War. During the secession crisis, he recruited a New York organization for real combat, and these "Fire Zouaves" soon showed a remarkable interest in the glory of military flags. Carrying what one observer described as "the most beautiful stand of colors" in the whole Union army, they vowed to "fight for these pieces of cloth till we die!" They also pledged that "we're goin' to have one more flag when we come back . . . the flag o' secession, nailed on the bottom o' this flag staff!"[7]

There were several differing accounts of what happened inside the Marshall House when the Zouaves crossed the Potomac on May 24, the day after Virginia finalized secession. But within a matter of minutes the primary result was clear—both Jackson and Ellsworth had been killed by a rapid exchange of gunfire. Ellsworth was immediately monumentalized in the North as the greatest northern hero yet. His body lay in state at the Washington Navy Yard and at a White House funeral, where the Lincoln family shed tears of grief. Even before his funeral train had made its way through New York State, prints were available that brought his image within northern homes. New songs were written to his memory, parents named their newborn children for him, and regiments named "Ellsworth's Avengers" swore retaliation for what most Unionists considered an act of murder. "By his blood," the editors of *Harper's Weekly* summed up, "all patriot hearts" had become "more closely sealed together."[8]

The stream of Confederate tributes to Jackson differed from those honoring the dashing Ellsworth. For the most part, southern newspapers and poets focused quite narrowly on Jackson's one defining action at the Marshall House and largely ignored the volatile past that might cause embarrassment to his cause. At times, it seemed Jackson would be little more than a name, which "little children, yet unborn" would "learn to lisp" just as they had learned the incantations of earlier revolutionary heroes like William Jasper of Fort Moultrie. Portraits of Jackson and plans for monuments to him were promised but never materialized. This hero was little more than an emblem, devoid of any but the most basic details of his life. While some Confederate newspapers

13. This northern image captures the climactic moment of the Marshall House affair, when James W. Jackson shot and killed Elmer Ellsworth for hauling down the Stars and Bars. Courtesy, Library of Congress.

sneered at Ellsworth for his "taste for gymnastics" and his "good many acrobatic tricks," Jackson was assumed to have been a "noble, frank, generous, and gallant" man whose primary motivation was defending his family. A local coroner's jury popularized the image that an average citizen had been wrongly assaulted through no fault of his own, concluding in its inquest that "the deceased came to his death at the hands of the troops of the United States, while in defense of his private property in his own house."[9]

Jackson's image was underdeveloped in part because he was not the only southern victim of the day. Unlike the single Ellsworth, Jackson left a wife and three daughters, who became the focus of a highly publicized fund-raising campaign to assure their support. And there was the Confederacy itself, which suffered "pollution" from the Yankee force that had crossed into Virginia for the first time that day. Yet perhaps the most important casualty in Alexandria was the Stars and Bars itself, which patriots claimed had been "stained for the first time" with the "blood of a martyr and a hero." As such, the Marshall House incident inspired among Confederates the same sort of solemn outrage and heated war spirit that the bombardment on Fort Sumter had spurred in the North. The centrality of the new national flag in this conflict lent it a decidedly mystical aura, and gave what poets called a "magic spell" to "that great deed" which Jackson performed when he was inspired "Almost to God like sacrifice!" The violent assault on the Stars and Bars shaped understanding of the patriot's death, as Confederates readied themselves to fight those whom one paper called "the insolent and invading hirelings and ruffians who seek to disgrace the chosen standard of a redeemed people."[10]

The flag-centered nature of the events could be seen in the earliest wire reports, which rhetorically focused attention on Jackson's willingness to allow his own body to endure humiliations that he would not allow his country's symbol to suffer. The telegraphic dispatch that spread the story informed readers that Jackson's corpse had been "cut to pieces" by a saber, just like a piece of cloth might be. Symbolically, the flag itself was "ripped to shreds" by the friendly hands of Jackson's family so that it could not be taken as a trophy by the Zouaves. Later, more detailed reports explained how Jackson cried out before shooting Ellsworth that he intended to take a trophy for the Confederacy in the form of a dead Yankee commander. These also reported how Jackson's body was "mutilated by repeated thrusts of the bayonet" and was left impaled by an upturned rifle to the floor for several hours. This degradation of his corpse was soon followed by a strikingly similar insult to the Stars and Bars. During Ellsworth's monumental funeral procession in New York City, the same bayonet that had pinned Jackson to the ground pierced an actual Confederate flag. Rebel cloth, like the rebel body, was dragged through the dust in humiliation.[11]

While Jackson offered up his own fragile body to insults intended toward his flag, the Stars and Bars lived on in revitalized form, reborn with renewed power everywhere it appeared. This process was not at all unusual in the ritual sanctification of sacred objects, as a recent study of American attitudes toward flags in the late-twentieth century explains. Caroline Marvin and James Ingle intriguingly argue that Americans have made their flags into quasi-religious totems, invoking the fiction that these emblems do not merely symbolize the larger collective community, but embody them. Through blood sacrifice of "real" bodies, usually those of soldier patriots, the material presence of cloth receives the sort of care usually reserved for a living, breathing presence. Once sanctified in this way, patriots are likely to regard physical insults to their sacred flag—whether expressed by burning it, cutting it, or even letting it touch the ground—with the sort of dread that can best be understood in religious terms.[12]

Confederates would no doubt have found concepts like the "totem" as a form of infidelity, if not outright paganism. Yet they elaborated through the medium of patriotic poetry and oratory similar understandings of how Jackson's blood sacrifice ennobled his flag and endowed it with special powers. As tributes to "our first martyr" circulated through the southern press, Jackson was lauded both for displacing his love of country onto the flag and for making an attachment to the physical object itself. In death, he acted out an earlier vow to "guard these matchless colors," which had been "given by hands divine." He had chosen to die rather than allow insult to the object, since, as the poet Henry Holcombe explained, his "patriotic heart / had pledged its faith" to the flag "as to a bride." Within these conventions, the flag become itself an agent in the struggle that lay on the horizon. As yet another poet predicted:

> Our Flag baptized in blood,
> Away, as with a flood,
> Shall sweep the tyrant hand
> Whose foot pollutes our land.[13]

Verse tributes lent power to the scene by associating it with death and rebirth and also by invoking one of the central ideals of Victorian America—the sanctity of Jackson's "home." By marking the Marshall House as a private refuge rather than a public place of business, Confederates misrepresented both the locale and Jackson's clear intent to precipitate conflict. His earlier defiance was softened by reports that placed him in a domestic scene and described his devotion to this banner in romantic terms. Poets explained how Jackson "loved his flag, and wished it saved, / He prized the beauties that it wore." From the very beginning, such verse tributes contrasted his death among his family to that offered up during combat. "Not where the battle red / Covers with fame the dead" did Jackson achieve his fame, one poem began. "Not with his comrades dear / Not there, he fell not there." Instead, his was a lonelier duty, though one no less important, that required him to stand up to an assault against his household. In this sense, the Zouave's invasion was particularly alarming, causing another poet to wonder, "How dare that base born rabble come / To trample in a freeman's home?"[14]

It mattered little if this idealized martyrdom fit the facts, since such tributes were meant to provide a model for future patriots. "Stand by your flag, like Jackson stood," a poet from Culpepper, Virginia, implored within days of the news. In Franklin, Louisiana, where eyes became "wet with briney tears" at the very mention of Jackson's name, the message was even more direct. "If we want to know how flags are loved," Miss Louisa McKerall told departing soldiers, "look at the manner the noble Jackson avenged the insult offered to that floating over his house." "He died to show us how to die / And ne'er before the foe to fly," a New Orleans poet added, while in Portsmouth, Virginia, one young woman told an audience witnessing a flag presentation ceremony, "There exists not a mortal man in Virginia who does not envy [Jackson's] fate, who will not emulate his example, and who would not rather die than live to breathe an atmosphere polluted by such moral and social lepers as the degraded and murderous wretches whose hands are bathed in his heroic blood." Georgia soldiers were told during another ceremony how Jackson had sought to "cleanse with his own blood our glorious banner from the contaminating touch of the foul invader." Texans even gathered at the historic battlefield of San Jacinto to honor a patriot who had been "murdered . . . for defending the rights of his home and his country."[15]

Across a thousand-mile span, Jackson's fate provided Confederates an inspiration and a warning. Those who took up the call to arms were taught that mortal sacrifice would result in fame and glory. Those who wavered heard another message that was equally pointed. Avoiding combat would bring shame and risk the safety of individual homes that the Yankees sought to disrupt. With an invasion underway, Union forces seemed ready to violate any households that stood in their way. Following Jackson's example was less important than launching a preemptive strike to meet the enemy at the border of the country, rather than at the threshold of one's house. The best way to save homes was to do what Jackson had not: to leave loved ones behind and to take the fight to the battlefield.

Confederates reduced the Marshall House transaction to its essentials, telling a melodramatic story of how a patriotic body was sacrificed for a flag that had protected a home. This account resonated with white southerners who were placing the same set of images at the center of hundreds of communal farewells for men leaving for battle. Both in the North and the South, most volunteers for this war could expect an appropriately elaborate send-off, usually at ceremonies where local women presented battle flags for the coming conflict. These festivities were particularly exciting for those living in the small towns that predominated in plantation districts and the southern upcountry. As an observer of a flag presentation in Mount Pleasant, South Carolina, remarked, "Such a demonstration being rare in this neighborhood animated every member of the community, who were gathered in liberal numbers." In other out-of-the-way places, from Wax Bayou, Louisiana, to Whippy Swamp, South Carolina, such transfixing rituals cumulatively involved hundreds of thousands of white southerners in tributes to locally raised regiments whose loyalties were pledged to locally made banners.[16]

These affairs received far more attention in the press than any other flag-related activity during the first year of the Civil War, despite their relatively formulaic nature. In both North and South, the speeches delivered at these occasions were published in full, providing textual scripts that were widely emulated during an extended process of military mobilization. After a gathering and perhaps a procession, the presenter of the flag would explain the motives of the gift and the expectations that it carried. These might also contain some more general reflections on patriotism, the justness of the cause, or the perfidy of the enemies to be repelled. The reply (or, more typically, the series of replies) registered communal appreciation and then expressed, with varying degrees of formality, a vow on behalf of those enlisted in the cause. After this verbal exchange, symbolic actions such as marching, singing, or blessing the banner rounded out what was typically an entire afternoon of activity.[17]

Press coverage of these ceremonies included extensive detail, suggesting that the ritual was just as important as the flags, which were usually described briefly. Presenters often explained to soldiers that the banners would help them to remember the day that they accepted the duty of defending their homes. "When you look upon this flag, its silken folds waving in the breeze, may this day loom up before your minds," one explained. Those receiving might predict, in reply, how the "day and the scene" of the actual presentation would be "depicted in our imaginations as the brightest and proudest moment of our existence." Memories of these celebrations were in many ways the primary purpose of the festivities, with the gift being not so much a single flag but a set of recollections that might be a source of comfort during the strain of battle. As one soldier asked, "Think you not that our nerves will grow stronger and our blows fall heavier as we glance upon that flag which awakens the thoughts and associations of this moment?" This banner, like others presented in similar ceremonies, marked the occasion rather than became its primary focus, as had been true in the first attempts to introduce the Stars and Bars in the early spring of 1861.[18]

As these flags memorialized community cohesion, they once more resembled totems, though not in exactly the same way that the Stars and Bars had been transformed by James Jackson's martyrdom. These flag presentations continued to mark the interaction of the sacred realm with a material form, just as the Marshall House episode had. But they also helped communities to recall particularly emotive gatherings. Emile Durkheim, the French sociologist, captured the manner and meaning of this process in the rituals that he considered early in the twentieth century. In one of the classic texts of modern social science, Durkheim explained how totem ceremonies captured fleeting expressions in actual artifacts, assuring that collective gatherings would not "dim and fade away if left to themselves." "Wild passions that could unleash themselves in the midst of a crowd" he wrote, were likely to "cool and die down once the crowd has dispersed, and individuals wonder with amazement how they could

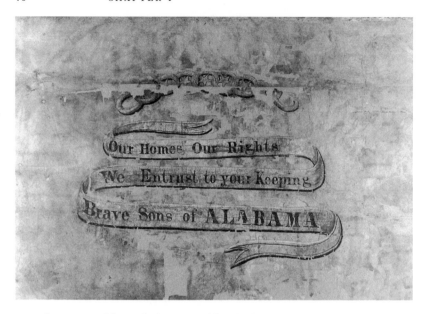

Our Homes Our Rights
We Entrust to your Keeping
Brave Sons of ALABAMA

14. The emotional farewells given to soldiers by local communities were made durable on regimental banners. The flags themselves often did not hold up that well, as this banner, recently identified as that of the Sixth Alabama infantry, clearly shows. Courtesy, Alabama Department of Archives and History.

let themselves be carried so far out of character." Yet "if the movements by which these feelings have been expressed eventually become inscribed on things that are durable, then they too become durable." The flag presentation rituals conducted throughout 1861 suggest that such insights might be applied beyond the context of this seminal work. Durkheim himself implied wider relevance in a series of suggestive remarks about the devotion that modern soldiers displayed toward their banners during combat.[19]

The insights of Durkheim are useful primarily in framing a central question: What sort of emotions and claims did participants in these local flag ceremonies strive to endow with a durable form? Flags captured the main themes of love, courage, honor, and duty with far greater brevity than lengthy orations could. Regimental colors given at these presentation ceremonies contained an extremely wide range of emblems, some drawn from previous militia traditions and earlier national symbols, others more recently adopted and circulated, either to represent a state or the new Confederacy. The titles or mottoes of the companies provided inspiration in some instances; at other times, images were drawn primarily from the imagination of designers.[20] Words were also quite common on these flags, making them more akin to secession banners than to those models suggested for a national flag or to later standardized battle flags chosen by army commanders. The regiment's name was nearly always included, and sometimes a date, either to indicate when the company was founded or when the flag was presented. And there was usually some sort of motto or charge, if not several. A good many such charges were in Latin, especially the increasingly familiar "Pro Aris and Focis," routinely translated for the uninitiated as "for our hearths and altars." Others stuck with the simple clarity of "God Defend the Right," "Any Fate but Submission," or "Liberty or Death." The seven-by-five-foot banner presented to the Adams Light Guard of Natchez, Mississippi, featured the regimental name, the date of its organization, and three other inscriptions: "Mississippi," to indicate state loyalties; "Deeds, not Words," to convey the traditional corps motto; and the final self-reflexive charge—"A Woman's Gift: Never Surrender It."[21]

As this last inscription indicated, gender was the primary means of organizing these acts of communal solidarity, as participants reminded one another of the duties men and women were expected to fulfill. An agreed-upon set of patriotic expectations required female participation, if only to reinforce the ancient distinction between male warriors and the "distaff" manufacturers of uniforms and banners. The popular conceit that women were above politics helped make their presence an assertion of communal willingness to come together after the divisive campaigns for president and then for secession. A female presence was also a powerful reminder of the stakes involved in defending southern homesteads against outside aggression. The domestic prerogatives of the slaveholding South had long been a powerful link between the politics of the household and larger national disputes over slavery and states' rights. As northern aggressors seemed ready to carry out the gravest threat yet to southern security, local women affirmed the need for active male protection and for patriotic unity of the entire white community. They often took a quite active role in asking for protection, self-consciously "breaking the bonds of female delicacy" to offer the sort of public speech rarely seen by women in the mid-nineteenth-century South.[22]

Women had long played a role in this sort of local flag culture, having been involved in community militia festivities on a regular basis. But the tone of those antebellum gatherings differed notably from those staged with the awareness of almost certain war. A presenter in 1861 looked back wistfully at the "merry throng in gala costume and gladsome spirit" that had gathered in previous years to hear "some proud heroine in accent tremulous" present "a gay standard to a gallant host." Such frivolity seemed increasingly inappropriate, though it did not cease to be a part of flag matters all at once. The giddiness that followed Fort Sumter tempted Atlanta schoolgirls, for instance, to bombard a miniature fort—complete with the Stars and Stripes—with their bouquets, as onlookers cheered them with wild applause and laughter. Other communities witnessed the same mock parading as in previous years, complete with the lighthearted cheers and ample feasting that had often made militia gatherings more like picnics than preparations for combat.[23]

15. This Union illustration, "Women Hounding Their Men to Rebellion," depicted a grudging acceptance of the important female role in sending their men to combat. *Frank Leslie's Illustrated Magazine.* Courtesy, Museum of the Confederacy, Richmond, Virginia. Photographed by Katherine Wetzel.

The looming presence of "dark and angry clouds" on the northern horizon turned most flag presentations into much more solemn affairs, however. Tears replaced laughter as speakers relentlessly reminded their listeners to expect "no holiday affair, but war! with its hardships, trials and danger." Looking out over the crowd in Natchez, Mississippi, a local clergyman proclaimed that this "was no idle, curious throng," but a group that had assembled from "a deep and earnest sympathy," which was "gushing up on every side of you" to send them into battle. When troops departed at the end of one such ceremony, female participants reportedly came to the "awful reality" that "what had heretofore seemed merely an imaginative scene was now a startling fact, a stern unpalatable fact, which needed strong nerves and brave hearts to stand the shock." The gravity of women presenting instruments of war intensified as conflict grew nearer. As one Tennessee woman put it near the end of 1861, "It would be difficult to render a compliment more delicately conceived, more potent in its moral influence, than for the women of their hearts to present them with a banner around which in the thickness of the battle, will cluster the fondest memories of their firesides."[24]

The best way of conveying heightened solemnity was to conjure up the details of patriotic bloodshed. Presenters reminded soldiers that flags would be present "in the hottest of the fight, when the leaden hail is falling thick and fast, and a deep mouthed cannon is belching forth its contents of destruction." Descriptions of the high costs of war often involved fairly gory images. A Georgia captain pledged that " the last drop of life giving current shall ooze from the warm fountain of life of each member of this little band" before they allowed their flag to be "trodden beneath the feet of the foe." In Arkansas, a presenter sketched an even more striking image, explaining how flags would "inspire your souls and nerve your arms" even when soldiers found themselves "marshaled before the booming cannon," as they became "exposed to the solid sheets of death." As if to reassure her listeners, she then contrasted the scene to the alternative, insisting "no wailings, no cries are equal to those of expiring liberty as she lies prostrate, bleeding at every pore." A Louisiana woman put her sentiments in verse, charging listeners:

> Let death to dust reduce your form,
> Let scars upon your persons be,
> But keep your flag, your country free.

Francis Bartow promised a group of Savannah women that soldiers would "fail to bring back to you this flag," only if "there is not one arm left among them to bear it aloft."[25]

Both the intimacy of figurative bodies and the feminine appeals to emotion could easily venture into imagery that later generations might consider erotic. After a certain "Miss Simpson" of Hancock, Georgia, imagined soldiers' "ardent pantings for the strife with the flashing eye and erect bearing," she was repaid in kind by "Lieutenant Reid," who assured her that his company would march to the beat of "the throbs of your heaving bosom" and the light of "your favoring countenances." In New Orleans, an even more highly charged ritual unfolded after officers of the Zouave battalion traveled to the podium to express appreciation to the "fair friends of the corps." They unsheathed their sword before a crowd given to frequent "cheers and hurras," after which each of the ladies responsible for the flag kissed these extended weapons, one by one. The reporter covering this scene remarked that "this manner of being dubbed a knight is in our opinion much better than the ordinary one."[26]

At first glance, nineteenth-century patriotism seems to be charged with romantic overtones absent in even the most emotionally charged patriotism of the early-twenty-first century. Young women during the Civil War heard appeals to "enkindle in your every breast the sparks of patriotism" and were encouraged "to stir its vestal fires till they burn and glow, that in their bright refulgent light you may bring your young hearts for sacrifice, and on their living, leaping flames you may scatter the fragrant incense of a fresh, virgin loyalty." Male devotion was similarly tinged with romance, with the soldier's homeland often portrayed as an actual lover. The poet William Gilmore Simms described the "sunny, sunny South" as a "land of true feeling" before depicting how he meant to "drink the kisses of her rosy mouth." After this lyrical consummation, Simms explained how "my heart swells as with a draught of wine," leading him to pledge his all to southern honor.[27]

One should be careful not to read too much into this language, however. If, as Paul Fussell has argued, irony was underappreciated by Victorians, one might similarly wonder whether men and women of the nineteenth century would have heard what to our own ear seem to be explicit sexual references. Simms's poem, for instance, immediately followed a passionate kiss of his homeland with a somewhat jarring image of a South that "brings me blessings of maternal love" and that "with strange fondness, turns her loving eye / In tearful welcome on each gallant son." Conjoining these disparate images of lover and mother suggest that Simms invoked a range of emotions and relations that existed between men and women rather than any specific one. This was common, as images of devotion to female family members often became blurred. "You are defending the homes and the firesides where you have been loved and cherished since the day when your first infant eyes opened to the sunny skies of our favored clime," one presenter reminded in giving soldiers a new flag. Such appeals defined male duty not in the expression of any particular act of affection, but in the attempts to repay the common nurturing that sons, brothers, husbands, and fathers alike had received from the women in their family.[28]

Feminine associations were powerful in any respect, extending past the inscriptions and provenance of these regimental flags to the very cloth used in their construction. "Its every fold shall tell, in terms more eloquent than tongues can speak, of the fair form that bent over it and the bright eyes that followed the fingers as they plied the very stitch," one Mississippi orator explained, continuing that "every thread shall be a tongue to chant the praise of woman's virtues and woman's worth." This elaborate praise sounded common themes that linked sewing with female devotion. A Texas woman reminded

soldiers that while their flag was "floating on the breeze," they should recall
that it had been "perfumed with the incense of woman's prayers." A regimental
commander in South Carolina predicted in receiving his company's flag that
"every rustle of its folds will be to us as music from home." And in Georgia,
one presenter was told that the Stars and Bars tricolor she had made would
bring memories of "your rosy lips, fair cheeks, and blue eyes." As if that was
not enough to make the connection, the captain added that "those glorious
stars" had taken their "lustre from your bright eye."[29]

One effect of giving flags such a feminine gloss was to elevate the importance
of protecting them from the "pollution" of enemy degradation or dishonor. A
distinct etiquette was worked out to guide actions that might keep pledges
sacrosanct. Sometimes this involved a simple directive that soldiers accept their
own deaths rather than see the flag taken, though at least a few authorized
soldiers to "rend its bars into shreds" if the only alternative was surrender. A
Virginian admitted that the flag "shall be returned, tarnished and torn" by "the
smoke and strife of battle," but insisted that it be "unsullied by desertion or
defeat." This symbolic sense of purity meant that the proud possession be
treated with respect normally reserved for religious objects. "No sacrilegious
hands must touch its sacred folds" one Colonel put it. A poet, who was also a
presenter, likewise charged:

> Long may this Flag wave;
> Without a blot to mar its fame
> Without a stain upon its name
> Its sons have for their holiest aim
> Our Southern rights to save.[30]

The notion of a flag's symbolic "pollution" or "purity" added yet one more
religious dimension to the sacred nature of banners. This was no mere figure
of speech. On several occasions, clergymen actually blessed these flags as holy
instruments, devoting the cause not only to community but also to God. Catholic priests seemed particularly inclined to perform such martial sacraments,
considering these banners to be "sacred emblems of the fatherland." Yet the
Reverend Benjamin Morgan Palmer, among the staunchest of Old School Pres-
byterians, also took part, reminding the New Orleans Washington Artillery
that they were engaged in a holy cause, "a war of religion against a blind and
bloody fanaticism" that would be decided "with the nations of the earth as
spectators and with the God of heaven as umpire." After consecrating the company flag to the favor of the Almighty, this celebrated minister left the soldiers
with the charge: "May the lord of Hosts be around about you as a wall of fire,
and shield your head in the day of battle!"[31]

In local ceremonies, white southern men and women encountered certain
themes of responsibility, purity, and duty not only by hearing charges and
replies, but through reading about countless such ceremonies as reported in

the southern press. Cumulatively, this extended exposure added a new dimension to flag culture that would, in time, influence the selection of a new national flag, which was born on the battlefield. Yet by late in 1861, some had grown tired of the repetition. The *Atlanta Confederate* complained in October that such ceremonies "fill up a large space in a paper," and besides, they were "not interesting to the general readers as they were when the war first commenced." Soldiers leaving home with cherished flags flying had undoubtedly received important preparation for war. But their initiation into combat would come with the actual shedding of blood under circumstances almost impossible to imagine without direct experience of battle.[32]

Themes first worked out at the local level were put to national use late in the fall of 1861, when the so-called Southern Cross made its first appearance as an official Confederate banner. The distribution of this famous battle flag drew upon earlier community rituals, joining key elements of departure ceremonies to a "grand review" of the Confederacy's main fighting force. After the war, details of this battle flag's "birth" became one of the set pieces of the Lost Cause, as stories of its design and adoption drew even more attention than had competing legends about the origins of the Stars and Bars. Postwar recollections smoothed out the details, and the imperatives of mythmaking offered a single narrative to replace the broad mix of competing agendas that shaped this episode. Yet as with the flag considerations made by delegates to the Montgomery Provisional Congress, there remains a contemporary historical record that shows a set of intertwining agendas that produced a Confederate battle flag destined for far greater fame than that achieved by the Stars and Bars.[33]

The Confederate reading public became aware of a new battle flag even before it had been unveiled to southern troops in Virginia. Soon after the victory at Manassas in late July, General P.G.T. Beauregard of Louisiana publicly complained that the Stars and Bars had nearly cost him the first major battle of the war. He carefully explained how during a key moment in that fight, colors carried by his own troops could not be distinguished from the Stars and Stripes of the United States army. After vowing to find a more distinctive replacement, he worked with William Porcher Miles and the War Department in Richmond to provide a substitute, and leaked hints of his progress to the press throughout the fall. He and General Joseph Johnston then engineered ceremonies that would be witnessed by thousands of soldiers in early December of 1861. By combining the presentation of flags with a spectacular review of the troops, these two commanders assured that an even broader audience would read about the new flag in press reports. Seizing on these bare details, later historians have taken for granted that the new battle flag was born of necessity, as army brass simply selected a new banner for narrowly practical reasons. Yet while pressing needs were clearly a part of the equation, there was more at stake than this usual explanation implies.[34]

There is little controversy that Beauregard's efforts on behalf of the Southern Cross were decisive, though it is equally clear that practicality was not his only concern. The Louisiana general's fondness for inspiring rhetoric and dramatic actions made him more interested than any other Confederate military leader in the motivational power of words and symbols. He demonstrated this repeatedly, whether in the extravagant praise he showered upon the troops who bombed Fort Sumter or in his note to mourners for the Confederate dead at Manassas, Virginia. The battlefield being but a short distance from Mount Vernon, he concluded that "their graves are beside the tomb of Washington; their spirits have joined with his in eternal communion." At times, Beauregard seemed more interested in how his stirring orders would be received by the public than with how they might accomplish specific objectives. Early in 1862, after his transfer from Virginia had been completed, he called on Confederates in the Mississippi Valley to donate their plantation bells to the southern cause, prefacing his order with past examples of church bells being melted down into cannon. While this plea inspired a considerable body of patriotic poetry, its practical results were more modest. His subordinates even had to issue subsequent instructions that admitted that many types of metal were useless. In Charleston, his third major command, Beauregard continued his patriotic pleas. As Union forces approached, he instructed citizens: "pikes and scythes will do for exterminating your enemies—spades and shovels for protecting your friends."[35]

Beauregard's flowery language annoyed many of his associates, even if it struck a chord among his sizable body of admirers. His melodramatic sensibility was used with perhaps greatest effect in linking his Southern Cross initiative with the women of Richmond, who were enlisted to construct twenty-five new battle flags in October of 1861. These first St. Andrew's Cross designs, which would eventually become the most famous Confederate flags, were made of silk rather than more durable cotton or bunting, guaranteeing that a new issue would be needed in a matter of months. Similarly, the three most famous artifacts from this period—the prototypes given by the "Cary Invincibles" to Confederate commanders—were probably not intended to be used in battle at all. Yet whatever the needs of the moment, Beauregard seemed aware that women had played a crucial role in flag culture and that they should be involved in any new flag choice. This mythic moment of symbolic creation retained the most powerful aspects from local ceremonies, namely, the sanctification of banners by southern women.[36]

One consequence of Beauregard's initiative was a burnishing of the reputations of Jenny, Hetty, and Constance Cary, whose own sense of patriotic drama made them natural partners in this birth of the foremost Confederate symbol. The first two Carys were sisters who had reportedly fled their homes in Baltimore to avoid punishment for having taunted federal troops with secession banners. When they moved to Virginia, they joined their cousin Constance, who herself had left Alexandria to escape contact with Union occupiers and the murderers of James Jackson. The Cary threesome soon became unofficial sweethearts of the southern army and paragons of southern female beauty. In presenting one of three original Southern Cross battle flags to General Earl Van Dorn, Constance expressed the hope that it might "one day wave over the recaptured batteries of my ill-fated home," a pledge that Beauregard repeated in receiving a similar flag from Jenny. The Carys also introduced troops to the song "Maryland, My Maryland," and thereafter gained entrance to the most fashionable Richmond social circles. Their wartime exploits made them among the most celebrated heroines of the subsequent Lost Cause tradition. In the process, these women became linked to the Southern Cross the same way that Betsy Ross would become associated with the Stars and Stripes late in the nineteenth century.[37]

Whatever Beauregard thought about providing an opportunity for female patriotism, he seemed intent to build on the womanly sanctification evident during community presentation ceremonies and on the floor of the Montgomery Congress. In forwarding the new flag to his troops, he did not merely praise the Carys or the "Richmond ladies" for their efforts. His orders instead made the women loved by each and every soldier central to an ongoing process of endowing flags with the associations of home. After hearing that "a new banner is entrusted to-day, as a battle-flag to the safe-keeping of the Army of the Potomac," his troops were reminded of earlier commitments:

> Soldiers: Your mothers, your wives, and your sisters have made [this new flag]. Consecrated by their hands, it must lead you to substantial victory, and the complete triumph of our cause. It can never be surrendered, save to your unspeakable dishonor, and with consequences fraught with unspeakable evil. Under its untarnished folds beat back the invader, and find nationality, everlasting immunity from an atrocious despotism, and honor and renown for yourselves, or death.

One reporter who witnessed this scene in person appreciated how a symbol blessed by women might become a new national flag. He told readers that since this Southern Cross had been "hallowed by the hands that made it," they should expect that it would eventually become "the banner of your country!"[38]

Beauregard's invocation of soldiers' earlier pledges to their women was accompanied by new themes. His proclamation, which appeared by telegraph in most Confederate newspapers, was read to troops in the midst of an imposing set of ceremonies that, in contrast to community rituals, drew from European traditions rather than American precedents. This imposing "Grand Review" featured the generals, who, reportedly accompanied by a hundred bodyguards, "rode at full speed from the right of the battle array to the left, stretching out more than a mile in length," as one newspaper correspondent described. The men marched together in huge numbers, fading into a "solid mass of bayonets" that "would glisten above the hill top" for those officials and female supporters who looked upon the scene from a distance. The new banners at the center of it all provided a focal point, as did the collective blessing by a Louisiana priest that Beauregard himself selected. The spectacle of the day, which featured charges offered and pledges made, provided one of the most memorable events of what was otherwise a placid fall and winter.[39]

Though such spectacles were also witnessed in the North, their pomp and pageantry had special appeal for Beauregard, who would soon be known as "Napoleon in Gray." The Louisiana general staged this unveiling of a new battle flag with a distinctively Gallic touch, no doubt aware that the tradition of presenting flagstaffs in grand reviews had begun with Napoleon Bonaparte and that flag concerns were being revived in new form by his nephew, the second emperor of France. Melding such traditions with more homegrown themes was difficult in a no-nonsense, overwhelmingly Protestant society of the American South. A young private who took part in the ceremony was probably not alone in his puzzling over Beauregard's decision to have "his confessor" offer a prayer with his *catholic badge* prominently displayed. While finding the ceremony "a very solemn thing," this soldier nevertheless admitted that he found even more impressive the brass band rendition of "Dixie," which had been a regular feature of the mobilization efforts of the previous spring. At this tune, "my blood almost boiled," he wrote his parents, showing how an American favorite was more likely to arouse stronger feelings than even the most carefully staged import.[40]

Given the timing involved, Beauregard's showy adoption of the Southern Cross involved something more than an attempt to bring imperial splendor to the Virginia army. His troops received their new flags at the very moment that this rising southern hero was tangling with the Richmond bureaucracy over who was ultimately responsible for the war effort. Very public disputes and recriminations involved Beauregard's determination that the country be represented primarily by its fighting forces, its commanders, and, by extension, a flag that could motivate soldiers and keep them safely identified. In this way, he contrasted his own sense of "patriotism, the highest civic virtue," with what he saw as the civilian preference for "office-seeking, the lowest civic occupation." However much Beauregard might have wanted to substitute his own vision of the country for civilian authority, his fiat would not alone make the military preeminent in the Confederate imagination. Symbols and ceremonies would help to place armies at the center of the southern cause, though this did not occur in the way Beauregard had worked to achieve. Shortly after the imposing Virginia flag ceremony, Jefferson Davis asserted his determination to keep the military subordinate by transferring Beauregard to the west and by continuing to keep close watch on this potential nemesis for the rest of the war. It would be left to later generals, who had less sense of spectacle, to bring glory to the new army flag and establish the preeminence of the Confederate fighting forces.[41]

The introduction of the Southern Cross was still important in beginning a process, which Beauregard continued to help along, that would establish a single resonant symbol for a country intent on achieving this goal. The ceremony solidified a trend toward new ways of presenting battle flags and sanctifying them. The *Charleston Mercury* had worried early in the war that "in the absence of any action on the part of the proper authorities, the fair sex, with their noble public spirit, have undertaken to supply the several regiments and companies with standards." This might be a powerful means of motivation, the paper conceded, but standardization and efficiency were severely compromised by leaving everything to be decided "according to the fancy of the fair donors." Commanders' orders for new battle flags reduced the variety and the confusion, in Virginia and across the rest of the Confederacy too. Soldiers usually accepted the practical need to send the array of locally made colors "ignominiously to the rear," as one former commander later remembered. In several instances, units even returned the gifts to the safekeeping of the donors, explaining the care they had taken with them thus far.[42]

Female patriots constructed some of the new army-authorized battle flags, though sewing circles became less important once mass-production of uniform regimental colors by machines began. Similarly, flag presentation rituals that did continue after the first year took place in the army camp, rather than in the public square of local towns. Ceremonies that had once helped to stir a community's imagination about war became a way of helping soldiers immersed in military routine to experience the comforts of home. These also allowed them to enjoy a day of flirtation and perhaps the beginnings of courtship. Female visitors could "break the monotony of the camp," as a South Carolina soldier put it in April 1862, describing the interest of soldiers rising to "fever heat" as they listened to a "beautiful girl, yet in her teens," deliver a "neat speech" before delivering a new army-approved flag to their care. In general, women were far more likely to be observers at these occasions rather than the meaningful participants they had been in communal rituals. There was little they could do to help men imagine the war. The world of battlefield danger, courage, and sacrifice became a male preserve, as the few female patriots intent on taking up arms had to disguise their sex and pretend to be men in joining the ranks.[43]

The diminishing role of women in producing flags did not altogether eliminate female associations with banners. Silk continued to be used in some of the most cherished banners, especially the handful of flags supposedly made from wedding dresses or other bridal clothes. The regimental colors made by Mrs. John C. Breckinridge and Mrs. Louis Wigfall used such materials, which attracted considerable press attention, drawing the focus away from local organization to the wives of prominent leaders. The real significance in such episodes had less to do with gender roles than with a basic reworking of the relation between localities and the expansive national community. A war that

16. After the first year of war, women typically presented flags under the supervision of generals, rather than in the midst of communities, as was shown in this picture of New Orleans ladies in the summer of 1862. *Harper's Weekly*, August 2, 1862. Courtesy, Michigan State University Libraries.

had begun as a fight for homes was becoming one fought by massive armies, carrying symbols that would nationalize commitments.[44]

If Beauregard realized the defects of the Stars and Bars at the battle of First Bull Run, soldiers who had experienced war for the first time learned a much wider range of lessons about flags. This first full-scale conflict of the Civil War introduced most participants to the modern realities of battle, an initiation that would be repeated for western troops at the battle of Shiloh the following spring. In both of these huge conflicts, flags helped troops to signal one another, to coordinate charges and retreats, and to indicate the desire for a temporary truce. Banners of the enemy proved to be the most desirable trophies. In addition to learning the practical role of colors in combat, soldiers participating in such large-scale battles became increasingly aware that dying for a flag was the epitome of wartime patriotism.[45]

The initiation of ordinary Americans into a world of Minié balls and battle flags played itself out both in the field of combat and in the cultural realm that gave meaning to killing and dying. Worlds of home front and battlefront were never so permeable as in the Civil War, when a ceaseless flow of newspapers and personal mail, both of which were largely free of censorship, kept up pre-war lines of communication. In the interchange of letter writing, newspaper reading, and patriotic poetry, a new cult of battle flags and flag heroism emerged. In these, the emotions brought forth by flags changed significantly. Pieces of colored cloth became less important in representing the new Confederate nation and more crucial to memorializing the transformative experiences of glory and of death.

Enlisted men and civilians both focused particular attention on standard-bearers, those men most closely associated with battle colors. During the rise of professional armies in early modern Europe, ensign-bearers faced execution if they failed to inspire their men, to always show bravery, or to treat their banners with respect and in compliance with a strict code of etiquette. Americans of the nineteenth century were less stringent, but they still expected those in charge of a company's colors to register a collective willingness to protect its flags, particularly those made by local women. Once the real fighting began, it was clear that this position was also the most dangerous assignment possible. Given the artillery and infantry fire that such flags drew as targets, to volunteer for the job of carrying them into battle was clearly an act of bravery. It was also an indication that regard for personal safety was a low priority. One Confederate manual of arms suggested that flag-carriers in America might also need assistance in maintaining the requisite bravery. While in camp, these men should keep within the outer chain of sentinels, this book suggested, and "if necessary," they should have "their eyes bandaged, that they may not witness the number and force of their adversary."[46]

A wide range of stories made the valorous, if not suicidal, deeds of color-bearers a recurrent theme in Civil War lore. Some considered flag-bearers reckless in their thirst for conflict. When an Arkansas company reached the Potomac River after a long trek eastward, its flag-bearer waded into the water to defy passing Union gunboats. This provocation did not lead to a naval assault, but it did show, as one comrade later remarked, "how green we were in knowledge of warfare." Naïveté was no excuse for a similarly misguided effort by another color-bearer to lead an infantry charge against Federal cavalry. Though this action showed "more bravery than intelligence or discipline," as a witness later recalled, it still led other rebel standard-bearers to follow suit, since they did not want "to be outdone." Luckily, most of the men in these companies did not follow, knowing full well that even the bravest foot soldiers were no match for charging horses.[47]

Skeptics might suspect that such accounts were a phenomenon of postwar mythmaking, produced only when a regard for the heroics of combat eclipsed the less romantic aspects of war. The pages of late-nineteenth-century veterans' magazines in both North and South were filled with examples of men who, one after another, picked up their colors and advanced them, only to be imme-

17. The death of a color-bearer conveyed a religious aura in both North and South during the Civil War. *Harper's Weekly*, September 20, 1862. Courtesy, Michigan State University Libraries.

diately shot dead as a consequence. Some of these appear a bit too dramatic to be believed. Yet as the historian John Keegan has noted when writing about the Napoleonic wars, soldiers on the field of battle willingly took on dramatic roles, acting out flag-related heroism according to cultural scripts that placed a premium on death-accepting exploits. Private letters and journals from the period of the Civil War, as well as frequent press reports, indicate that those charged with the colors mostly lived up to the very high expectations that they accepted in taking on a dangerous job.[48]

Flag-related exploits were not limited to those designated as color-bearers. Soldiers who captured a banner from the enemy were also recognized for their bravery, as were those who defended flags that flew over entrenched positions or forts. In Charleston Harbor, a quartermaster earned a moment of international glory by replaying the famous scene of Sergeant William Jasper, who had risked his life in saving a fallen Fort Moultrie flag and attaching it to a cannon halbert in 1776. A Confederate sequel to this mythic episode from the American Revolution was set in motion when a cannonball shot through the fort's main flagstaff in the summer of 1863, killing a soldier below. An unnamed quartermaster then responded in a way that suggested his awareness of Jasper's own rescue of the Revolutionary flag in the exact spot nearly a century earlier. A British reporter, who did not mention the Jasper precedent, explained how this anonymous hero "immediately sprung forward and seized the fallen flag, tore it from its hold and leapt on to the traverse." Then, the soldier outdid Jasper himself by becoming a human flagpole, withstanding "the heavy fire immovable, until a jurymast was rigged and raised in the place of the shattered staff." The reporter on the scene considered this action "one of the most gallant feats" of the campaign, and his accompanying illustration of this scene was featured on the front page of the *London Illustrated News*.[49]

Not surprisingly, such larger-than-life heroics inspired patriotic verse, which served to heighten expectations of flag valor and to shape how combat was waged. One of the most explicit tributes to a standardbearer emphasized his exuberance and youth, in contrast to the more seasoned reserve of his comrade:

"Dost thou see the foe outnumbers us?"
A veteran calmly said;
The youthful soldier laughed aloud,
And gaily shook his head.
Then onward rode him to the fray,
Before the cannon's mouth,
Waving aloft, exultingly,
The banner of the South!

This song's conclusion showed this color-bearer's death, as might have been expected. But it chose to stress the satisfaction that resulted from his constant faith, willing sacrifice, and continued idealism: "The gallant boy lay on the

18. The daring attempt to keep the Confederate flag waving above a Charleston fort in 1863 reenacted the scene by William Jasper at nearby Fort Moultrie during the American Revolution. *London Illustrated News*, June 6, 1863. Courtesy, Michigan State University Libraries.

field," it observed, though there was "A smile upon his mouth" and "to his death-chilled breast he clasped, / The banner of the South!"[50]

Dramatic martyrdoms provided an incentive for all soldiers to care about the colors and to follow them forward into fire. They also served to remind soldiers of their responsibility for maintaining the flag once the chosen standard-bearer was killed. One Confederate poem depicted sequential sacrifices in verse: "The bearer falters—bleeds—he dies! / But ere to earth they slowly shrink, / Another grasps the staff—they rise!" An even more memorable image was produced in a northern poem that showed how "brave lads" who saw the color-bearer fall leapt "from the ranks . . . eagerly / Like groom to meet a bride." Margaret Junkin Preston pursued the theme of voluntary martyrdom, taking her listeners where "The steady colors tossed aloft / Their blood-red trail of light." In her story, the brother of a dead bearer picks up the fallen flag. Shouting, "God help me sir— I'll bear this flag / To victory or death!" he was then killed himself. Those who found his body after the battle noted "his face still wore / A look resolved and grand" and, more importantly, he "held a riddled flag close clutched / Within his shatter'd hand."[51]

Such poems, and the anecdotes that echoed them, nearly always ended in the fatal wounding of the flag-bearer. The main purpose of such mordant verse was to equate bravery with accepting death gladly. As the war continued, the fearless patriotism of color-bearers remained a major theme. During the Seven Day's campaign around Richmond, for instance, four different "boys" were killed while advancing the flag of the first South Carolina Volunteers. The oversized blue palmetto flag they carried was soon retired, in part because the commander considered it was "too conspicuous and costing too many lives." A Texas cavalryman also contemplated retiring his unit's colors after three men had died in its defense, noting that he "would want no brighter monument than this faded flag to decorate my parlor walls" if he lived to return to civilian life.[52]

Poetry, anecdotes, and illustrations alike placed flags at the center of the most decisive of all battlefield experiences—the actual moment of death. Victorians were acutely concerned with the details of a person's last moments, signaling as they did the passage from earthly existence to the afterlife. Earlier Christian notions of a "good death" had been democratized by the nineteenth century's "grief culture" and assumed particular importance during the Civil War. As Drew Faust has recently written, loved ones who could not be present at this fateful moment had an obsessive need to know the particulars of a soldier's death. Cues for the fallen's state of mind during the very last second of his earthly existence was particularly important for those who were immersed in a culture that discussed all aspects of mortality much more freely and with greater pathos than we do today. For a flag to be present at this moment imaginatively situated the soldier within a larger national community that he had pledged his life to defend. The flag could even serve as a proxy for a family member. A northern poem made this point explicitly, depicting a flag-bearer asking at his moment of death to "tell them gently how I died," noting that he had eight times saved "that fair flag" that "my sister helped to make."[53]

In dramatizing the death of a single individual, American sentimentalists put a human face on the mass suffering of modern war. These melodramatic scenes also gave a new role for the flag, which became a comforter and a celebrant of last rites as well as a shroud for burial. John H. Hewitt, one of the Confederacy's most prolific songwriters, explained how the flag had become the object that would:

> lead our battalions through carnage and fire,
> While the dying its beauty shall bless;
> And beneath its proud folds shall the free soul expire,
> While his lips the bright galaxy press.

In a later effort, Hewitt addressed the flag directly, registering the country's appreciation for the dignity it lent to the last moments of its citizens:

Over Secessia's dying sons,
Thoust droop'd thy bloodstained crest;
Witnessed the soldier's trembling prayer,
Before he sunk to rest.

This song, written late in the war, also thanked the flag for cheering those saddened by the conflict, though it was left ambiguous whether those who were fatally wounded or those left to mourn were more in need of comfort. The flag seemed to comfort them both, as it "flapt away the weeping dews" after having "mixed with them thy gory tears."[54]

The Civil War was not unusual in producing battlefield verse, since from the days of Homer through the twentieth century, combat has repeatedly called forth literary expression. Artists in successive periods have focused on the tools of war to capture the details of fighting. Typically, however, such efforts have focused on instruments more closely related to the business of killing enemies and defending one's own body than were those flags that appeared so frequently in the American imagination of the mid-nineteenth century. Ancient tributes to spears and shields were followed in modern times by such weapons cults as that of the bayonet in France, the machete in Revolutionary Cuba, and the AK-47 in Mozambique, whose national flag contains the image of this machine gun. There was no counterpart to this in the American Civil War, where popular attention did not focus on Sharpe's rifles or on rifled cannon, but on banners and, to a lesser extent, on drums and drummer boys. In this context, the inspirational poetry of the Civil War, with its stress on the nobility of dying and of following the flag and the music of battle, is noteworthy. The waving of banners and the marching to music represented the most purely patriotic aspects of war, while such activity also provided a fair rendition of the accelerated nature of Civil War combat. More powerful and accurate weapons, and the tendency, prior to 1864, to fight in the open, helped to make the quick charge on the field the prevailing image of this conflict, just as the trenches would conjure up the experience of World War I.[55]

As for the development of Confederate symbols, the growing prominence of battle flags meant a decline in some of the prestige associated with the civilian Stars and Bars. For a brief period in the fall of 1861, the same national flag that had inspired James Jackson's martyrdom became widely celebrated for being tested on the field of battle. One poem described this transformation by addressing the Stars and Bars:

Oh! lately but the flag of Hope
Thou hadst a prouder title won;
The battle flag! that dared to cope
With odds that e'en the brave might shun.

Service under fire at Fort Sumter had given immediate glory to "thy unfamiliar folds," this verse continued, while "thy latest field," in the battle of Virginia in midsummer, "has made thee sacred" and "taught us how to die, not yield." Another poet agreed, explaining how being "covered with glory at Bull Run" had made the "two crimson stripes" of the Stars and Bars "painted with the heart-blood of the free," while it caused the "eleven stars" to be "lit by patriot fires."[56]

The emergence of distinctive battle flags redirected some of this cultural energy away from the national Stars and Bars and toward new army symbols, particularly the Southern Cross unveiled in Virginia. Two months after the appearance of this flag, a Louisiana soldier praised the new flag by implicitly contrasting its origins with the national standard selected by Congress. This Southern Cross was special because

> Twas born amidst the battle glare, amidst the Artillery's roar
> Twas born while Southern steel repelled the invader from our door;
> Twas born while rushing squadrons drank deep of the crimson wave.
> It is the perch of Victory
> The Standard of the Brave.

This comparison was drawn even more boldly by an anonymous poet who noted that the Southern Cross was "No silken toy to flaunt in joy / When careless shouts are heard," as the Stars and Bars had been. In contrast, "Where thou art borne all scathed and torn," this poet concluded: "A nation's heart is stirred."[57]

One paradox of Civil War patriotism was that the only accomplishment more celebrated than dying for the cause was achieving victory on its behalf. This preference for winners explains why the victorious army, generals, and flags of Virginia were so much more inspiring than their comparatively hapless counterparts in the western theaters. By the spring of 1863, the *Richmond Enquirer* considered it "no disparagement to other great Generals and gallant forces" to recognize that Robert E. Lee and the Army of Northern Virginia had become nothing less than "the most famous Chief and army on earth at this day." Lee had none of the interest in symbols or flags that Beauregard had displayed and was clearly "not given to parades merely for show," as a subordinate later recorded. Yet merely by having "stood so often and so long in the tempests of fire," no other flag could claim to "fly higher" or "glow with a purer lustre" than that of the Army of Northern Virginia. It was hardly a coincidence that at this very moment, when the Virginia army was at the height of its success, Congress chose to place the distinctive diagonal Southern Cross associated with this force on a national flag that replaced the Stars and Bars. By situating a Southern Cross upon a larger field of white, this new flag, soon dubbed the Stainless Banner, established martial service as the highest national ideal.[58]

If anyone rivaled Lee in the popular imagination, it was Thomas J. "Stonewall" Jackson, whose cult grew to monumental proportions during the first two years of war. It was Stonewall's example, not any of the flowery directives like those issued by Beauregard, that was responsible for the combination of fear, awe, respect, and devotion that he received from his troops. As John Esten Cooke put it shortly before his leader's death, "to follow General Stonewall" was considered "a thing to tell to children's children." Jackson helped to embody the resolution, to use Cooke's words, that "the flag of the Republic must be borne aloft in triumph tho' the dearest and most precious blood of the Southern land be poured forth like water." Stonewall Jackson's own death, coming from a mistaken shot of his own soldier, was itself a testament to his insistence that even though "the field may be strewn with the flower and pride of the whole South," what was important was that "the red cross flag is floating still."[59]

Since Jackson's death came shortly after the adoption of the Stainless Banner to replace the Stars and Bars, his funeral in Richmond was one of the first appearances of this new emblem. The image of a general's coffin draped by a decidedly martial image drew considerable notice at the time and helped fix the reputation of the new national flag as a symbol of the warlike religiosity that Stonewall epitomized. The adoption of this more distinctive national flag followed a prolonged discussion by the press and by Congress on how best to replace the Stars and Bars. The debate over the appropriateness of the Southern Cross as a national symbol, and the subsequent role this symbol played in hastening Confederate consolidation, deserves attention in a chapter of its own. But before turning to this issue, it is important to recognize that the reputation of the St. Andrew's cross came more from its status as a battle flag, whose glory depended on actions on its behalf and from sacrifices it had drawn forth, than from any other single factor. In making a standard of war into the prime national symbol, Confederates were saying something important about the centrality of blood sacrifice to their collective sense of identity.[60]

The image of Stonewall Jackson's flag-draped casket reveals a larger pattern when placed in the context of two years of mounting sacrifices for the Confederate cause. In 1863, as in 1861, the patriot body was named Jackson, but Stonewall's corpse wore a soldier's suit of gray, not the blood-spattered clothes of a civilian innkeeper. The change in the actual design of the Confederate national flag was obvious; the shift in the metaphorical colors of war was more subtle, but no less important. By the time a new flag was chosen, few patriots were dying alone in the streets of southern cities and, as a result, Confederate public culture focused its attention on armies and enlisted men rather than on isolated patriots standing alone against armed invaders. The number of deaths in any one of the gigantic battles of this war eclipsed the total number of civilian casualties over four years. In understanding this sort of war, the story of James William Jackson, and of the Stars and Bars he died for, became increasingly irrelevant.[61]

CHAPTER FIVE

The Southern Cross and Confederate Consolidation

CURRENT CONTROVERSIES OVER the X-shaped Southern Cross rarely involve its specific design. What makes arguments so charged is a fundamental disagreement on what the Confederacy stood for and how its flag has been used, not on what elements of this banner were originally meant to convey. Yet for us to grasp the debates that occurred over the Southern Cross in the early 1860s, and to understand how this symbol stirred faithful hearts to action, we must examine its details more closely. White southerners subjected the particularities of this diagonal cross design to careful analysis during wartime, arguing among themselves about what sort of symbols would inspire ordinary citizens to endure hardships and even death. In considering whether the Southern Cross should become an official national emblem, sharp disagreements were aired about the use of explicitly Christian symbolism. Arguments over a cross flag, which began during the Montgomery convention, continued for over two years. In a process that became far more contentious than the selection of the Stars and Bars, editors pushed the question of a new national flag on a largely uninterested Congress, whose failure to adopt a new banner undermined its already declining prestige.

The associations of a cross design changed markedly over the first two years of war. The religious message that had been intended at the outset remained strong, though this became less controversial as the flags basic uses changed. The distinctiveness of the Southern Cross flag, which owed less to the American past than did the Stars and Bars, was another important part of its appeal. Despite the obvious differences between it and the Stars and Stripes, the Southern Cross retained the most popular elements of an earlier flag culture, especially the red, white, and blue colors it contained and the representation of each of the country's member states with a five-pointed star. Yet the most important associations of this symbol had little to do with Christianity, change, or continuity. Instead, the emotional power of the Southern Cross depended primarily upon its adoption as a battle flag late in 1861. When the Southern Cross was placed as the defining feature of a new national banner, the colors of war signaled the fundamentally military nature of collective purpose. As congressmen and other civilian leaders faltered in their effort to shape the national imagination, commanders and soldiers who had made this Cross famous nurtured national commitments and sustained national morale.[1]

By 1863, the Southern Cross had consolidated Confederate symbolism on a basis of martial religiosity. Congress chose a national flag that honored its most famous army at the same time it selected a national seal that invoked earlier military themes. These two icons together broadcast the southern struggle for existence through armed conflict to supporters of the cause at home, to enemies in America, and to potential allies abroad. The emphasis on martial themes was a mixed achievement. While the Southern Cross inspired support for the war through regular combat, it proved unable to ignite further political separatism once the Confederate armies had been soundly beaten. In this way, this emblem was no match for the American flag, whose more expansive associations conjured up martial experiences without being reduced solely to a war symbol. The convergence of martial themes of fighting for a holy cause continued through the growing use of the Southern Cross in the last years of war. The diagonal design that was first adopted in Virginia would be the most recognizable southern emblem by war's end. Its popularity, which outlasted the Confederacy, caused later generations to assume that there had never been more than a single rebel flag.

After stars and stripes, crosses were the most popular element in the Confederacy's initial consideration of national symbols. Beginning with the first two designs presented to the Montgomery Congress, nearly a fifth of all entries in the informal flag competition contained this symbol in one form or another. In addition to the twenty-two citizens who offered crosses in their suggested designs, another nine wrote letters that formally objected to this Christian emblem. In sum, nearly one out of every three entries addressed either the benefits or the liabilities of featuring the most familiar of all religious symbols on the new country's national flag.[2]

Two intertwining issues emerged in this early period that would continue to influence considerations of the Southern Cross. The most heated disputes pitted those who wanted to capture the sustaining power of a widely shared religious faith against those who wanted to keep religion and politics separate and to avoid alienating those outside the Christian community. But the earliest enthusiasts of the Southern Cross also injected themselves into the more general debate over the proper degree of continuity and departure that shaped the early weeks of the new government. Most who supported cross banners claimed these would be "utterly unlike" the flag of the United States, taking great pride in this "original and peculiar" idea.[3]

Pleas for this distinctive cross symbol were made in the same range of media that carried calls to retain the Stars and Stripes. Christopher Memminger of South Carolina gave this Christian symbol a powerful history during the first and most influential flag speech made to the Provisional Congress, three days before Walker Brooke made his own tribute to the American flag. Going farther back in history than the American Revolution, Memminger referred to the Roman emperor Constantine, who had placed the cross on his banners after receiving an instruction to do so in a dream. This fourth-century visitation resulted in Constantine's conversion to Christianity and his command to the Roman army to inscribe the initials of Jesus Christ on its shields and its "labarum" banners. Aware of the link between this gesture of faith and Constantine's decisive victory at the battle of the Milvian Bridge, Memminger suggested that Confederates would achieve similarly happy results by making their own symbolic pact with God. To blunt the legendary appeal of the Stars and Stripes, he offered up the Latin motto *In hoc signo vicnes*, the words that had promised Constantine "in this sign we will conquer."[4]

Memminger added more peculiarly southern concerns to this ancient legend. He claimed in this same speech that a cross flag would show the world that it was "by the aid of revealed religion" that Confederates had beaten back abolition and "achieved over fanaticism the victory which we this day witness." Memminger and others who wanted the sharpest break from American norms hailed the conjunction of distinctiveness, Christian faith, and defense of slavery in a Southern Cross flag. George Bagby, one of the earliest and most passionate advocates of this design, called out early in 1861 for southerners to "tear from the national flag the fifteen stars which the despots of the North have attempted to sully with the imputation of barbarism" and to "give these stars a double brilliance by forming them into a cross." This gesture, he promised, would produce an "emblem of that pure and holy religion which has been reviled, trampled and spit upon in the interest of Abolitionism" and might ward off "the mercenary hordes of the North would fain deliver over to the sword of the invader and the pike of the negro insurrectionist."[5]

The connection between the slavery controversy and the avowal of Christianity in a cross flag would have been clearer to participants than to those looking back from today's perspective. In contrast to the South's status as the Bible Belt of later years, the slave states in 1860 did not boast a larger church-going population or a particularly greater emphasis on theological orthodoxy than other American regions. The Confederate case for being a new chosen people of God rested on a narrower basis, which Memminger suggested in his emphasis on the triumph of "revealed religion" against abolitionists. In this reference to the scriptural defense of bondage, he sounded a common southern refrain that the Bible was the best means of establishing slavery's basic legiti-

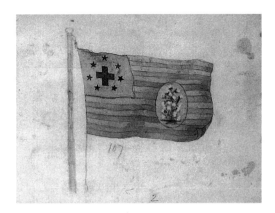

19. A wide variety of cross design appeared among the flags offered in Montgom-
     ery. These three were suggested by P. J. Anderson of Montgomery. Courtesy,
     National Archives.

macy. Southerners repeatedly charged that the abolitionists were abandoning God's word and ignoring that slavery had been a sanctioned institution both in ancient Israel and in early Christian Rome.[6]

As Confederates considered putting a cross on their national flag, they were pursuing other ways to identify their new country with evangelicalism. The antebellum period had witnessed a remarkable spread of Protestant organization that convinced many evangelicals to make their governments more self-consciously Christian. Some saw the framing of a new constitution by the Confederacy as a welcome opportunity to launch a new nation united by a common religious tradition. The Montgomery convention did insert a "faith clause" in its preamble and even toyed with such evangelical issues as the banning of mail on Sundays. The pattern would continue with a range of thanksgiving days, public sermons, and army revivals over the course of the following four years. Christianity came to function, as the historian Drew Faust has explained, as the "most fundamental source of legitimation" for Confederate nation-builders. The belief that God was on their side lay at the heart of the new country's image of itself and its role in human history.[7]

The case for a Christian, anti-abolitionist flag was brought into the popular culture by St. George Tucker's "Southern Cross," one of the most widely re-printed flag songs of the secession crisis. While this poem, which George Bagby published in the *Southern Literary Messenger*, did not sway the Provisional Congress to adopt a religious emblem, its words remained popular throughout the war, and one paper even ventured in 1863 that "no song has a better title to be our national song." The song's success no doubt owed something to its use of the "Star Spangled Banner"'s melody, though its striking use of religious imagery was probably even more impressive to its listeners. "Like the symbol of love, and redemption its form," the song explained, the new flag would give the "promise of peace, or assurance in war!" Like Memminger and many other advocates of a cross flag, Tucker invoked the example of Constantine's labarum, which had converted devotion to a Christian redeemer into military victory. Its chorus also offered a distinctly hopeful promise that the "Cross of the South, which shall ever remain, / To light us to freedom, and glory again."[8]

Tucker's song also featured an array of powerfully negative images that recalled classic Christian themes. Recalling a recent attack on New England Puritans in his own novel, Tucker explained: "How peaceful and blest was America's soil, / 'Til betrayed by the guile of the Puritan demon." The same intolerant Puritanism that had stifled dissent in colonial New England now "lurks under virtue, and springs from its coil / To fasten its fangs in the life blood of freemen." Tucker called for "each heart that can feel" to "crush the foul viper 'neath liberty's heal!" in order to combat this subversive intruder into the New World garden of innocence. His last verse turned even more violent, ending a song that began by invoking harmony and love into a violent warning that promised "Defiance to tyrants, and death to their minions!"[9]

Despite the backing that Southern Cross banners received in speeches, editorials, and this widely quoted verse, the Montgomery convention chose the Stars and Bars after four weeks of consideration and then practically eliminated all crosses from consideration for over two years. The first public opposition to the design came not from Jeffersonian skeptics of orthodox religion, since the number of unbelievers had declined markedly between the time of the Revolution and the outbreak of the Civil War. Instead, it was religious practitioners of various sorts who criticized the cross as a national symbol. Francis McMaster, a Presbyterian, considered that placing a cross on a flag would be a "Papal sign"; the editor James DeBow, himself a Baptist, thought it "reminiscent of Catholic rule" that had "too much to do with the machinery of the Dark Ages." Others suggested that adopting the cross as a national emblem was sacrilegious. "This is a sign of good will from God to man," one writer to the *Charleston Courier* explained. Since the cross was "too sacred to wave as the sign of political contest," there was "no propriety in battling under that sacred symbol for earthly fame or power." Still another objection reluctantly admitted that the Yankees were Christian too. "This contest is not with the Saracens," it pointed out, "where the sacred cross would have been very appropriate."[10]

The most vociferous protest came from Charles Moise, a thirty-six year old who described himself as "a southerner of the Jewish persuasion." His six-page letter to the Montgomery Convention was among the earliest flag-related communications addressed to that body. It spoke for Jews across the state to protest what Moise considered "the attempt to encapsulate religion with government." His objection, which would be echoed for the following two years, was that "the flag of a country ought certainly to be regarded with affection and reverence by all classes of people composing the nation." Clearly, he then explained, "this cannot be the case if the symbol of a particular religion is made the element of configuration." Though apparently never published, Moise's letter was addressed to each member of the South Carolina delegation. Its contents became well known to the other Confederates who submitted their objections to the Congress, and the letter seems to have played a major role in the resulting hesitancy to adopt a Cross flag thereafter.[11]

Some might find it odd that Jewish concerns were taken so seriously by leaders of a slaveholding South that is often assumed to have been a bastion of Protestantism. Yet stereotypes aside, the roughly twenty-five thousand Jews living in the Confederacy in 1860 were a significant presence, with some of them holding major positions of importance within the new government. Charleston Jewry had especially strong claims to be taken seriously. This community had constructed one of the earliest synagogues in British North America, while its peak population of five thousand made it the largest Jewish community in the United States until those of Philadelphia and New York surpassed it in the 1830s. The history of Moise's own family bore out his letter's claim that "Jewish citizens had stood by the state in every crisis" and that they had nurtured strong feelings about their home. Descended from refugees from the Caribbean, Moise had been raised by the only Jewish Charlestonian to practice law successfully in the antebellum period. His own great-uncle, Myer Moses, had gloried as early as 1806 that Jews considered South Carolina to be no less than a "second Jerusalem" and that they were "proud of being sojourners in the promised land." Other Carolinians praised their Jewish brethren for their fidelity to slavery. The same week that Moise sent his letter, the *Charleston Mercury* argued that Jews "too well understand the Old Testament" to be "carried away by the false philanthropy of a spurious fanaticism" of Yankee abolitionists.[12]

However one might measure the impact of Moise's intervention, any sort of sustained dissension among whites would have been crippling at a time when national unity was crucial. Alienating even a small group from the fight ahead was bad policy; there were too many other things that might go wrong without stirring strong negative emotions with a divisive flag. Letters sent to Montgomery made this clear, agreeing with Moise that the cross was "not appropriate for a Flag of an entirely national character" and echoing his concern that it conveyed "too sectarian an aspect" to be chosen. Exactly how the Congress made its final choice, or how the opposition of Moise and other Jews was factored in, remains unclear. Miles later explained that there was nothing particularly controversial about an overtly religious flag but that the congressmen had voted against it for "looking like a pair of suspenders." The evidence suggests otherwise. Jewish concerns seemed to have shaped symbolic issues even after the Southern Cross became the battle flag of the Virginia army. When Robert E. Lee became commander of the Army of Northern Virginia, he made no effort to change Beauregard's cross design. Yet he designed his own headquarters flag as if to balance the field of religious emblems. A unique arrangement of stars on this banner, which is now held at the Museum of the Confederacy, apparently represents the Ark of the Covenant, which sealed the ancient Israelites' pact with God.[13]

Even before the Southern Cross became an emblem of the Virginia army, some Confederates were intent to place a cross design on the official national flag. William Porcher Miles led the way as chairman of the Committee on the Flag and Seal, making the replacement of the Stars and Bars his "pet hobby" by late in the summer of 1861. Miles welcomed Beauregard's complaints about the confusion caused by the Stars and Bars at the battle of Manassas, probably hearing echoes of his own warnings against the "military solecism" of emulating the colors of a probable enemy. The need for a distinctive battle flag presented him an opportunity to introduce his own agenda of weeding out former loyalties from Confederate culture.[14]

During the Montgomery convention, Miles had tried to make the Southern Cross more palatable to its opponents, especially those who objected to its clear Christian connotations. He self-consciously opted for the St. Andrew's cross of Scotland, which featured a diagonal design, admitting that his choice of this model was a way to assuage "the religious objections about the cross" that would have followed a more recognizable upright St. George's cross of England. He had hoped that a cross presented on its side would "not stand out so conspicuously" and that it might be accepted as a "heraldic rather than an ecclesiastical symbol."[15] When it became clear that the opinions of his fellow congressmen would not be changed by this modification, Miles and Beauregard instead sought authorization for new army flags from the War Department. They obtained permission not because of the merits of their particular design, but because the department concluded that selecting a flag should be the prerogative of individual commanders. Other generals soon followed in adopting their own symbols, and some, such as Bishop Leonidas Polk, incorporated even more recognizably religious versions of the Christian cross symbol.[16]

Confederate newspapers joined Miles in his call to make the Southern Cross the official national flag. The day before the battle of Manassas raised the issue of combat confusion, the *Charleston Mercury* claimed to "speak the sentiments of three-fourths of the Southern people" in its opinion that the Stars and Bars "has not only failed to satisfy, but has greatly disappointed them." Pressure soon mounted against what the *New Orleans Delta* called "the hybrid bunting" that had been "in use during our transition state from attempted to confirmed independence." By the beginning of 1862, Bagby concluded in the *Messenger:* "everybody wants a new Confederate Flag," since the derivative one was "universally hated." In all three instances, the new Southern Cross battle-flag was urged as a national standard. This flag drew the support from a wide range of the press and also from at least two groups of Confederate women, who each organized petition campaigns on its behalf. In part as a result of this advocacy, there was a sharp increase in the numbers of designs presented to the Provisional Congress late in 1861 and early in 1862, though there is no way of calculating how many of these offered overtly Christian symbolism (see table 5.1).[17]

Complaints against the Stars and Bars were predictable. As John Daniel put it, "That which was thought its chief recommendation" (namely, its resemblance to the American flag) had become "its scarlet sin." The writer L. Virginia French explained that the question boiled down to whether Confederates should "forever be a nation of imitators," borrowing their flag from the Union and such songs as the "Marseillaise" from France. Others argued that the trouble was that the Star Spangled Banner was no longer worthy of imitating. Once "associated with some brilliant deeds achieved by Southern arms," this flag had become "eternally identified with all that is vile, odious and execrable," as a correspondent of William Porcher Miles put it. Calls to change the Confederate flag often acknowledged that the time had come to relinquish all those feelings for the United States that had lingered through the process of disunion. One

TABLE 5.1
Flag and Seal Petitions to Congress and Actions Taken, 1861–1863

	Number of Flag Designs	Number of Mottoes or Seal Designs	Number of Representatives Presenting Designs	Actions Taken at End of Period, with Date of Vote
February–March 1861	26/99[a]	5/10[a]	17	March 4: Unofficial adoption of Stars and Bars
December 1861– February 1862	19	0	9	February 11: Committee proposes "Four Star Flag" February 14: Congress passes resolution ceding decision to Permanent Congress
February–April 1862	28	3	16	April 19: Committee proposes "Sun Flag"; full Congress postpones action
September– October 1862	8	3	7	October 13: House and Senate fail to agree on their respective seal suggestions
January–May 1863	16	8	18	April 18: Adoption of C. S. Great Seal May 1: Adoption of Stainless Banner

[a] The first number from Thian; the second represents those designs, submitted but not presented, that are held in NA-CFD.
SOURCE: Raphael P. Thian, *Documentary History of the Flag and Seal of the Confederate States* (Washington, D.C., 1880).

petitioner to Congress early in 1862 found it regrettable that "the Black Republicans" had stolen a flag "as well as everything else that pertained to the late Union." He realized there was little choice but to accept the situation, however. Another concluded that since "the despot Lincoln" appropriated the flag to his "vile purposes," only one option remained—to "eke out something unique" as a true replacement, not a pale imitation.[18]

Despite a seeming groundswell for change, there were still problems with the Southern Cross, the only design that ever rivaled the Stars and Bars in the popular imagination. The most serious objections related to its overt Christianity, though John Daniel, the crusty editor of the *Richmond Examiner*, also pointed out that this seemingly original design was in fact a mere copy of the flags of other European powers. Continuing opposition to the cross frustrated George Bagby, who dismissed the objection of Jews as a "a feather weight in the balance." Once placed on a flag, the cross would give no more offense than those on the steeples of churches, he argued, while the benefits would be immense. Southerners would "fight under it and for it far more bravely and lovingly than under any other banner" since it was "what their hearts want." A short time later, the editor Joseph Addison Turner offered another reply to such objections. "We are as far removed from piratism, superstition, or fanaticism as any man can be," he wrote, "and yet we regard the effort to place the cross upon our national flag as all-important."[19]

Advocates of a new flag had to address another criticism—that there was an actual Southern Cross constellation that could not be seen in the Northern Hemisphere. Memminger had invited this complaint when he invoked this well-known feature of the southern skies during his first flag speech before Congress. Bagby went farther, arguing early in 1861 that this celestial Southern Cross would lead Confederates "the way our march of empire tends." He elaborated on expansionist aims a year later, just as the geographical criticism of the Southern Cross grew most intense. "The truth is we *shall* see the Southern Cross," he boasted, arguing that the Amazon forests were "the natural heritage of the Southron and his domestic slave." When the new proslavery republic reached its ultimate extent, the "soldier of civilization shall behold the Cross, like that upon his victorious banner, burning welcome from the skies."

Discussion of a new national flag was energized by the *Richmond Daily Dispatch*, which ran a series of influential articles that appeared the same week that Beauregard unveiled the Southern Cross battle flag to troops in Virginia. An anonymous contributor from Georgia explained in three successive articles in the *Dispatch* why neither the St. Andrew's cross nor the Stars and Bars were fit symbols for the new country. This writer rejected the St. Andrew's cross primarily because of its lack of emotional resonance, noting that at that point it had "no solitary association in the history of our people, nor root nor fibre in their hearts." The Stars and Bars had the opposite problem, since it recalled exactly those aspects of the past that needed to be expunged. "We have endeavored to put our new wine into fragments of old bottles," and now "bottles have burst, and the wine has been spilled." Whatever might be attempted, the problem remained a fundamental one. "We will never get rid of the taint of that old flag," since it was "like a marriage ring after a divorce for infidelity. When we hate the marriage, we hate all its mementos."

These articles suggested that symbols that represented the form of government through a federation of stars be rejected and replaced by those that might appeal to "the heart of the people" directly. This notion that flags represent the national community echoed the French decision in 1848 to keep the tricolor even after a change in government, since it had come to stand for the people at large, rather than a particular political regime. For Confederates to venture a similar project required a new discussion of common values and traditions that had been muted since the Montgomery Congress chose to reassemble the Stars and Stripes into the Stars and Bars. The *Dispatch* writer made a fundamental departure from American flag conventions in suggesting that "our land itself" should be depicted on a flag that made the sun a signal of the warmth of the Confederacy. "No broader foundation could be laid for a nation's love and loyalty," this writer claimed, without much to back up such a sweeping assertion. "The dying soldier, lifting his last expiring glance to the rising sun on its folds, would find the symbol of hope to his country in the FLAG OF THE SUN."[20]

These articles moved the topic of flags beyond the choice between the status quo and the Southern Cross by asking Confederates to consider what design best captured the national spirit. Such a charge made a return to the issue of slavery all but inevitable. Bagby himself responded to the *Dispatch* articles: "If we want a truly symbolical flag, let us have a big black splotch, signifying the nigger, on a white field, signifying the cotton field." The comment was not intended as a serious suggestion, since Bagby, a wry humorist throughout his career, remained firm in his commitment to the Southern Cross. Yet whatever his intention, his comments were not unique. Bagby seemed as surprised as anyone when a flag model placed in the window of the *Dispatch* offices included a black stripe in reference to the "peculiar institution." Seeing this, he wrote to the *Charleston Mercury*: "Hah! How would a buzzard sitting on a cotton bale, with a chew of tobacco in his mouth, a little nigger in one claw, and a palmetto tree in the other, answer? Nothing could be more thoroughly and comprehensively Southern." Bagby planted his tongue firmly in his cheek, thinking that such attempts to capture the southern spirit were ridiculous. Yet another writer for the *Mercury* soon was more serious in providing a sketch of a black-and-white flag whose colors would convey "our faith in the peculiar institution," and that would become, if adopted, "an enduring mark of our resolve to retain that institution while we exist as a free and independent people." Congressmen paid little heed to this or to other murmurs about moving toward such an explicitly proslavery gesture. They recognized, as they had early in 1861, that embracing slavery openly would hurt the Confederacy beyond its borders.[21]

Congressmen took up other types of suggestions from the press, though never with the same energy that they had displayed in Montgomery. The Provisional Congress itself made one more attempt at a flag before its year term ended, offering a field with four stars that obliquely evoked the diagonal Southern Cross. Yet these four stars were too well disguised, leaving one critic to note, "Perhaps they mean something, but people will have to be told what their meaning is." Such a halfway measure was quickly ruled a failure, and the Provisional Congress entrusted the new permanent Congress the responsibility for a new national flag.[22] A reconstituted Committee on the Flag was not able to do much better. A few weeks after the permanent Congress had begun, there emerged what one paper called "a rare abortion of shields, crosses, triangles, and an eclipsed sun." Clearly inspired by the *Dispatch* suggestion of a sun, this flag substituted a single sun for stars, and even had a hint of a cross in the background, though again this element was too disguised to really stand out. The obliteration of stars invited immediate cries against "consolidation," a charge that actually meant something at a time when the Confederate government was drawing criticism for imposing conscription and martial law. This "sun flag" too was withdrawn just a short time after its unveiling.[23] Rumors circulated a few months later that Congress was moving once again toward disaster, considering a flag that featured a chain made from as many links as there were states. The southern press immediately registered its disapproval, preventing Congress from issuing a report and preempting what would surely have been endless remarks among northerners about the chains of despotism and slavery.[24]

The reinvigoration of flag debate that began in the winter of 1861–62 marked a shift both in topics and in the manner of deliberating upon the choices. Congressmen no longer gave "flag speeches" as they had in Montgomery, and they often seemed annoyed by the growing public outcry for a new flag. When the matter of symbols reappeared in the late summer of 1862, Senator Albert Gallatin Brown grumbled about "throwing away a whole day" on such matters while the "army is wasting away like snow before an August sun." This reluctance of politicians to debate symbols meant that the press was obliged to explain why flags mattered in the first place. "These outward signs and symbols of nationality, small as they seem," the *Richmond Dispatch* wrote in January of 1862, were "really of vast importance, and a Flag to fight under, and to learn to love, is now almost our greatest need." The *Dispatch* itself, as the most widely circulated paper in the Confederacy, published a steady stream of letters on the topic and emphasized the importance of new designs, while it also displayed several models in its Richmond window for citizens and other members of the press corps to observe and comment upon. The public space for considering flag designs thus moved out of a political body and into a print network whose center lay in the increasingly important world of the Richmond media. Comments about flags sometimes flowed in from elsewhere, especially from Charleston, but the journalistic node of Richmond, which by 1864 featured no fewer than ten separate periodicals, transmitted most of what was going on with flags to the rest of the country. Reports and opinions by Richmond papers or Richmond correspondents for other journals were picked up across the country as an incipient metropolitan press guided the consideration of what national symbols should be, and, by extension, how national purpose should be defined.[25]

The press became strongly critical of Congress for its haphazard campaign to come up with a replacement for the discredited Stars and Bars. Throughout the spring of 1862, there were mounting questions about the "taste" and "judgment" of southern elected officials and fears that they might "fix another abortion on us," to quote the editor of the *Richmond Examiner*. It seemed to him that "public taste cannot be compelled" and that delay might even be preferable to the product of the "secrecy and haste" that had produced the first flag in Montgomery. Most others were less patient, urging Congress to relinquish their authority by creating a "committee of women" to complete the task, or simply by seeking the help of "two or three gentlemen who are competent in the premises." By the fall of 1862, the *Savannah Morning News* entered the debate, charging that the country's lack of "ingenuity and taste" was especially pronounced in Congress. The *Richmond Enquirer* continued to think that symbols were "a matter of some importance" in that they provided men with "a symbol to rally round" that might be considered "somewhat mystic and divine." But even so, it wanted something soon, and was happy to lower its expectations to anything that might "contain no anomaly or stupidity."[26]

The carping tone of the press captured a wider sense of discontent and crisis. The *Southern Illustrated News* reported that public exasperation was widespread, as the people grew "tired of looking at the poor imitation of the stars and stripes which floats from our public buildings and military posts." If the decline in poetry to the Stars and Bars was any indication, this was indeed the case. The symbolic impasse that persisted through 1862 and the early months of 1863 exacerbated a more general problem of representation. The competition between the national flag and the Southern Cross could be seen in illustrations that featured both of these emblems intertwined. Having two widely hailed flags, one for their government and another for their largest army, could not equal the power of having one banner that united civilian and military commitments, as the Star Spangled Banner did for the Union.[27]

Congress finally adopted the Southern Cross on a national flag in 1863, though few were willing to praise this much-delayed action. A later writer colorfully summed up conventional wisdom that "a blind hog does sometimes find an acorn." Few ventured that Congress should be praised for elevating this symbol, since it had merely been accepted, after much foolish delay, a flag made famous by the country's true heroes—those men who fought and died beneath this symbol in war. In a growing number of battlefields, as well as in an expanding body of popular verse, "soldiers have died with one last look upon its dear cross," the *Richmond Enquirer* explained. "In the hour of victory," the flag had seemed "transfigured into something God-like, when the rapturous shouts of our Southern soldiery shook its folds like a storm." Since the Southern Cross had acquired most of its power as a war banner, it was clear to the *Southern Illustrated News* that this flag, which had been "made by Richmond ladies," had much earlier become "through baptism of blood and fire, the national ensign" regardless of the delay by politicians in recognizing this fact.[28]

General Beauregard chimed in to praise a flag that had been "consecrated by the best blood of our country on so many battle-fields." His earlier predictions that the cross would eventually become the leading Confederate symbol finally materialized, not least because of his own efforts to spread the banner into armies beyond Virginia. After taking the design west with him in 1862, he then introduced it to troops under his command in Charleston. After his favorite design was included in the Stainless Banner, the process of symbolic consolidation continued. Versions of the St. Andrew's cross were adopted by the navy, by forces in the Trans-Mississippi, and by much of the Army of

Tennessee. By the middle of 1864, the only major Confederate force fighting for a flag that did not contain a cross was William Hardee's unit, which still bore a blue standard with a white disk in its center. In comparative terms, this made the battle flags of the Confederate armies far more regular than those of their Union counterparts, whose individual corps did not witness the same sort of convergence toward a common battle design.[29]

Though official actions was crucial in the spread of the Southern Cross through Confederate armies, the southern public associated its power with the sacrifice of more ordinary patriots. The work of politicians, editors, and even generals was ignored by the *Richmond Examiner*, which gloried that the Southern Cross had been a "spontaneous creation of the war, chosen without an advocate by the soldiers." This was untrue in the strict sense, since Beauregard, Miles, and the Richmond press had worked assiduously to promote this distinctive flag. But such a claim recognized that the Southern Cross had entered a special category of symbols not through any abstract discussion about national ideas, but through the accumulation of voluntary deaths.[30]

Less than a month after the Confederacy adopted its new national flag, Henry Hotze, one of the most important Confederate propagandists in Europe, joined the image of the Stainless Banner with that of the British Union Jack and proceeded to paste the two banners on "every available space in the streets of London." Sensing a pro-Confederate "people's movement" in the wake of Stonewall Jackson's death, Hotze mass-produced placards of the two flags in order to "impress the masses with the vitality of our cause." As Parliament prepared to revisit the question of Confederate recognition later that summer, Hotze recognized an appropriate moment to begin a concerted effort to sway the loyalties of the British public.[31]

Hotze knew that membership in the international community was not a process of self-selection and that claiming nationality was worthless without diplomatic recognition. This Swiss-born southerner edited the *London Index* and took on a range of cultural projects to help the British to determine "whether a new Power is really added to the family of nations." Deciding whether a people had created a nation was not just an "etymological puzzle or even a philosophical speculation," as he put it in 1863, but was "the gravest practical problem which a statesman has to solve." As foreign leaders debated this crucial issue, Hotze sensed that a flag designed primarily for its own citizens might also find favor beyond its borders.[32]

This international context influenced Confederate flag design in a negative sense, by discouraging any overt reference to slavery. The case was different with in the matter of a national seal, which Hotze would eventually procure for his government. This matter elicited a debate over the nature of national symbols that ran parallel to the more popular flag discussions. Congress turned its attention to the question during the fall of 1862, causing the press to become

20. Seal designs generated a series of congressional debates between the fall of 1862 and the early summer of 1863. The Confederate House and Senate proposed similar designs (facing page, top and bottom) to represent the current struggle, differing only in the choice of an ancient or modern scene. After press complaints about these and subsequent suggestions, Congress finally agreed upon the last seal pictured (above), which featured the image of a warlike George Washington and appealed to God with the motto "Deo Vindice." This selection complemented the themes of martial religiosity also evoked by the Stainless Banner. Congressional designs from Raphael Thian, *Documentary History of the Flag and Seal of the Confederate States*, courtesy, Duke University Special Collections. Great Seal of the Confederacy, courtesy, Museum of the Confederacy, Richmond, Virginia. Photograph by Katherine Wetzel.

"all agog" in trying to choose a seal that would elicit respect from those doing business with the rebel government. As the molders of Confederate opinion argued among themselves about competing designs; their debates took up the matter of what might be the most credible means of representing the country abroad and on paper, rather than on the field of battle and through cloth, as had been the case with their flag debates. In doing so, they would add another dimension to what was becoming a recognizably unified symbolic program.[33]

Suggestions for Confederate seals began in the Montgomery Congress, though these never touched the popular imagination as flags did. No one expected this insignia to be a matter of mass enthusiasm or the subject of patriotic verse, any more than the Great Seal of the United States had been in the years since its selection in 1782. A seal would not need to encourage citizens to risk their lives for cause and country, but would be judged according to its ability to convey dignity and power to the world and perhaps also to furnish a motto like "E Pluribus Unum" that might express a central national idea. Distilling the essence of the nation into a single design and motto was still something that could agitate editors and congressmen. As the country contemplated an emblem that might be "the exponent of its individuality, its pursuits, its position and importance among the nations of the earth," as one Richmond paper put it, difficulties were certain to arise.[34]

Both houses of the Congress prepared for an imminent diplomatic exchange by suggesting new seal designs during a short session that met in September and October of 1862. Yet while hopes for international recognition drove their actions, melodramatic themes from home informed their suggestions. The versions of House and Senate each featured an archetypal Confederate man and woman in respective roles as defender and defended from invasion. The House set the scene in classical times, though it took the liberty of substituting a wreath of cotton for the traditional laurel. It made its point clear with an accompanying motto "Pro Aris et Focis," which had also been a common inscription on regimental banners. The Senate chose a translated version, "Our Homes and Our Constitutions," and a correspondingly modern scene, believing that "the history of this revolution was of sufficient dignity to originate symbols." Both examples intended to honor the efforts of ordinary citizens in achieving independence.[35]

Journalists who were already perturbed over flag matters were quick to condemn both these designs. Each was criticized for being too heavily laden with the theme of conflict and war, which made them inappropriate for a country that might someday hope to exist in peace with the rest of the world. As the *Charleston Mercury* warned, seals needed to avoid subjects that conveyed "a transitory state" and should remember their future use when the country was "in a condition of well-established repose." Another common criticism was that these designs were just too busy. John Daniel of the *Richmond Examiner* wondered if Congress thought it "was manufacturing a vignette for a counterfeit bank note" in its selection and condemned the crowding of images as a "Yankee Doodle apparatus." Considering himself an expert on such matters, this former diplomat warned that the country was in danger of becoming "the laughing stock of the whole official world" if it did not choose something more dignified. This hapless first foray into seal design elicited the same type of scorn for the talents of congressmen that had greeted their flag efforts. "Condemnation and ridicule" of the grouped pair was "universal and well-merited," the *Charleston Mercury* reported, while editors of the *Charleston Courier* concluded, in what seemed a general assessment, that congressmen were "smitten with a special access of incompetency when they touch the subject of flags or seals."[36]

Daniel's *Richmond Examiner* had taken an early lead in considering the seal, setting down some basic principles early in 1862, at a time when most papers were calling for a replacement of the Stars and Bars. The paper argued for a "single noble object" capable of gaining respect abroad and attracting the "affections of the nation" as no "absurd allegorical picture of many figures" ever could. As a round of suggestions in the press proceeded, most stuck to this suggestion of a single principle or defining characteristic of the new country. Among the possibilities were a plow or a collection of crops to represent agriculture or a magnolia or a sun to suggest tropical lushness. What must have been the least likely symbols of the Confederacy was a preference for the American buffalo by both the *Richmond Examiner* and the *Charleston Mercury*. There was not anything particularly "southern" about this beast, these two papers conceded, but it was undeniably "noble in form, powerful in make, is American, and is distinct in form from any other animal."[37]

Early in 1863, a suggestion by Senator C. C. Clay of Alabama showed that seals could provoke controversies as volatile as those raised by flags. Presenting an idea first devised by Secretary of State Judah Benjamin, Clay argued that the "cavalier" should be featured in order to "indicate the origin of Southern society." He pointed out that not only were southerners a "nation of horsemen," but that this figure would remind the world that their ancestors had been gentlemen. Given the festering class divisions already apparent in the Confederacy, the identification of the country with the wellborn was not very good politics. The press was quick to denounce Clay's "ideas of caste" and the notion that those "few families" that could trace actual cavalier descent should be set up with the "pretension" of being the truest representative of the new Confederacy. Congress itself backpedaled, including in its final report an explicit disavowal of the "division of society into two orders," which it considered (apparently leaving aside the issue of slavery) as "inconsistent with Confederate institutions."[38]

Senator Clay had suggested almost in passing that the best model of a horseman was the equestrian statue of George Washington, which had been erected outside the Virginia state capital building in the 1850s. Since Washington's image did not touch off the same sort of class tensions, newspaper commentators quickly pressed forward the notion that this Virginia hero should appear on the national seal. As both the founder of the first American nation and a leading southern slaveholder, Washington had figured as a potential national symbol earlier. Some had even hoped that the new Confederacy might adopt the title of the "Republic of Washingtonia." The choice of the Richmond statue drew out other themes as well. This was one of the most martial presentations of Washington that had ever been attempted, portraying him as a general fighting for independence, in a way that struck a chord with Confederates who were doing the same in the 1860s. The statue also recalled Jefferson Davis's presidential inaugural, held on Washington's Birthday and delivered to the public while he stood standing beside this massive sculpture. To make this link visible, the Congress chose to engrave the date of this occasion, February 22, 1862, directly onto the seal itself.[39]

As for the seal's motto, there had been some concern that Latin should be avoided, so that soldiers could recognize immediately what they were fighting for. Editor Daniel dismissed this argument, noting that "dispatches of the Government are not addressed to soldiers" but to "foreign nations." His respect for Latin as a "universal language" was echoed in Congress; as one representative reminded his colleagues, "the motto on the seal would be sent to countries beyond the sea, where our language was almost unknown." After some debate, Congress placed "Deo Vindice" on the seal, which can be roughly translated as "with God as our defender." The primary rival to this short, easily remembered phrase, might have raised a more general ruckus from those who wanted something to appeal to the common people of the Confederacy. After quoting Livy, Horace, Justin, Cicero, Plautus, and Tacitus, Senator Thomas Semmes of Louisiana suggested: "Deo Vindice Majores Aemulamur." If chosen, this would have proclaimed to the world: "Under the guidance and protection of God we endeavor to equal and even to excel our ancestors."[40]

The invocation of God in "Deo Vindice" did not make a particularly good fit with Washington, who was not well known for his piety. Yet it did complement the Southern Cross, which had been placed on the national flag just a few weeks later. Religious mottoes had been urged earlier as a way to "invoke the blessing of God as a constant prayer." A proponent of this idea insisted that "the nation that knows God, He will honor," and hoped that "other nations will admire and may be led to similar acknowledgment" after learning of the "sincerity of our nation and conduct." With the proper words, even the Yankees might be shamed into "less of hostility" toward an avowedly pious people. As the Confederacy was nearing the peak of its military success, registering twin appeals to God—one on a flag and another on the seal—seemed a means of bringing about a decisive turn toward permanent independence.[41]

With the nearly simultaneous adoption of a flag and seal, Congress established a world of Confederate symbols that proved surprisingly popular even with the hypercritical Richmond press. Together, these two emblems echoed each other's messages in featuring symbols of martial religiosity, albeit in slightly different forms. The God of battles and of pious generals was seen in both the seal of Washington on horseback and on the various flags containing the Southern Cross. In the first, Confederates drew from the example of the American Revolution, while in the latter, more recent experiences of Civil War combat were the main theme. Europeans who might have wondered what this rebellion was all about no longer had to rely on mere words. Symbols too conveyed different aspects of increasingly common themes.

The matter of the seal remained a special case, since engraving required more expertise than cutting and sewing pieces of cloth. Aware of the lack of skilled engravers within its borders, the Confederate State Department arranged for the casting of the seal in Great Britain, despite the call by some newspapers to patronize home industry. Ironically, as this overseas commission proceeded, Confederate diplomacy foundered, and boasts that the country had acquired "a highly creditable signet to affix to our first treaty" soon rang hollow. The Emancipation Proclamation, set in motion the day before the first seal was proposed, effectively ended all Confederate hopes for European assistance. When the seal finally arrived in Richmond sixteen months after its adoption, it lacked the accompanying hardware that would have been necessary for it to function properly. As a result, even though its design had been seen and praised on both sides of the Atlantic, there were very few impressions made from it during the Civil War years. Its Latin appeal "Deo Vindice" did circulate in popular culture, becoming as well known as the image of Washington on horseback. When first selected, this plea for divine recognition was seen by some as a way of finding common ground with potential foreign allies. The stark reality was that Confederates had far more cause to hope for God's intervention than for that of even the most sympathetic earthly powers.[42]

Confederates went about celebrating their second national flag in much the same way as they had greeted their first. They strove for a suitable nickname while placing the new symbol at the center of a body of patriotic verse and music. Such efforts helped to complete a decisive shift in the meaning of the Southern Cross, as original concerns about its divisive religious messages and inaccurate geography vanished from public discussion. The new national flag became known as the Stainless Banner, as both the familiar cross and the large field of white became linked to larger themes of popular patriotism. Attention to the elements of this new flag redirected interest to a civilian flag once more, even though martial themes still prevailed. Although the second national flag was more popular than the discredited Stars and Bars, regimental colors still held pride of place in the Confederate imagination.

The decision to make more than half of the new national flag entirely white returned some Confederates to the question of race. The *Savannah Morning News* argued that the preponderance of white would make clear to the world that "we are fighting to maintain the Heaven-ordained supremacy of the white man over the inferior or colored race." It even predicted that the new banner would be "hailed by the civilized world as THE WHITE MAN'S FLAG." Such expectations proved premature. "Purity" did become the primary association of this banner's whiteness, and at a time when the Union turned to a war of emancipation, this resonant color could not help but conjure up something of the fears about "amalgamation" that were a part of American culture in both North and South. Yet the sort of overt reference to slavery and race that the Savannah editor expected did not become a major theme in the published record of commentary and verse. The opposition that most Confederates took to African

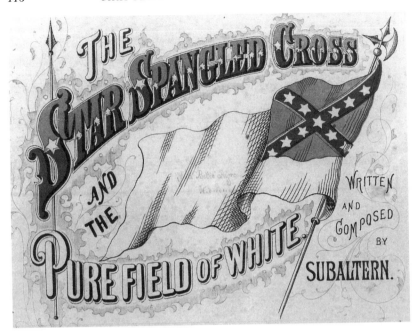

21. "The Star-Spangled Cross and the Pure Field of White" addressed the second national flag of the Confederacy, more popularly known as the Stainless Banner. This flag's distinctive feature was the Southern Cross in its top corner, which linked the national cause to the most celebrated Confederate fighting force. Courtesy, Duke University Special Collection.

American freedom hardly needed overt expression. Yet the tendency to skirt this theme in patriotic poetry recalled the earlier caution of risking international isolation and the alienation of southern nonslaveholders.[43]

Most reflections on the flag's whiteness and "purity" took up religious rather than explicitly racial themes. A decisive moment here was the prominent display of this second national flag at the funeral of Stonewall Jackson, a leader associated far less with slaveholding than with Presbyterian piety and fierce war-making. Just as important was the way the religious meaning of "holy whiteness" fit into a larger program of appeals to God. One of the best known tributes to the new flag, suggestively titled "The Star Spangled Cross and the Pure Field of White," made indirect references both to the motto "Deo Vindice" and to affirmations of a cross battle flag:

We will stand by the Cross and the pure field of white,
While a shred's left to float in the air
Our trust is in God who can help us in fight,
And defend those who ask Him in prayer.[44]

Religious themes achieved an even more sustained expression in Margaret Junkin Preston's "Hymn to the National Flag" of 1864. This Virginia poet had plenty of her own flag experiences to draw upon. Her request that the flag "tell the price at which we purchased / Room and right for thee to wave" recalled the turmoil within her tightly-knit family. Her Unionist father, the Reverend George Junkin, fled Virginia after personally burning a Confederate flag that students of Washington College raised over a campus where Junkin served as president. Both Preston's husband and her brother-in-law, who was none other than Stonewall Jackson, chose a different path, joining the Confederate army with the conviction that the rebellion was the best expression of God's will. In addressing the Confederacy's new flag, Preston also evoked the sacred nature of the cause, asking the banner:

> Shelter Freedom's holy cause,
> Liberty and sacred laws,
> Guard the youngest of the Nations—
> Keep her virgin honor bright.

Evoking each of this flag's three colors, she continued religious themes. "In the cross of heavenly azure / Has our faith its emblem high" she wrote, while "In thy field of white," was "the hallowed / Truth for which we'll dare and die." The last color deserved special comment, and a series of exclamations: "In thy red, the patriot blood," she cried out "Ah! the consecrated flood! / Lift thyself! resistless banner! / Ever fill our southern sky!"[45]

Junkin's effort provided one example of the military orientation of the Southern Cross, which first gained fame as a battle flag. In contrast to Tucker's secession-era verse, the Southern Cross after 1862 was usually depicted as a tool of combat in efforts that merged themes of religion and of sacrifice. The Cross was as likely to be shown as "the soldier's beacon-light through toil" as "the lode-star of the Christian brave," though in many instances, it was seen as both. Constantine's example continued to be invoked, as did the history of cross battle flags that appeared when the "Queen-galaxy of heaven" appeared "on shield / Of bold Crusader." The poet Henry C. Alexander hearkened back to the time when the European faithful embarked on the quest to drive the infidels from Jerusalem, noting that the same "sacred form" of a warlike cross "once more shines, / From standards thickly prest and stained with gore" in America.[46]

In a range of these efforts, it was the death of soldiers rather than of a divine savior that mattered most, and it was national independence rather than eternal salvation that was accomplished through blood sacrifice. A cross flag testified to these patriotic martyrdoms, while it also gave Confederates a symbol that was powerful in and of itself, just as the crucifixion had given Christians a cross to memorialize the earthly suffering of the Son of God. The Christian cross was about a saving faith that was distinct from national glory, of course.

But the cross of Jesus and the Southern Cross for which soldiers died both invoked a system of sacred martyrdom. The work of René Girard and others suggest that the aura of organized war would probably have achieved a religious dimension through the ritual actions of extreme violence even without an explicitly Christian symbol to mark it. But for Confederates, there was no need to bolster an emblem of civil sacrifice by comparing it to explicitly religious symbols, as has often been done in modern military cemeteries that place crosses and flags side by side. The twin totems of Christianity and nationhood were combined at a formal level by those who died so that a new Confederate nation might live.[47]

Geographical connotations of the Southern Cross also followed the increasing emphasis on war. References to the skies of the southern hemisphere or even of the states that each of the stars represented ceased to be a part of public dialogue. The Southern Cross became instead associated with such bloody locales as Manassas, Antietam, and Fredericksburg. As the Alabama poet A. B. Meek put it in a series of poems in 1864, "the flag of the Cross, / With its stars all aglow" inhabited a world defined by the valor of its troops. "Thrice it shone on grim Manassas," he wrote,

Like a meteor from afar;
Through Virginia's mountain passes,
It was aye our guiding star;
Sharpsburg's blood-shot eyes beheld it,—
Richmond with her Seven Days;
Chickamauga's breezes swelled it,—
Charleston still its folds displays.[48]

In a range of creative expressions and on a growing number of battlefields, the Southern Cross flag referred not to national ideas, but to recent national experiences, especially those bloody military clashes that transfixed Confederates. The shift in emphasis occurred as military leaders, especially those in the East, became "critical agents that engendered unity and hope" among Confederates, as Gary Gallagher has recently put it. Since few actual images of these inspiring generals were available to print-starved Confederates, the inclusion of an army emblem on the national flag was crucial in broadcasting visually the importance of martial principles to national ideals. The compound of army and nation on the Stainless Banner was in this way as important as the compound of Christianity and soldierly sacrifice achieved on all variants of the Southern Cross.[49]

Soldiers, generals, and the flags they fought behind became crucial elements of the Confederate experience. Civilian leaders were quite willing to cede cultural authority to the military, even if the ultimate control of elected officials remained sacrosanct. Senator Louis Wigfall lectured his colleagues that there was "no antagonism between the army and the people, for the army is the people" and that "the people of the Confederacy compose the army." The *Richmond Enquirer* was even more pointed. In discussing what made this new country really tick, this paper urged readers in the middle of 1863 to focus their attention on its fighting forces. It was in the armies that "the heart of the country beats, and there its pulse must be felt," it explained. It added for emphasis: "whosoever reads only the newspapers, and listens only to the politicians, knows little of the Confederate States of America."[50]

The final wrinkle in the story of the Confederacy's quest for a national flag showed how decisively military principles had replaced nationalist ones. While the Stainless Banner satisfied the press and the populace alike, commanders judged its design to be as deficient as the Stars and Bars in terms of its practicality. Naval officials objected that the emblem's predominantly white field hindered its visibility at sea. Others were concerned that this flag was unrecognizable on land when the winds were calm and, worse yet, could be mistaken for an all-white flag of surrender or truce. Adding either a red or blue stripe to the design, while retaining the Southern Cross in the corner, became a common suggestion to remedy this defect. Opinion was split among the Richmond press on the wisdom of such a change, as the *Sentinel* endorsed the modification late in 1864 for its "warmth and richness of expression" and the *Whig* denounced any effort to alter the flag as "mere childishness." One contributor to the *Whig* early in 1865 called the entire discussion "puerile and ridiculous," since this attention to detail looked past the fact that "the question really is, are we to have a nationality at all?"[51]

There was more than grim desperation—and no little humor—to this final attempt to stave off defeat by changing a flag that might be mistaken for a white surrender flag. The debate itself also showed how both advocates and critics of the change used a common set of criteria. Transmitting something important about the country had become less important than a narrower set of goals, all related to the military aspects of war. One writer complained that the "gingerbread decoration" of adding a stripe would "make the Flag resemble those sentimental Banners presented by young ladies to volunteer companies at the commencement of the war." Those lobbying for the change, however, had no such intention of reducing the dignity of the flag, as they gathered endorsements not from civilians but from generals and naval officers. In doing so, they emphasized exact proportions of the new flag as much as the addition of a color to the end. Though the question revolved around a government flag and not a combat banner, military needs were still judged to be all-important.[52]

Well before 1865, the Southern Cross had become the preeminent Confederate symbol, beginning a career that would make it one of the best known of all American icons. As it spread to a variety of army flags, to naval colors, and onto the government's Stainless Banner, this St. Andrew's cross could also be seen in a range of other media, including Confederate money, stationery, and sheet music. In the late summer of 1862, the Richmond press advertised brass, silver-plated badges that included this icon as its defining feature. A bit later, the X-shaped design began to appear on the buttons of army uniforms. A pattern primarily designed for use on colored cloth moved onto a wide array of other material.[53]

How the proliferation of crosses ultimately mattered is difficult, though important to assess. From the first days of the Confederacy, a wide range of commentators claimed that a widely recognized symbol might translate into a decided Confederate advantage. William Howard Russell predicted that an emotionally satisfying flag would stir popular energies and might even prevent the restoration of the Union. Others argued that a gesture toward God would bring Providence to the side of the new country. Nearly everyone who designed, sewed, or waved a flag or composed a poem, speech, or prayer on behalf of a banner believed, whether they said so explicitly or not, that their actions were meant to help win a war and establish a new country.

The stunning and near total defeat of the Confederate rebellion raises hard questions about the ultimate value of such symbol making. Gary Gallagher makes a valid point in saying that evaluating Confederate nationalism should involve the question of how the Confederacy was able to fight for so long, and not just why it ultimately lost. From this perspective, one might say that defeat came in spite of the vibrant expressions of flag-related patriotism rather than because of any inherent weaknesses in these expressions. Such an approach seems sensible, if not taken too far. This formulation cannot resolve how an apparently vital commitment to country ended in total collapse, as a federal army in 1865 established little more than a cobweb occupation of the former slave states. How army flags and the cause they represented were surrendered merits extended consideration on its own. But before we leave behind the story of the Southern Cross, it is worthwhile to ask how this most powerful of all rebel icons was involved in the transformation from a defiant culture of flag waving to a solemn culture of flag furling. Understanding Confederate flag culture as it relates to this emblem can help us to move beyond trying to establish it as a net positive or net negative in the quest for Confederate nationhood. Specific attention to the themes associated with the Southern Cross can help instead to identify larger cultural processes at work.

As we search for these sorts of larger patterns, the nineteenth-century notion of consolidation provides a way of appreciating some of the countervailing and at times contradictory forces that marked the popular patriotism of Confederate flag culture. Recent historians have used this notion of consolidation to explore the range of ways that mid-nineteenth-century Americans expressed unease with rampant individualism and sought new ways of building social order and collective identity.[54] Confederates themselves used the term frequently, though in several varying senses. Politicians such as Jefferson Davis often used the notion to critique the Republican party for apparently disregarding federalism and nationalizing all issues, including the all-important matter of slavery. Some of this was disingenuous, since slaveholders throughout the 1850s increasingly turned to an active federal government to protect their interests. Consolidation in this political sense would continue within their own Confederacy, as leaders in Richmond built a central state that was in some respects more centralized than that of Lincoln's Union.[55]

Confederates also recognized positive aspects of a consolidating unity, however, especially when they considered social and cultural matters. Most defenses of southern slave society were based on the notion of an organic order, where bonds of mutuality established reciprocal duties and rights that depended on one's status in society. Drawing contrasts to the atomistic free-labor North, writers like George Fitzhugh, Henry Hughes, and George Frederick Holmes heralded the South's dense social network that, at least in theory, valued collective stability over individual rights. During wartime, a corresponding cultural sense of consolidation came to the fore, as citizens sought ways to bind themselves with one another and to their country's larger purpose, through literature, art, and, as we have seen, a unifying set of symbols and experiences. It was widely acknowledged that a new national community was in formation and that gaining independence would require the active involvement and enthusiasm of a great portion of the white population toward common goals.[56]

In this last sense, flags reflected not just the achievement of Confederate consolidation, but were a signal means of helping to bring it about. These symbols and the passions they inspired organized different themes in a single object and, in the case of the Southern Cross, brought disparate themes of sacrifice, faith, commitment, and pride within a single field of expression. Their design generated a sense of corporate identity, while celebrating it provided an important focal point to establish a sense of transcendent purpose. The multimedia flag culture that lasted through the Civil War helps to reframe the negative judgment that a group of prominent historians reached in a collective effort to understand "why the South lost." A major conclusion of a book by this title was that "the Confederate nation was created on paper, not in the hearts and minds of its would-be citizens." The increasing attention given to print culture in the formation of nationalism makes this dismissive tone toward mere "paper identities" problematic; unifying texts and media, we have come to learn, are an important part of what makes imagined collective identities possible in the first place. When one appreciates how cloth and silk symbols bound the ideas expressed on paper to Confederates' "hearts and minds," there is an even stronger basis for reconsidering the achievements of flag-based popular patriotism.[57]

Though Confederate symbols and flags might have increased the intensity of certain themes involving religion and sacrifice, they narrowed the grounds of affiliation, especially in the case of the Southern Cross. The metaphor of consolidation helps to clarify how the emphasis given to battle flags and war passions made a resulting patriotic corpus more dense, while at the same time and through the same process, it resulted in a mass that was more compact and less capacious than it might have been without this consolidation. A national flag with overwhelmingly martial connotations had been an option for Confederates from the outset, when one designer sent the Montgomery Congress a chessboard pattern to represent the "battlefield of war" and another sent a sickle to summon up the likelihood of death beneath the folds of a new national flag. These suggestions, which were largely ignored, failed to look past armed struggle and provide a point of inspiration for future peace. The Southern Cross was considerably more powerful in witnessing death, rather than just symbolizing it, during its service as the preeminent battle flag of Confederate soldiers. But the diagonal cross was still self-referential in drawing attention to the means of the conflict—of fighting a holy war that required great sacrifice—and largely ignoring what this country might be if it actually won its independence and charted a course for the future. The notion that nationhood depended as much upon God's favor as on unquenchable patriotic desire tinged the Southern Cross with an element of fatalism, as several poetic tributes made explicit.[58]

The Southern Cross was an emblem of war both because a multimedia flag culture drew out these themes and because it was used, in almost all of its various manifestations, primarily to push an armed struggle forward. A full accounting of where and under what conditions the Southern Cross flag was raised, displayed, or waved is impossible to accomplish with any degree of certainty, though it seems clear that the battlefield was the symbol's primary home. Some suggestive evidence from a Union prisoner of war in 1863 bears this out, and reminds us that the most meaningful point of comparison was between Confederate flags and the Stars and Stripes of the Yankees. "One might almost travel from one end of the Confederacy to the other" without spotting a single Southern Cross outside the armies, this prisoner, Robert Kellogg, explained in the midst of his narrative. In contrast, he continued "at the North, the 'Stars and Stripes' are floating from nearly every prominent public building, and often-times from private dwellings." The flag frenzy that followed Fort Sumter had helped northerners to nurture an "all-pervading appreciation" of a symbol that seemed to represent "everything that is just and true" in flying nearly everywhere one looked. The Star Spangled Banner reached where few public symbols could, becoming nothing less than a "household idol in every Northern home." In the ways that they used their flag, Unionist families set about "imbibing a strange love for it, that will tell upon their devotion to country in their future history."[59]

The Southern Cross, by contrast, waved primarily over armies in its battle flag version, and over government buildings, military fortifications, and urban newspaper offices as part of the Stainless Banner. This flag could inspire reverie in those spots where it regularly appeared. As George Bagby walked past the Richmond capitol building late in 1863, he was "struck anew" with the beauty of the national flag flying there and moved by a "secret exultation of the heart for the proud day of our deliverance, when that standard shall be known in all lands as a symbol of a noble cause triumphant through the agency and the heroism of a great people." "Somehow," he reflected, "our beautiful flag, streaming on high, and relived by the sapphire back-ground of the clear sky, always inspires hope." The difficulty was that southerners had a fairly limited range of opportunities for such patriotic communion, while their northern neighbors would have had a difficult time keeping the American flag altogether out of their field of vision. It may have been that Confederates lacked the cloth and the manufacturing resources to match the North's flag flurry. Resistance flags seemed to festoon every available space of southern cities during the secession crisis, while the Stars and Bars also flourished early in 1861. Yet the Stainless Banner and the Southern Cross seemed to have been displayed with less abandon. A few days after Congress adopted the second national flag, John Daniel was outraged that the first copy of this design appeared over a theater he called a "place of amusement," where he thought it had become no more than a "clap-trap advertisement of a showman." The "presumptuous impertinence" of this civilian initiative was unusual enough to merit comment from Daniel, who hoped that thereafter the flag would be respected by appearing only in those official contexts that were consistent with its dignity and honor.[60]

Southern Cross flags that were flown, whether in front of armies, above buildings, or in the streets, were likely to have been placed there by those engaged in conflict. Occupied areas under Union rule also witnessed plenty of defiant banners, while in some civilian settings like churches, the Southern Cross was used to keep local Unionists at bay. But these emblems seemed to have been used more in battle and to defy authority than in reaching into other aspects of Confederate life. As the battle flag became increasingly associated with male warriors, the important female role in the first expressions of Confederate flag culture diminished. The Southern Cross was unable to retain all of the civic associations of a truly national flag since it was a "newly-constructed emblem" that had "too weak a hold on existence" to match the power of the Stars and Stripes, the prisoner Kellogg explained. "To live," he explained, a flag "must be planted in the hearts of men" and then "thoroughly tested, and made to show its adaptation and fitness for the wants of men, before it can be readily received by them calling forth their love and veneration."[61]

In trying to rival the power of the Stars and Stripes, Confederates were reaching for a goal that was moving ever higher and ultimately beyond their reach. American flag culture at the beginning of the Civil War had rested on an overwhelmingly martial basis, with battlefield associations providing much of what was most special about the Star Spangled Banner. The Southern Cross would have a similar effect among its followers, who by the end of a war that had witnessed countless deaths on its behalf. But by that time, the Union flag had already become something more. Patriotic Unionists like Robert Winthrop of Massachusetts sensed that there was "a magic in the web" of a transformed Stars and Stripes, which suddenly seemed to have entered all areas of life, from the parlor to the church to the windows of what seemed to be every home. Once war began, this ubiquitous cloth presence seemed to Winthrop to have "an answer for every question" and "a solution for every doubt and every perplexity." In the matter of flags, as in that of nationalism more generally, the intensity of Confederate passions tells only half of the story. What also needs to be considered is that how an even deeper and more developed cult of the Stars and Stripes helped lead the Union to victory.[62]

CHAPTER SIX

Treason's Banner and the Colors of Loyalty

CONFEDERATE FLAGS were rebel flags, a fact that added an important aspect to their emotional power. Waving a banner of rebellion thrilled many Confederates. Daring to throw off their former government showed their willingness to "tread in the paths of their forefathers," who had defended their rights by shedding blood in an earlier revolution. Those loyal to the federal government saw the matter differently, of course. All the defiant emblems of rebellion repulsed Unionists and filled them with a mixture of rage and sickness. In a range of media, northerners created a counter-Confederate flag culture that portrayed banners as visual evidence of treason. Such efforts imbued these symbols with a set of satanic associations that would survive the end of war and lay the basis for the attack upon rebel symbols that has occurred in our own time.

As with all civil wars, America's crisis of Union elevated questions of allegiances to paramount importance. There was uneasiness on both sides about how loyalties might be aligned, and how these might either hold or falter. Flags provided a means of reassurance, since they projected inner convictions into a public stance. This would be especially important for women to engage in, since their absence from the battlefield made their true allegiances difficult to gauge. The question of patriotic commitments would involve flags when it came to African Americans as well. Taking up the colors of the Union showed the willingness of slaves to become partners in a cause that combined their own freedom with the Union's salvation.

Showing one's true colors in cloth was at the heart of Civil War patriotism, both on the field and behind the lines. It provided women a chance to face down the Yankees with as much emotional intensity as their men showed under fire. Yet flags that were associated with a nation and its armies could channel passions as well as incite them. Black soldiers who took up the American flag to fight against treason did not pursue more personal acts of retaliation and revenge against their masters. However bloody the Civil War was, freedom came in the United States in a much more orderly way than some had imagined it would. Similarly, the massive chaos and carnage of the Civil War never spun completely beyond the control of a highly structured and immensely powerful military. Rebel flags played a part here, if only in showing that resistance under the metaphorical colors of a black banner would not be a part of white southerners' cause.

In the fall of 1865, Professor Francis Lieber perused the collection of Confederate flag designs recently captured by Union troops. He was not impressed by these artifacts, which had been sent to the Montgomery Congress in the spring of 1861. In fact, he was appalled. This bundle of letters and designs reminded Lieber why he had left South Carolina a few years earlier. His move from a professorship at South Carolina College to one in New York had given him the freedom to express support for Union and opposition to slavery. His experience as a leading Union publicist and a codifier of war rules then gave him new opportunities, which shaped his aesthetic judgments as well. In the early months of peace, flag designs drew out his emotions and provided him gut-churning evidence that the southern rebellion had been characterized by "reckless impudence, faithfulness, and . . . ruffianism." Whether considering the "repulsive" crescent, the "unsightly" all-seeing eye, or the palmetto, which he dismissed as a "scrubby ugly, would-be palm tree," these offerings appeared to him as uniformly perverse. In a lengthy diatribe to a friend, Lieber could scarcely contain his contempt at the "want of taste, of rudeness, of coarseness and puerility displayed in these designs." His reaction made clear that what Confederates had lauded as soaring patriotism became damning marks of treason when seen through the eyes of a Unionist.[1]

It is unclear how Lieber's former South Carolina colleagues would have reacted to his virulent response. Those who produced Confederate symbols expected such hostility from their enemies and at times even seemed to welcome it. Secession banners clearly conveyed messages beyond southern borders with inscriptions like "Don't Tread on Me," or the Latin version, "Noli Me Tangere." Regimental standards often echoed the same themes, and even the Southern Cross could be used as a warning, as the defiant closing lyrics written by St. George Tucker had shown. National flags have traditionally been one of the most effective ways of signaling hostile intent to enemies, especially in their invocations of national armies willing to protect a country from harm. For Confederates, flag culture that was first and foremost directed toward its own citizens was also part of a larger set of symbolic practices intended to unnerve the Yankees. The suggestion of William Gilmore Simms to dress soldiers as

Indians was one such example of conscious intimidation of invaders, while the bloodcurdling "rebel yell" provides a case that was actually put into practice.[2]

The rattlesnake that appeared in Confederate iconography showed the mixed results that attempts to intimidate enemies yielded. South Carolinians were especially fond of the "venomous heraldry" that Lieber singled out for its "despicable absurdity." It seems clear that those Carolinians who circulated this image intended not just to threaten enemies, but to hearken back to the symbolism of the American Revolution and specifically to recall that snake Benjamin Franklin had first made famous in his instruction to the colonies to "Join or Die." By picturing the snake wrapped around the palmetto, Confederates redrew the map and signaled that the coming crisis pitted the South against the North, rather than rustic colonials against the British. While usually wrapped around a tree, the snake used in secession symbolism was also shown in more violent poses. Several secession prints presented a snake striking out with its fangs exposed, registering a collective willingness to inflict harm on those who tested southern boundaries. One patriot who lobbied for this snake's inclusion on the national seal declared that its rattle promised "certain death" to those who disturbed it, while another emphasized that the snake displayed the "generosity which does not strike without warning."[3]

This rattlesnake motif gave southerners a way to glory in their aggression and to experience the thrill that came with willful subversion. Predictably, however, the symbol also gave northerners a ready-made image of southern treason. Serpents had long been a potent image of evil within a Judeo-Christian tradition that linked them to the temptation by Satan in the Garden of Eden. In American iconography, snakes had been repeatedly used to represent any dark force that needed to be strangled in the clutches of a vigilant patriot or crushed underneath his foot. In the wartime North, the serpent image represented both disunion and Democratic "Copperheadism." In the Confederacy, abolitionists were most likely to be cast in the role of viper. The seal adopted by Mississippi in 1861 showed such a wily serpent underneath a magnolia tree that threatened an eagle's nest on top; the nearby bale of cotton on the seal put this story in full perspective. Given the widely negative depiction of the snake image, Unionists naturally focused their attention on those rebel banners that used them. "Down the traitor's serpent Flag," one northern song cried out in 1861, before promising "death to the wretch o'er whom it waves." Snakelike treachery soon became part of a set of diabolical images that would predominate in the Union depictions of Confederate emblems. These reassured the North that rebels were in league with the devil.[4]

The Stars and Bars did not provide such easy fodder to the Union, even if this symbol too acquired strongly negative associations. At first, a few northern newspapers even complimented the Confederacy's first national flag, seemingly flattered by its imitation of the Stars and Stripes. Samuel B. Morse, a leading New York Democrat, suggested that the symbolic deconstruction of the American flag be taken even further, with the North and South evenly dividing the Star Spangled Banner between themselves. Soon enough, the attack on the colors flying above Fort Sumter changed the tone of northern comment. The Stars and Bars abruptly conveyed far more aggression, especially after the Confederate Secretary of War made an incendiary vow to place the Confederate banner above the capitol in Washington and perhaps carry it even farther north. His rhetorical flourish, made just as hostilities began, might have fired the southern heart. But like secessionist use of the snake, the gesture had serious repercussions in the North. The possibility that a disunionist flag might lead a war of conquest caused even those who had been sympathetic to the South to suggest a preemptive strike. In Boston, Edward Everett condemned this threat to raise a newly hostile Stars and Bars while heatedly warning that "red hot cannon ball and shells" might soon be in the streets of northern cities. Though Everett had defended slaveholders for years, he changed his stance quickly once a hostile flag promised that rebels would soon be "battering my house about my ears."[5]

Over time, northern publicists proved to be as interested as their enemies in loading the Stars and Bars with specific meanings. Several linked this "triple-barred emblem of hell" with the same set of satanic themes they had seen in the rattlesnake, the devil, and Jefferson Davis. Charles Drake, a Unionist from St. Louis, took a different approach, lambasting the "bastard banner, of strange and meaningless device" for leading a rebellion that was "more causeless than the history of modern civilization has disclosed." Others poked fun at how rebels had "made a flag from a rag / Torn from a cotton bag / By a privateering crew." To many who were loyal to the Union, nothing summed up the insignificance of the Confederate cause better than its embrace of a diminished American banner. This was clear in the design of a patriotic envelope that showed Jefferson Davis leading a "piecable secession" with only a remnant of what had once been a great and glorious flag. Collectively, such images made up a counter-Confederate flag culture that would be important both during the war and in subsequent years. Like Confederate attacks on the Stars and Stripes, these efforts contained both trivializing caricatures and more passionate denunciations.[6]

The North held a decisive edge in producing and circulating visual images that conveyed Unionist ire toward rebel emblems. No southern periodical could match the range of illustrations in magazines like *Harper's Weekly* and *Frank Leslie's*, both of which produced several memorable parodies of Confederate flags and seals. Nor were there any chromolithographers in the South who could rival efforts such as the *Fate of the Rebel Flag*, a striking depiction of a fiery Stars and Bars that streaked the skies above a sinking boat that God himself had destroyed. Patriotic envelopes were a partial exception to the sectional discrepancy in publishing resources, since these mass-produced pictures circulated freely in both North and South during the early years of war. Even

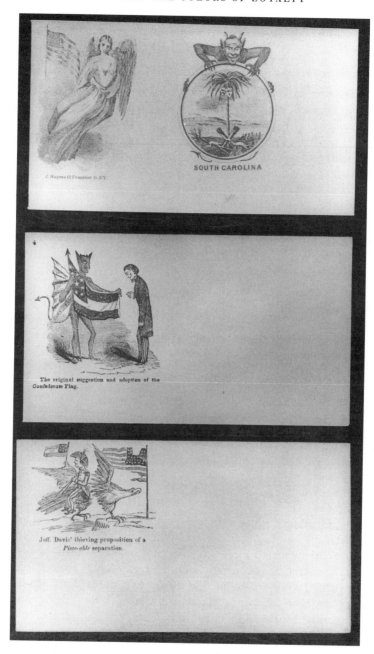

22. Patriotic envelopes helped Unionists to portray the satanic influence on rebel emblems. The bottom image, also from a patriotic envelope, poked fun at the Confederates' attempt to tear their own flag from the Stars and Stripes. Courtesy, American Antiquarian Society.

so, there seemed to have been a much greater variety of these envelopes made by northern printers. While both Unions and Confederates used this new media to glorify their own cause and its symbols, there were many more examples of negative portrayals of rebel flags on these envelopes than there were attacks upon the Stars and Stripes.[7]

Slavery was tied to the Stars and Bars less often than some might assume. The primary negative association of Confederate symbols was with treason, in part because white southerners had consciously distanced their emblems from slavery, their country's most controversial institution. From time to time, illustrated magazines prominently placed Confederate flags above slave auctions and decrepit plantations, making an obvious statement about the proslavery intent of the rebellion. The most extended attempt to link the Stars and Bars with bondage came not from the North, however, but from an English poet, who condemned the "sinister bars" that confined "dusky mistresses." Not only did this verse compare "Hell's black rag" with piracy; it issued an antislavery ultimatum, instructing

> Take it down—it taints the air
> With odours from the Slavers' lair.
> Pull it down—for well the people
> Know it's round the Devil's steeple.[8]

Illustrators generally paid less attention to the Southern Cross than they had to the Stars and Bars, though there were a few attempts to show how the diagonal design of this new flag mimicked the crossbones of the pirate's banner. Poets proved more attentive to how this symbol might discredit the southern rebellion. Several pointed out its hypocrisy, while others poked fun at its pretensions. One writer castigated the "sacrilege" of taking up a holy emblem for "the land of the traitor and the slave." Picking up on the theme of the actual cross constellation, this writer warned that "God never set that holy sign / In deathless light among His stars / To make its blazonry divine / A scutcheon for thine impious wars."[9]

From the perspective of northern flag culture, the most troubling aspect of any rebel flags was not anything specific about their designs or symbolic schemes. What mattered most was that these emblems threatened the Star Spangled Banner. One poet captured this sense of outrage about Confederate flags by cursing those who came "near the sacred banner / With their foul and flaunting rag." For others, the presence of a rival to the beloved American banner generated melancholy rather than anger, and one verse even offered up conciliation to southerners, asking, "What is the value to you or to me, if stars are torn from the flag of the free?" George Root's fabulously successful "Battle Cry of Freedom" displayed both memorable brevity and steady resolve in crying out "down with the traitor / Up with the star!" The chorus of a later version of this same tune captured how most northerners responded to the waving of Confederate colors. "Hurrah for the Union, / Hurrah for the flag" it shouted. "Down with the traitors, / And the cursed rebel rag!"[10]

Confederate flags suffered direct physical assaults as regularly as they were attacked in print and in song. Rebel pieces of cloth were typically ripped to bits, though there were also incidents in which secession banners were burned so that their "ashes [became] a part of the mud of our streets," as the Unionist *Louisville Journal* approvingly reported. Frances Peter noted how both sides took part in attacks upon their enemies' banners once war began. A cycle of such activity took place in her native Lexington, Kentucky, where federal soldiers early in 1862 tore up and divided a secession flag that had floated over the local college. When rebels took the city that fall, they shot a man who refused to raise their Stars and Bars flag on the courthouse and then forced a prisoner of war to do. After a female Confederate sympathizer trampled on a Union flag on Main Street, rebel soldiers attached it to a horse and dragged it behind them in the dust. During their preparations to evacuate the city late in 1862, these southern troops made sure to take all their flags with them, depriving Yankees of symbolic retaliation.[11]

As these episodes made clear, flags did not just motivate Confederates and Unionists; they furnished the means through which patriotism could be acted out in the first place. For soldiers, this required little active initiative. As Francis Pickens told South Carolina troops departing northward to Virginia, enlisted men were taught that "wherever the Confederate Flag floats, there too is our country, now and forever." For enlisted men to desert their colors not only demonstrated a lack of patriotism; it constituted a betrayal of duty that could be punished by death. The case was different for civilians, whose actions to rally to national symbols and to defend them was mostly voluntary. Waving banners in streets and from homes allowed citizens outside of the army to display their true colors through symbols they could themselves construct.[12]

The collective and personal merged in such civilian use of flags. Whether one waved a flag or hoisted it above the house, the use of a national banner signaled solidarity with soldiers and shared commitment to the cause. Those who flew the wrong flag or who refused to fly the right one could often be singled out for attack, as James Jackson's fate in Alexandria made clear. Though his transfixing death at the Marshall House was an extreme example, Jackson was hardly the only civilian to be involved in flag-related violence during the secession crisis. The office of the *Palmetto Flag* newspaper in Philadelphia was besieged by a mob until it waved an American flag from its window, while the Reverend William J. Anderson was driven from California for refusing to fly the Stars and Stripes above his church. Secessionists trying out new flags were often forced to move south of the Potomac, while those Unionists who insisted on keeping the Stars and Stripes aloft often fled north. At first this was in response to popular pressure. Soon enough, however, military officials also took part in monitoring the loyalties of residents.[13]

Neither the Union nor the Confederacy developed a clear set of policies about civilian display of treasonous emblems. A few commanders considered the flying of rebel banners an extremely serious violation. On the Kansas plains, General Samuel Curtis castigated an entire community for "quietly and exultingly resting under the flaunting rebel flag" that had been raised in their midst. His outrage focused more on this town's failure to remove a polluting emblem than on the individual or group responsible for raising the symbol in the first place. Curtis wanted to follow the example of Napoleon, who he claimed had responded to a similar situation by "sacking and burning" an entire city. Though he did not have authority to pursue such a collective punishment in Platte County, Kansas, he made clear his preference that such "breaches of public confidence" be followed by "such terrible consequences as to deter the people from their repetition."[14]

A much wider range of activity was seen in large Confederate cities, where most civilian flag clashes occurred. Baltimore, the largest city in the border South, witnessed the most regular use of rebel symbols to defy the Union. The attack on northern troops by a pro-Confederate mob in April of 1861 and the strength of secessionists in the legislature convinced federal officials that martial law was the only means of keeping the state in the Union. As such measures were implemented, General Benjamin Butler announced that the display of any "flag, banner, ensign or device" in Baltimore would be considered evidence of "a design to afford aid and comfort to the enemies of the country" and would subject the violator to arrest. In justifying his regulations, Butler argued that disciplining disloyal citizens would spare loyal supporters of the Union a more indiscriminate application of military force. Looking back at measures introduced by Butler and by James A. Dix, one writer proudly concluded that through such loyalty policies "tranquility was maintained; dangerous persons were prevented from doing mischief; incendiary papers were silenced; the rude were taught good manners," and, most importantly, "the Federal supremacy was maintained throughout the state."[15]

New Orleans, an even larger city, rivaled Baltimore in the number of flag-related incidents. Federal action here followed a somewhat different pattern, since secession had to be overturned rather than prevented. Those wielding hostile flags or threatening Union colors were not only likely to be controlled and confined, as was the case in Baltimore, but were threatened repeatedly with direct bodily harm. Prior to his efforts in Maryland, James Dix had turned his eyes to the mouth of the Mississippi, instructing revenue officers; "If anyone attempts to haul down the American flag, shoot him on the spot." His rousing instructions, which became a famous Unionist slogan despite never having been carried out, signaled a federal determination to protect and then to restore national supremacy at the mouth of the continent-draining Mississippi River.

During the naval attempt to bring New Orleans under Union control, flags were considered markers of sovereignty rather than symbols that might merely incite subversive activity. After a landing party of marines hoisted the American colors above the federal mint, Admiral David Farragut vowed to fire upon the city if the flag was lowered. A hostile crowd defied his order, and replaced the emblem with a Confederate standard. Had not federal gunships been temporarily disabled, an all-out naval bombardment of the city would have been the immediate federal response.[16]

In the aftermath of this volatile transfer of power, Ben Butler joined the same flag-related regulations he had issued in Baltimore with much swifter punitive action. While implementing martial law there, Butler charged William Mumford with treason for his part in removing the American flag from the mint and then ripping it to shreds. A military court quickly sentenced Mumford to death, leading to one of the most famous executions of the Civil War period. Late in 1862, Jefferson Davis judged this act to have been a simple murder and threatened Butler with execution as a war criminal if captured. The defense of Mumford and others who suffered for flags continued to be a part of Confederate public relations, though those who attacked the enemy flag would never be as important as James Jackson of Alexandria, who had died for his own country's banner. In both cases, Confederates saw the same pattern of a federal despotism that based patriotism on coercion rather than affiliation. Stories circulated throughout the southern press about sailors court-martialed for refusing to sing national songs. Baltimore garnered steady attention, becoming known, with a nod toward Russian rule of Poland, as the "Warsaw of America."[17]

As is often the case in protests made against foreign invasion, women had a particularly important role to play in defying Yankee authority. They clearly recognized their power to confront their enemies with the emblems of the Confederate rebellion. Several cities witnessed battles over red-and-white dresses or bonnets that were arranged to recall the pattern of the Stars and Bars. Butler successfully thwarted the attempt of New Orleans women to make an actual Confederate flag by requesting the leader of a "sewing bee" to appear before him. Having learned of this secret group of patriots from a slave who worked within the household, Butler requested this rebel flag for his own use during Fourth of July festivities. Threatening to send soldiers to retrieve it if his request was refused, he inspected the flag and indicated that "I don't want any more and I wouldn't make any more if I were you." Given his notorious "woman order"—which threatened to treat rebel women as "ladies of the street"—this thinly veiled threat seemed to have accomplished its purpose.[18]

Up the river in Baton Rouge, Sarah Morgan resolved for quite different reasons to cease taunting Union troops by wearing Confederate colors. The young woman was initially gleeful that Butler had extended his ban on rebellious symbols to her hometown. Eager to demonstrate her patriotism, Morgan

23. Confederate women taunted federal occupiers with rebel colors, as this contemporary portrayal, "A Female Rebel in Baltimore," showed. *Harper's Weekly*, September 7, 1861. Courtesy, Michigan State University Libraries.

welcomed a new opportunity to "devote all my red, white, and blue silk to the manufacture of Confederate flags," and she boldly pledged in her diary that "as soon as one is confiscated, I will make another, until my ribbon is exhausted, when I will sport a duster emblazoned in high colors!" She soon did exactly that, creating a "great excitement" with a miniature Stars and Bars she wore pinned from belt to shoulder. As Morgan went out a second day however, her attitude changed, as she reached the "painful conclusion" that she was "unnecessarily attracting attention by an unladylike act of defiance." Disgusted with herself for acting too aggressively, she vowed to consign her flag to the parlor mantle and not to display it again in public. Morgan's change of heart resulted in part from her own uneasiness about violating gender conventions, an issue she confronted throughout the war. But in this episode, a changed perception of Union officers also played a role, as her "newly acquired sentiments" were triggered by the "refinement and gentlemanly bearing" of men who "bigoted narrow minded people" had convinced her were "unworthy of respect or regard." Their restraint was praiseworthy, she noted privately, and even "set us an example worthy of our imitation."[19]

The popular press had not prepared Morgan for the "gentlemanly" officers, since it routinely presented Yankee occupiers as crude "ruffians" filled with spite and hatred. Again and again, southern newspapers presented soldiers frustrated by military defeat exercising their anger in the torment of southern women and children. A typical story focused on one Baltimore woman whose brother in the Confederate army had made her "an object of especial venom among the Yankees." After being "narrowly watched" by authorities for weeks, she was one day seized by a federal soldier who, after "throwing her violently to the pavement," then "tore open the bosom of her dress and took from thence a Secession flag." This Yankee defiler of womanhood did get his comeuppance, the story related, but not before adding to a long list of similar violations of female sanctity. As the Baltimore graphic artist Adalbert Volck suggested in his image of the "search for arms," federal efforts to root out Confederate flags required officers at the very least to peer within normally inviolable realms of domestic life. In the extreme cases, even more invasive acts were perpetrated, as flags hid within the clothes of both black and white women were snatched out by Yankee despots.[20]

The level of federal hostility toward Confederate flags was exaggerated for effect. As in other aspects of Union policy toward civilians, myths often were more powerful than reality. Yet whatever the threats to their actual physical safety, women who had the courage to stand up to federal officials performed patriotic deeds comparable to those of their men. Snippets of news from occupied areas detailed how flags were "smuggled down the street by the aid of crinoline" so they might be saved from capture and sent behind Confederate lines. A teenager from Savannah earned praise by pledging her resolve that "in spite of everything but chains, I intend to wave my banner." Others bragged about being imprisoned, or even shot at, after taunting Union troops with their flags and handkerchiefs. These boasts drew an analogy between male soldiers' sacrifice and women's loyalties to the colors. The refusal of other Confederate women to walk beneath American flags hung out in occupied cities did the same.[21]

Women's defiant flag-waving was distinct from those death-accepting actions of soldiers in battle. Feminine associations kept a whiff of romance in rebel colors, as was clear in one poetic connection between the "tints of our

24. Adalbert Volck, a pro-Confederate artist from Baltimore, displayed Union
pettiness in their attempt to "search for arms," as he titled this print. From
War-Sketches. Courtesy, Duke University Special Collections.

national flag" and the "rosy lips," "blue eyes," and "white arms" that watched
the war from the home front. This evocative image of a living female tricolor
helped assure men that neither the "heartland" nor the hearts of southern
women could ever be conquered, since "each heart is a breastwork, the foeman
will find, / When these are the Ensigns unfurled to the wind." Southern wom-
en's steadfastness was important to morale, this poem suggested, even if female
defiance was never as widely celebrated as the willing deaths of James Jackson
or of soldiers in the field. The interaction between female dress and the colors
of flags presented female patriotism in conventional and outward terms that
might be no more lasting than the latest fashion to appear on the streets of
Baltimore. Reports that some civilians flew flags only to prevent the attack of
armies further suggested that these emblems did not represent core convictions
when used away from the battlefield.[22]

In a civil war that blurred the cultural distinction between civilian and combatant, defiant flags could bring brave women and enlisted men face to face.
John Greenleaf Whittier's famous lyric "Barbara Frietchie" dramatized the most
famous episode where this reportedly occurred. This depiction of the Confederate invasion of Frederick, Maryland, during the fall of 1862 showed that
female hostility toward unwelcome forces was not limited to the occupied
South. Whittier's heroine—who was a matronly gray rather than an attractive

rose, white, and blue—was supposedly provoked to action by the arrival of the "silver stars" and "crimson bars" of waving Confederate banners. The ninety-year-old patriot produced a confrontation by waving the Stars and Stripes out her attic "to show that one here was loyal yet." After a failed attempt by a southern soldier to shoot this flag from her hands, Frietchie responded with a line that would enter a corpus of patriotic poetry that survived well into the twentieth century: "'Shoot if you must my old gray head, But spare your country's flag,' she said." In the verse, Frietchie's bravery inspired Stonewall Jackson to order his troops: "'Who touches a hair on yon gray head, / Dies like a dog! March on!,' he said." The sympathetic portrayal of the rebel general was an odd gesture for Whittier, himself a veteran abolitionist. But while the poem acceded to the martyred Jackson's postwar popularity in the North, it also made clear that Frietchie and the flag were nobler still. They had successfully appealed to Jackson's conscience, drawing forth a "shade of sadness" and a "blush of shame." Here, feminine influence worked to defy enemies and to elicit just the sort of meek humility on which a successful reunion under a common flag would depend.[23]

Unionists in the Confederate heartland were given considerably less discretion than Frietchie was in choosing which flags they might wave in public. Adoption of an alien enemies' act late in 1861 gave official sanction to what southern vigilante groups had already established—a determination that traitors to the new country would suffer penalties every bit as serious as those imposed by the United States on its civilian opponents. As rumors swirled about possible opposition to the new Confederate government, the display, or even the possession, of an American flag was often enough to elicit reprisal. A Union flag found at the quarters of the German Turner Association in Richmond, Virginia, forced the group to respond to the "grave charge" of treason in the spring of 1862. Their explanation, which did not remove all suspicion, rested on the history of the flag (which supposedly had been made three years before secession), on the group's demonstrated support for the Confederacy, and on their excuse that the failure to destroy the symbol was "more a matter of neglect than of intention." No such explanations were attempted by East Tennesseeans who had sworn their hostility to the Confederacy on the American flag before burning railroad bridges. They were executed swiftly, and thereafter Confederate officials in this Unionist stronghold carefully reported subsequent displays of American flags to their Richmond superiors.[24]

The activities of a Unionist group in Confederate Atlanta, recently brought to light by the historian Thomas Dyer, suggest some of the reasons why sympathizers did not simply destroy flags that constituted such powerfully incriminating evidence. Cyrena Stone, a native of Vermont, clearly knew that her possession of a small Stars and Stripes was dangerous, especially since her husband, a suspected Union sympathizer, had already fled the South. She accordingly took great pains to conceal her prized American flag in jars of fruit and in her sugar container. Her wartime writings indicate that she considered this object worth the trouble and the risk, not least because of the powerful emotions it drew from her wider Unionist circle. In the spring of 1864, she took out the "forbidden thing" at the request of a close friend, who had earlier received from Stone a small sketch of the emblem. The visitor then "bowed her head, and kissed its beautiful folds—reverently, as if it were some precious friend lying dead before her." Acting out what surely was one of the most intimate flag dramas of the war, the two friends then quietly sang the "Star Spangled Banner" together, anticipating the time, just a few months later, when Stone would be able to wave her flag openly, to the cheers of the thousands of Union soldiers who marched through occupied Atlanta.[25]

Earlier in the war, a man from Salem, Massachusetts, who had resettled nearly thirty years previously in Nashville, harbored a much larger Star Spangled Banner, measuring a full thirty-eight by nineteen feet. He was unable to keep this prize possession secret, and when word of it reached the Texas Rangers stationed nearby, they resolved to burn his house if he did not relinquish it. Luckily for the elderly man, his friends were able to protect him for more than a week, at which time Yankee troops arrived and took Nashville as the first Confederate capital to surrender to Union arms. This unnamed patriot shared his tribulations with the officers, who not only received his gift of the flag, but allowed its former protector to raise it above the Tennessee capitol building. "With my own hand, in the presence of thousands, I hoisted that flag where it now floats, on the staff which has trembled with the fluttering of treason's banner," the man wrote his daughter. With this momentous actions, he confessed, he was "ready to lie down with my fathers of the heroic age" and to "go home to God, for I know He is about to give my people rest."[26]

While some bided their time until the Yankees arrived, Caroline Seabury, still another New Englander adrift in the Confederacy, took more active efforts to seek the protection of the American flag. Her odyssey began in 1862, when she was dismissed from a teaching job in Columbus, Mississippi, because of her suspicious Yankee lineage. Her decision the next year to leave a state where she had lived for nearly a decade was no easy matter. Traveling through hostile territory, she struck out for the Mississippi River; when she spied the first United States flag she had seen in two years on this waterway, she recorded in her diary, her "tears fell thick and fast." In order to catch the attention of a passing boat, Seabury pasted together her own American flag from white notepaper and blue and red silk remnants. Waving the colors from a cottonwood stick, she attracted a friendly boat, which picked her up and carried her to safety. As she moved toward Union lines she admitted that words could hardly describe the "feeling of security" as she had "once more . . . over me the emblem of a strong government—not the flag of a distracted anarchy—where confusion ruled and reigned—in the struggle for power."[27]

The case of southern Unionists dramatized that the matter of flag-waving loyalty could not be boiled down to a simple question of rival sections. Within the Confederacy there were many unwilling to bid farewell to an American standard. The internal divisions—based on former residence, class, border state ties, and previous political affiliation—would fundamentally influence the outcome of the war. And there was a larger group than white Unionists whose wartime experiences would involve working out a whole new relationship to the Star Spangled Banner. As black southerners faced American patriotism, the stakes were high, since the end result of the war depended, to some extent at least, on which set of national symbols slaves would strive to make their own. [28]

What would be the colors of black loyalty during a war to preserve the Union? Late in 1861, Frederick Douglass was not so sure. "When I join any movement," the former slave wrote to a friend, "I must have a country or a hope of a country under me—a government around me—and some flag of a Northern or Southern nation floating over me." That had still not happened when Douglass made these remarks, as the U.S. government under Abraham Lincoln had yet to place emancipation on its wartime agenda. Though frustrated, Douglass expected more from the North in time than from a southern nation formed by worried masters. Even so, the image of his flaglessness appropriately conveyed the dilemma of being surrounded by a sea of hostile banners.[29]

The patriotic allegiances of African Americans had been an issue well before the American Civil War. As slaves, black men and women experienced a "state of war continued" that had begun with their initial forced transportation to the New World. As "internal enemies," slaves caused constant anxiety for imperial officials, who knew that enormous profits came at the price of sporadic slave rebellions. Thomas Jefferson had the volatility of slavery in mind when, in one of the most influential passages on American slavery ever written, he suggested that "if a slave would have a country in this world, it must be any other in preference to that in which he is born to live and labour for another." His reflections on the loss of patriotism by Virginia slaves was no mere speculation, since several of his own Monticello workers fled to the British during the Revolution, preferring to live freely in a monarchy rather than remain enslaved in the new American republic.[30]

There had been a number of black patriots during the American Revolution, of course, and there would be other famous black military contributions, nurtured within free African American communities as a means of claiming membership in the national community. Such contributions were rarely rewarded with equality, however, and many black slaves and their white abolitionist allies developed a cynical view of American patriotic tributes to their purported land of liberty. The most uncompromising opponents of slavery considered the United States Constitution a "covenant with death and a pact with hell."

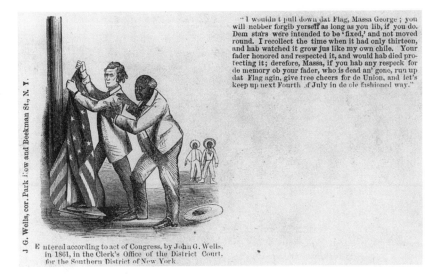

"I wouldn't pull down dat Flag, Massa George; you will nebber forgib yerself as long as you lib, if you do. Dem stars were intended to be 'fixed,' and not moved round. I recollect the time when it had only thirteen, and hab watched it grow jus like my own chile. Your fader honored and respected it, and would hab died protecting it; derefore, Massa, if you hab any respeck for de memory ob your fader, who is dead an' gone, run up dat Flag agin, give tree cheers for de Union, and let's keep up next Fourth of July in de ole fashioned way."

Entered according to act of Congress, by John G. Wells, in 1861, in the Clerk's Office of the District Court, for the Southern District of New York

J. G. Wells, cor. Park Row and Beekman St., N. Y.

25. A Union patriotic envelope enlisted the aid of an elderly slave to argue against a master's betrayal of the Stars and Stripes. Courtesy, the Southern Historical Collection, University of North Carolina, Chapel Hill.

Douglass himself was hopeful of a different future, but he too was unsure whether the Fourth of July could really be meaningful to African Americans. The country's flag, many felt, was poisoned by a close association with slavery. The British poet Thomas Campbell provided a lasting vocabulary to this connection in 1838, writing an epigram to the American flag that explained that its stripes "mean your negroes' scars!"[31]

African American distrust of the American flag was not just about symbols. Throughout the 1850s, federal agents directed the full force of their government against vulnerable black communities, whether in overseeing the capture of suspected fugitives in the North or suppressing the raid that abolitionist John Brown made on Harpers Ferry. On the high seas, this flag was complicit in bondage in another way, disguising illegal efforts to bring even more Africans to the United States. Black men were excluded from the army and thus denied the chance to prove their patriotism under fire. The aftermath of secession did little to change the sinister associations that this primary symbol of white America held for many blacks. Two weeks after the bombardment of Fort Sumter, an anonymous African American writer explained how the Star Spangled Banner was the symbol "of our bitterest and most malignant enemies." Given Lincoln's reassurances to loyal southern masters, this writer announced: "Withered forever be the hand, and paralyzed the arm of the colored American who lifts up either in support of the Federal Flag." This curse would be lifted, he added, only when whites recognized "the justice of our claims and the greatness of our sufferings."[32]

Ignoring the depths of disaffection felt by African Americans, white Unionists and Confederates both figuratively enlisted slaves in their cause. A Unionist image printed early in the war put unlikely words into the mouth of a slave who counseled his "Massa George" to give the American flag the respect it deserved. "I recollect the time when it had only thirteen" stars, the elderly black man says, adding that he "hab watched it grow jus like my own chile." Serving as a link to the earliest days of their common country, he reminds his master of previous family loyalties and of the need to "give tree cheers for de Union" to show he still held "any respeck for de memory ob your fader." Such messages of "darky loyalty" did not go unanswered by Confederates, who all along had claimed that their institution was the best means of promoting slaves' true happiness. The *Charleston Mercury* early in 1861 carefully showed how black workers constructing fortifications around Charleston had gathered around the flagpole to cheer the palmetto and sing "Dixie." As the war dragged on, newspapers drove this point home both through numerous anecdotes of slaves' fidelity and a few portrayals of slaves proudly waving the rebel standard.[33]

Flag-waving, even in those instances where it might have occurred, was an outward display that, like so much in the relations between whites and blacks, masked what was going on beneath the surface. Confederates worried a great deal about the inscrutability of their slaves. Southern African Americans had little reason to be forthcoming, since violence seemed a likely consequence of even the slightest deviation from subservience. Such guardedness gave white Yankees as well as white southerners cause for alarm. Knowing that the United States government had helped to keep blacks in chains, some feared that pro-slavery theorists might have been right to boast that black southerners would protect their masters in times of crisis. Even if he remained skeptical of such claims, Lincoln's private secretary John Hay was still worried how the "linked shouts of Union and Liberty" would be received by what he condescendingly called the "dull sounds of the waiting contraband." Anticipating the Union invasion of the Atlantic Coast, Hay wondered whether slaves would "consider the constellated banner of the kind invader the promise of a vague and traditional good" or whether "the incessant teaching of a degraded life-time associate it with everything the childish mind knows of cruelty, rapine or ravage."[34]

The gradual embrace by African Americans of Union patriotism, and particularly of the United States flag, was dramatic to those who were uncertain how the story would turn out. Acutely aware of past broken promises, African Americans themselves were careful to avoid taking sides too early. A few black abolitionists in the North ventured some initial hopes in the late spring of 1861, suggesting that it might be a fallacy to claim this was a "white man's war" strictly about "their flag, and their constitution." By the end of that year, William P. Powell told a group of fellow black abolitionists in New Bedford,

26. While not yet waving national flags, these African Americans waved copies of the Emancipation Proclamation while celebrating on January 1, 1863. Courtesy, Chicago Historical Society.

Massachusetts, that "never in the history of our unfortunate country have the Stars and Stripes been held in greater veneration by Abolitionists, even by colored men, than now." Once regarded with "utter contempt," this patriotic symbol "never looked more beautiful, more hopeful." Even so, few African Americans were willing to embrace the Union cause without conditions. As a black poet put it at the time, they seemed less concerned with pledging devotion to the flag than with making the request that "Starry banner, wave for me" and "Break the bonds of Slavery!"[35]

Slavery became inextricably linked to the war for Union at least by the fall of 1862, when Abraham Lincoln announced his plans to move against slavery in areas under rebel control. This decree may not have liberated many slaves, as critics at the time noted, but it changed the basis of the war, making it monumentally good news for even those African Americans not affected directly by the proclamation. In rural Virginia, slaves hoisted copies of the proclamation as if they were banners, while in Union-occupied Portsmouth, a group of black women celebrated the news by destroying Confederate flags. Such actions were steps toward flag-waving patriotism rather than a full-fledged manifestation of it. In Philadelphia, Robert Purvis was amazed to hear himself praising the "Star-Spangled Banner," remembering how, as a veteran Garrisonian and critic of the United States, he had long railed against the hypocrisy of the American flag. African American expressions of patriotism were still tentative, which was understandable, given the fierce backlash among many Unionists that Lincoln's initiative had provoked.[36]

In Port Royal, South Carolina, more certain commitments were made to the American flag during an Emancipation Day celebration that has received widespread attention ever since it took place. This occasion, which centered on a presentation of flags to the First South Carolina volunteers, was not the first patriotic celebration in the occupied Sea Islands. But unlike the Fourth of July festivities six months earlier, national flags at this event were not merely flown above the heads of black South Carolinians, but placed, with great fanfare, directly into their hands. Though superficially similar to earlier ceremonies involving white soldiers, this presentation did not affirm local community ties but announced the forging of a new alliance. This alliance was more complicated than a simple conversion of blacks to the American cause. For this partnership to work, white Unionists needed to redeem the flag not only of its history but of the unsuccessful attempts just a few months earlier to place black soldiers in the army through a coercive draft.[37]

The order of the day in Port Royal dramatized the complicated intersection of parties and interests involved in the new Unionist alliance. The tone was set by a prayer and a poem, both read by white Yankees, and then the reading of the final Emancipation Proclamation by David Brisbane, himself a former slaveholder. This document, though subdued in tone, unexpectedly abandoned the idea of colonizing slaves outside the United States, which had previously been central to Lincoln's vision of the aftermath of slavery. It also put forward a tepid, though no less significant, endorsement of using slaves in the U.S. army. Such a shift, which would have been noted by those in the audience, lent meaning to the next event, as representatives of the New York Church of the Puritans unfurled a banner inscribed with the words "The Year of the Jubilo is Come!" This silk flag demonstrated that the change in war was not just a matter of "military necessity" from an opportunistic government, but a willingness of the northern public to make emancipation part of a new dispensation. While these flags were officially received by the white abolitionist Thomas Wentworth Higginson, the black audience interceded, registering their own acceptance by singing "My Country 'Tis of thee, / Sweet land of liberty / Of thee I sing!" As Higginson said at the time, this action "made all other words cheap," and apparently caused most of the whites in the crowd to dissolve into tears.

While this musical interlude was for many the "life of the whole day," it did not end the patriotic transactions that marked one of the most dramatic flag ceremonies of the whole war. Higginson followed the stirring song with another white interjection, explaining how the merging of love of country and aspirations of freedom had to be accepted with responsibilities and duties char-

27. Port Royal, South Carolina witnessed one of the most dramatic flag presentations of the war when, on January 1, 1863, the Stars and Stripes announced a
new alliance between slaves and the Union. *Frank Leslie's Illustrated Magazine.*
Courtesy, American Antiquarian Society.

acteristic of caring for a sacred flag. With "the most solemn words" he instructed Sergeant Prince Rivers that "his life was chained" to the colors and
that "he must die to defend it." Rivers, who had been chosen as the regimental
flag-bearer, looked him in the eye and responded "Yes sar" when Higginson
asked, "Do you understand?" Then, with what one white reporter mocked as
the "broad patois of the plantation," Rivers turned to address the four thousand
blacks present, generating the most enthusiastic response of the day. Whatever
their accent, the Sea Island community had already internalized the flag-centered patriotism of the larger country and were ready to support leaders who
voiced it. Nearly a month before the ceremony, a Florida recruit had elicited
the same "immense applause" from a black audience in saying of Confederates:
"de fus' minute dey tink dat ole flag mean freedom for we colored people, dey
pull it right down, and run up de rag ob dere own."[38]

What transpired in South Carolina was "watched with microscopic scrutiny
by friends and foes," as Higginson later put it. The association of "contrabands"
with patriotic song was jarring to many whites, since, as a reporter for *Frank
Leslie's* noted at the time, black faces would have been associated by most
whites with the minstrel stage and its banjos rather than with blacks accepting

military flags while singing patriotic hymns. The spectacle of Port Royal, and those involving black soldiers that followed, were as much about changing the perception of American symbols as of changing racist stereotypes, however. Men who could have been claimed as property just hours before gave new meaning to lyrics praising the "sweet land of liberty" and the "land where our fathers died." The tune of "My Country 'Tis of Thee" had already seen plenty of modifications, beginning as a Jacobite song of rebellion before being made into the British anthem "God Save the King." With words that had been republicanized in the 1830s, former slaves would make this hymn a song of revolution, just as schoolchildren in the Sea Islands had for "The Star Spangled Banner" performance they prepared for the Fourth of July. Unlike Confederates, these black southerners did not need to change words to change meaning; a radically different context imbued songs, as well as flags, with an entirely new significance.[39]

The commanding general in South Carolina expressed his wish at the end of the New Year's Day celebration that "flags for negro regiments would continue to arrive until the whole South should lie under their shadow." While falling short of this goal, flags did become over the course of the next two years every bit as central to the wartime experience of African Americans as they were to other Civil War participants. Presentation ceremonies in free black communities across the North recalled the same rituals that white patriots had witnessed in 1861. Black women took a central role in making and presenting the standards at the center of the events, yet because of the relative poverty of many African American communities, they also engaged in elaborate campaigns to raise the necessary funds to purchase materials. There are several descriptions of these flags in the contemporary press that also show how themes were altered. One transformed the seal of Virginia and its motto, "Sic Semper Tyrannis" into a scene of a black Union soldier bayoneting a Confederate. That of the famous Fifty-fourth Massachusetts Regiment featured a cross with Constantine's motto, "In Hoc Signo Vicnes," affixed to it. In presenting the standard, Governor John A. Andrew of Massachusetts claimed, in what might have been an intended slight to the Confederate Cross, that this unit was the first to carry a Christian banner in this war, making blacks in this sense "the real leaders of the nation."[40]

The attachment of black soldiers to their flags was, like that of their white counterparts, was consecrated as much by combat as by the rituals that preceded it. Less than a month after their New Year's Day celebration, the South Carolina volunteers carried "the regimental flag and the President's proclamation far into the interior of Georgia and Florida," where they captured a Confederate flag in the process. Other African American troops would prove as enthusiastic as any soldiers in protecting their color-bearers, in developing lasting ties for their regimental colors, and in taking enemy standards as trophies, for which several were awarded Congressional Medals of Honor. When a Louisi-

28. By serving in the Union army, slaves made the Stars and Stripes into a beacon of freedom and helped to assure the defeat of rebel banners. This contemporary lithograph featured a Confederate flag beneath the feet of a black soldier and just beside the broken manacles of slavery. Courtesy, Chicago Historical Society.

ana unit was deprived of an irregular banner that white officials dismissed as a "pettiecoat" flag, they petitioned up the chain of command to reclaim it.[41] All of this dramatized how, despite unequal treatment, black troops entered Union service as citizen-soldiers and as full participants in the flag culture of the Union cause. The patriotic tenor of their service should not be assumed, since the usual method of enlisting soldiers in slave and postemancipation societies had depended on coercion rather than consent.[42]

The service of black soldiers in federal armies was observed from the outset by the white southern public, whose doubts about the loyalty of African Americans also included suspicions about their capacities and courage. The service of "colored troops" became a focal point for abolitionists, southern slaves, and the country more generally, and the test of devotion would be the defense of the country's flag under fire. African Americans were willing to take up this challenge, singing,

> Oh! give us a flag all free without a slave
> We'll fight to defend it as our fathers did so brave.
> . . . So rally, boys, rally, let us never mind the past.

The rest of the war would justify the remarks of the sergeant of the Fifty-fourth Massachusetts Regiment, who noted the "school of the soldier" seemed the "only means by which the collective power of the negro race can be brought to bear on the civil and political affairs of the country."[43]

After 1863, African Americans developed what they saw as a deeply personal stake in which set of colors would emerge triumphant from the war. While a soldier's uniform usually gave protection to whites, it sealed a death sentence for many blacks. And it was not just the fate of the black soldier that mattered, but that of their families and loved ones. At Port Royal, one of the color-bearers acknowledged this fact, reminding his listeners that "not one in that crowd but had a sister, a brother, or some relation among the rebels still." A short time after their ceremony, M. L. Maimi sounded similar themes in a letter to his wife. This biracial Connecticut soldier shared with many of his comrades the sentiment that Confederates had raised "their rebel rag" with the purpose that "freedom should die." Though his wife urged him to come home, he explained that all Unionists had committed themselves to "shed the last drop of their blood in defense of the starry banner that is to be the symbol of freedom to all, whether white or black."[44]

Maimi was willing to sacrifice his body for something more fundamental than either his flag or the progress of his race. He had those he loved most in mind, knowing that Confederate victory would make them even more physically vulnerable than he was in uniform. "If these Southern demons conquer," he told his wife, who was also of mixed descent, she would be forced to "bow down to them and become their slaves or perhaps some white man's mistress, not an honored wife, loved and respected by her husband, but a mere plaything, to be cast aside as soon as he discovers a fresh victim to administer to his beastly lusts." With stakes this high, Private Maimi vowed that he would return "a free man, of a free country and a free flag, and my brothers free." Short of accomplishing this, he would gladly suffer death, a commitment shared by the more than 170,000 black soldiers who would by the end of the war wear the Union blue.[45]

For most ordinary individuals, the issue of Civil War loyalty turned upon which flag one followed and which government one pledged to support. In this, there was a clear choice between alternatives: either defend the Stars and Stripes and the Union or fight for a Confederacy represented by the Stars and Bars, the Southern Cross, and then the Stainless Banner. Leaders of the two warring governments faced more difficult decisions, however, in establishing their own official commitments to common flags rather than distinctive ones. Agreement about two symbols—one all black and the other all white—ultimately led to an underlying consensus between Americans about a common set of war rules. Shared conclusions reached by Confederates and federals about these banners helped to shape the conflict and to keep the passions of war from becoming altogether uncontrollable.

Calls to raise a so-called black flag were a distinct subtheme in wartime commentary. Like resistance banners, national flags, and battle standards, this emblem pre-dated the Civil War, going at least as far back as the pirate ships of the Spanish Main. References to this pirate's emblem appeared as a fantasy among those Confederates convinced that only bold resistance and retaliation would achieve victory. Paul Hamilton Hayne of South Carolina roused listeners in one widely reprinted poem:

> Up with the sable banner
> Let it thrill to the War-God's Breath
> For we march to the watchword—Vengeance!
> And we follow the Captain—Death!

Defiant editors of the *Charleston Mercury* responded to Union transgressions— whether it be the invasion of coastal plantations or the execution of Mumford in New Orleans—with similar calls to raise the emblem of war to the death. Federal recruitment of African American troops in 1863 led to a new depth of anger and resolve in meeting black men in blue with the black flag. In determining how African American soldiers might be treated, the *Mercury* insisted until the end of the war that "the skull and crossbones" should become "the insignia of the Southern battle flag." If the snake had provided rebels with an emblem of their own subversion during secession, the black flag subsequently became the most powerful image available to avid supporters of southern independence.[46]

What did all this mean? The black flag was usually not an actual piece of dark cloth, though there were scattered reports that the South's "fairest daughters" had, from time to time, brought out their black silk to prepare for a new stage of combat. At least one Congressional Medal of Honor was awarded to a Union soldier who captured a black flag that was, in all likelihood, merely a railroad marker. Mostly, however, the image worked on the level of metaphor, standing for a conscious departure from the rules of legitimate warmaking. Both sides invoked this powerfully charged emblem from the outset, though it was subject to a range of meanings. Northerners condemned the Confederate use of privateers to molest Union shipping as a turn to black flag piracy, an association that Lincoln himself extended by initially calling for the execution of all sailors captured on such vessels. As the land war shifted attention to territorial armies, the black flag became shorthand for the policy, often threatened but rarely openly used, of "giving no quarter" or "taking no prisoners." By executing all who surrendered rather than capturing them, those "raising the black flag" announced that they would not expect mercy either. Most of these calls came from southerners determined to do what was necessary to repel invading armies. The Black Flag Riflemen of New Orleans, for instance, required both that its soldiers "neither give nor ask quarter on the soil of Louisiana" and that they furnish their own rifles and hunting knives to achieve their ends.[47]

Proposals to wage war under this metaphorical banner generated considerable attention from policy makers. Lincoln faced a particular paradox, since his government fought a regular war against a group it defined as traitors who had forfeited all protections of international law. In both the case of the "pirates" captured at sea and the rebellious soldiers taken on land, the Union avoided risking an escalation that seemed capable of spinning beyond control and did its best to institute a series of prisoner exchanges and regular truces.[48] Confederates debated not only how to respond to perceived transgressions by their enemies but also engaged in an internal argument about what might result from pushing beyond the limits of combat by regular armies on the field. The high costs of raising the black flag were well known. Editors of the *Savannah Morning News* realized that this "demoralizing banner" might be an inspiring idea, but it was a "double-edged sword" that would deprive their soldiers of protection at the same time it announced a newly ferocious purpose. In the immediate aftermath of the Emancipation Proclamation, the paper warned against a practice that would take the country "back two thousand years before the light of Christianity and civilization dawned upon the world." It seemed clear that such "foolish talk" was already hurting the cause by recklessly defying European opinion. Though the use of black Union soldiers convinced even this paper that the black flag might eventually be necessary, the Richmond government did not give any of these suggestions serious consideration. Officials ignored pleas to raise the banner, even as officers in the field were often accused of implementing it directly, especially in the notorious Fort Pillow incident, where Confederates were reported to have executed black soldiers rather than take them prisoner.[49]

Legitimate flags with agreed-upon protocol were one means of providing a framework for war that the black flag threatened to destroy. The workings of these symbolic rules were articulated with particular effectiveness by none other than Francis Lieber, that fierce critic of Confederate emblems who had begun the war by praising the Stars and Stripes as a "piece of floating poetry." In addition to expressing such fairly typical kinds of wartime patriotism, Lieber wrote the first important American contribution to international law, which, among a great many other topics, explained how proper flag use might structure combat. He prepared the way with his opinion on guerrillas late in 1862. This set of guidelines, written at the request of the Lincoln administration, distinguished legitimate partisan bands, authorized by their government and deserving the protection accorded soldiers, from self-constituted bands, who lacked formal government sanction and were thus, in Lieber's opinion, no better than common outlaws. The determining feature, he explained, would be the wearing of a uniform or some other distinguishing emblem to mark soldiers from civilians. Without this outward sign, those engaged in hostile activity would receive none of the protections usually accorded belligerents.[50]

Lieber's comprehensive code of war, issued in 1863, shifted the emphasis on identifying marks of service from uniforms to flags. Not surprisingly, he denounced the practice of giving and receiving "no quarter," popularly known as "raising the black flag," considering it "against the usage of modern war." More interesting was a set of strongly worded statements on unacceptable uses of other flags in combat situations. To take up the national standard of the enemy for deception was nothing less than "an act of perfidy" and thus worthy of execution, his code established. Using the white flag of truce to gain a similar unfair advantage was even worse, since "so sacred is the character" of this signal that Lieber insisted that efforts to compromise its sanctity were "an especially heinous offense." In each of these instances, the proper use of pieces of cloth distinguished socially accepted violence from undiscriminating barbarism.[51]

Lieber's code indicated through a series of negations one important aspect of Civil War flags—their simultaneous status as emotional symbols and as specific signals to guide the business of war. This has been appreciated in the case of soldiers' use of their own standards, since the same cloth that inspired patriotism was also a practical tool used to coordinate troop movements. Yet flags of the enemies held two different meanings as well. While opposing banners might have stirred considerable anger, these emblems still helped both sides to play by the same rules and to differentiate friend from foe. Paradoxically, Lieber seemed to realize that regular use of battle flags, even when wielded on behalf of what he considered an illegal rebellion, was a vital part of legitimate and honorable combat. Compared to symbols that promised vengeance or tried to deceive, clearly marked flags were objectionable in a less fundamental way. Lieber's opinion, then, betrayed a grudging respect for Confederate soldiers who played by the rules and fought behind the flags they believed in. When Confederates surrendered their battle flags, Unionists would experience a similar sense of both relief and respect, seeing how martial decorum discouraged Confederates from taking up a flagless pursuit of guerrilla warfare.[52]

The white flag of truce was another example of how legitimate war depended on an agreed-upon use of common symbols. This emblem had long been a routine part of war making, allowing both sides to suspend hostilities so as to assure lines of communication, to allow proper treatment of the wounded and burial of the dead, and to permit travel and communication between enemy lines. From the earliest days of the Civil War, Confederates and Union forces each made regular complaints that their opponents were violating these conventions. Officials of both sides accused spies of carrying very small white flags with them, not to signal a cease-fire but to be used falsely as a claim of protection if captured. In other instances, charges were leveled that truce flags were not allowed and that troops knowingly shot the bearer of a white flag for spite. There were even accusations that soldiers had raised white flags to open their enemy's vulnerability, firing once defenses were relaxed, or even had used the pretense of a truce as an opportunity to take prisoners of war. None of these questionable practices ever received official approval. In responding to charges, both sides sought the high ground, simultaneous denying that anyone in their forces was guilty of these actions and repeating accusations against their opponents.[53]

Leaders resolved that white flags would be used properly and that the black flag of indiscriminate killing would not be used at all. Such conventions of flag restraint became effective, however, only when ordinary soldiers internalized them during the course of doing battle. A soldierly flag culture that emerged during the war itself had less to do with patriotism or nationalism than with playing by the rules. Fighting fairly was a means of gaining the respect of one's enemies, even while there remained passionately felt differences about which flag and which cause should triumph in the end. In this, a shared warrior culture began to link enemies together and even rivaled those ties that bound soldiers to their respective civilian populations.[54]

At no time was the need to honor shared symbols more important than at the moment of final surrender. When Confederates showed the white flag for the last time and gave up their battle colors, Unionists responded with relief and, in a few cases, a degree of respect. Those who hated the rebellion still appreciated how Confederates had held to martial decorum and the promise of their final white flag by renouncing guerrilla warfare. Southern disavowal of irregular resistance after 1865 has tempted many historians to suspect the insufficiencies of Confederate nationalism. Perhaps it is more accurate to see this as a logical result of prior decisions to wage a legitimate war through a regular army. Observing such rules may have doomed political independence for the Confederacy, but it was of utmost importance in helping white southerners return once more to full membership within the United States. At the very least, it showed that even though there had developed separate patriotic flag cultures within both the Union and the Confederacy, there was also a shared martial cult of battle emblems that would eventually provide a basis for reunion.[55]

For even a few civilians to go outside the regulations of "civilized" war could have profound consequences, as John Wilkes Booth's assassination of Abraham Lincoln made clear. This episode of unregulated civilian passion provided a crucial exception to a surrender mostly characterized by soldierly order, restraint, and a willingness to end hostilities after armed conflict had produced a clear military victor. Instead of waving either a Confederate flag or a black one, Booth staged his final act of vengeance with the Stars and Stripes in mind. A few months before the fighting had stopped, Booth expressed bitter anger at how Lincoln had made the "once bright red stripes" of the American flag to "look like *bloody gashes* on the face of Heaven." Later, in this professional actor's most famous scene, Booth became literally wrapped up in this same emblem, catching his foot on a red, white, and blue banner as he leapt to the stage of Ford's Theater. Immediately before his death in Maryland, some heard him cry out, apparently in reference to the torching of the barn where he hid: "one more stain on the old banner!" Booth's retaliation against those who had changed this flag's meaning was unique. But other Confederates shared his realization that rebel colors mattered less in 1865 than an American flag that had just survived what would be its greatest challenge ever.[56]

CHAPTER SEVEN

Conquered Banners, Furled and Unfurled

WHEN FIRST CAST TO THE WIND, Confederate flags heralded the future. Their main purpose was to lead people forward, whether into radical action, onto the world stage of nationhood, or into the midst of battle. A multimedia flag culture sustained popular patriotism by promising Confederates that they would eventually be a sovereign nation at peace with the rest of the world. Yet the more these emblems were used, the more they evoked the past as well. Civilian flags reminded southerners of the excitement of secession and of early attempts to rival the Stars and Stripes. Homemade regimental colors testified to female support of the cause and to the pledges young men made to protect their communities. Those unveiled on the field of battle brought memories of the spectacle of their presentation and their subsequent christening in combat. Even before the Confederacy was a lost cause, its patriotic flag culture was commemorative in these important respects.

The most searing experiences Confederate flags recalled for southerners were those that involved bloodshed. In this, combat banners occupied a class by themselves. These relics of the battlefield had "once danced in the breeze of death," a wartime article from the *Southern Illustrated News* explained in trying to reckon with their mystical aura. Those regimental colors taken from enemies stirred more complicated responses than those defended from capture. A trophy banner reminded soldiers of a hated opponent while it also testified to the fact that "the blood of our best and bravest" had been poured out to take such a prize. While cannon roared and confusion reigned, seizing an enemy banner or defending one's own stirred a frantic competition between troops to achieve the symbolism of victory as well as the substance. For soldiers, winning became defined as much by a shared martial flag culture than by the fate of the national cause. When the smoke cleared, tattered pieces of cloth testified to how the deadly sport of war moved hearts and established memories that would remain long after underlying goals had been forgotten.[1]

After the surrender of armies, the battle flags of Confederates looked only one way: toward the past. What had become the prime symbol of a defeated Confederacy became a Conquered Banner, which generated a range of cultural expressions among white southerners facing defeat. These battle-scarred emblems kept their focus on the martial aspects of the war and on the valor of soldiers, while they obscured the more controversial aspects of a conflict that had involved immense political consequences. After being furled for several decades, these banners returned to public prominence largely stripped of their nationalist messages. Waving Southern Crosses in the late-nineteenth century allowed white southerners to establish a certain vision of the past without compromising their basic loyalty to the larger country. Yet even as the associations of this rebel flag with treason virtually disappeared, its associations with slavery and racism eventually made it what it is today—one of the most controversial emblems in all of American culture.

An appreciation for battle flags was shared among Civil War soldiers, who developed an understanding of combat colors that would outlast the end of hostilities. Even before surrender, this martial flag culture subordinated nationalist ends to more basic matters of battlefield victories and defeats. Less warlike cloth had already helped individuals to make an emotional bond with their country's cause, and the associated flag culture stitched together soldiers and civilians in a single community of feeling. The use of flags in combat, on the other hand, formed a distinct class of warriors, which included enemies and allies in a common imagined brotherhood of martial principle. Flags used in this sphere owed less to theatrical conventions than to sport. The competition that flags established in battle had the capacity to establish respect between enemies, even though adversaries' primary objective was to kill those who flew the opposing symbols.

From the beginning, victories and defeats marked with flags involved highly charged issues of pride and honor. One of the most intricate flag transactions involved one of the war's very first conquered banners, that famous Star Spangled Banner that flew above Fort Sumter in April of 1861. Though badly outnumbered and aware of his need to withdraw, federal commander Robert Anderson hoped that his troops might be allowed to salute this oversized flag and carry it with them when they left. He was able to negotiate these generous terms, both because of poor communication among Confederates and because the first rebel party to land at the fort misunderstood flag etiquette. Charlestonians thus witnessed an unusual spectacle of the huge enemy flag being reraised above a fort that had apparently surrendered, and then honored with an unusually high number of cannon salutes. After the banner was marched out with pomp and pageantry, Confederate commander P. G. T. Beauregard

29. Union prisoners of war in Missouri were forced to relinquish their flag, laying it on the ground beneath the Stars and Bars, as this illustration showed. *Harper's Weekly*, October 19, 1861. Courtesy, Michigan State University Libraries.

publicized this as a magnanimous gesture toward a defeated foe. He perhaps sensed that conciliatory actions might lessen some of the anger that Unionists felt about the humiliation of the bombardment that had preceded this ritual.[2]

As war took its toll, Confederates rarely showed such respect and restraint, proving themselves as willing as their enemies to capture banners and to hold troops as prisoners of war. They would routinely require surrendering soldiers to lay down their standards as trophies, adding these to the Union banners taken during the heat of combat. In several instances, pieces of enemy cloth were carried through Confederate lines on horseback with the explicit purpose of whipping up the enthusiasm of southern soldiers. They were also paraded through Confederate towns and then torn apart to provide civilians with their own tokens of victory. Those captured banners forwarded intact to the Confederate capital were treated with only slightly more respect. Several of them were displayed in Libby Prison, the home for those Union officers who had been taken as prisoners of war. This practice reminded Yankees that their colors, and not just their persons, had been captured on the field of battle.[3]

Wartime conventions made taking an enemy banner in combat nearly as heroic as defending or dying for one's own flag. Confederates were less organized than the U.S. army in honoring such actions, initially leaving it to newspapers to praise soldiers who captured Union colors. Editors took particular interest in those emblems that were meant to insult the Confederacy, such as the one given to George McClellan to float over Richmond or that huge banner apparently intended to be placed atop a reconquered Fort Sumter. Later, the Confederate Congress established a "roll of honor" so that "gallant captors" who displayed "dash and valor" could expect "the grateful appreciation and future emulation of their admiring countrymen." Though some of these captured Union flags were taken to Richmond, many more were kept as souvenirs, either by the men who took them or by their commanders. As one official put it, "Nothing is more difficult than to make officers send up these trophies, which the men seem to regard as their own." Until the end of the war, Confederates were more likely than Federal troops to present flags to individual commanders or leaders, as even President Davis and General Lee departed from the official policy that insisted all captured trophies be treated as government property.[4]

The U.S. army kept more careful track of enemy banners, awarding a Congressional Medal of Honor to all who either captured a Confederate flag or saved their own colors through some exceptional act of heroism. The expectation of a medal for flag-related patriotism became so routine that one soldier retrospectively petitioned for one to honor his bravery in smuggling a Union banner out of Texas during the secession crisis. Private James O'Riley of Indiana received a commendation for "sallying out" to meet a color-bearer and then "running him through with his bayonet." Sergeant James Carney of the Massachusetts Fifty-fourth became the first black American to be similarly honored by carrying his regimental flag a half mile back from Fort Wagner. Though he did so with a bullet in his leg, he was able to earn lasting fame with his dramatic boast that his flag had "never touched the ground." Private Charles Stevenson of Ohio earned a single medal for the dual heroics of saving his own company flag and then tearing up a rebel banner with his own hands.[5]

As ever more flags were taken, surrendered, and retaken, Civil War combat came to resemble organized sport. This tendency intensified during the last year and a half of war, when competing armies engaged in a virtually uninterrupted series of battles. Early in 1864, Confederate General John Bell Hood issued a formal protocol for captured flags, which he recognized as the "most valuable trophies of war." He advised his men in the Confederacy's largest

30. The flag, carried by the Twenty-eighth North Carolina Infantry, is a striking example of how battlefield inscriptions changed the appearance of combat banners. Courtesy, Museum of the Confederacy, Richmond Virginia.

western army to keep fighting even after Union colors had been taken, instructing them to tie these captured flags around their waist or to send them with the wounded to the rear. Early the next year, Hood himself seemed to mistake such outward signs of victory for the true situation. Writing to his superiors, he defended his troops at the battle of Franklin by noting that, contrary to Yankee reports, his soldiers had only lost thirteen colors while taking "nearly the same number." His suggestion that the conflict could thus be seen as a draw was a total misrepresentation of what was clearly one of the most disastrous setbacks of the war. Hood's own resignation a few weeks later made this perfectly clear.[6]

Hood was not alone in allowing the competitive action of flag capturing to obscure his perspective during the closing months of the war. Late in the Petersburg campaign of 1865, a handful of federal soldiers displayed their desire for medals by seizing the hospital flags that departing troops had been left behind. Surprisingly enough, taking hold of these red banners earned the same honors that had been given to soldiers obtaining genuine regimental colors under far more dangerous circumstances. Other Yankees chose to relinquish claims to a medal altogether, subjecting trophy flags to what one officer called a new "passion for tearing them into bits to send home as relics." In some instances, this seemed to be a means of keeping a personal trophy for oneself. A more common practice was to send pieces of flags as presents to loved ones at home, effectively reversing the direction of flag presentations, which had flowed the opposite way in 1861.[7]

Regimental banners also kept score by listing the names of engagements directly on their cloth. Union officials formalized the practice of battlefield inscriptions early in 1862, reasoning that troops whose "meritorious" service was thus recognized would "regard their colors as representing the honor of their corps—to be lost only with their lives." Those deprived of this distinction would, by contrast, "not rest satisfied until they have won it by their discipline and courage." Attempts to stir troop enthusiasm through adding battle names to their flags were reintroduced in the fall of 1864, as a means to "excite the energy and soldierly pride" of their troops that faced a final push to victory.[8] Confederate officials emulated these practices, issuing orders in the summer of 1862 that all commanding generals were to enter "in some conspicuous place" the names of every battle that regimental flags had survived, regardless of how the troops fared. For both sides, flags thus became visible histories of specific battlefield encounters.[9]

At the center of the martial flag culture were banners endowed with actual battle scars. Regimental colors that had been shredded by bullets and cannon, stained in smoke, and soaked in the blood of their defenders acquired distinct physical features that lent cloth a nearly human presence. The "glorious, tattered flag" of one Alabama unit bound all of its members with "a delicate chain of affection," according to a soldier who wrote home in 1862. A North Carolina soldier explained two years later how "the soiled and tattered colors borne by our skeleton regiment" had become "sacred and dear to the heart of every man." He was sure that "no one would exchange it for a new flag." A southern visitor to Port Royal reported the same pattern was evident among Union soldiers. A unit that carried its "old worn, battle-stained, shot-riddled" flag seemed to walk "more proudly, and filed by in more solid phalanx, it seemed to me, looking at no one, but soberly following that flag."[10]

The marks of veteran emblems lent them a recognizably dramatic aura that was a key to their emotional power both during and after the war. The writer John Esten Cooke realized this better than most, using the changing appearance of flags and of the soldiers who carried them to chart the progress of the war. In the first rush of enthusiasm, Cooke wrote in 1865, "gaily clad volunteers marched gallantly through the streets" as crowds cheered and "the new flags, shaped by fair hands, fluttered." Before long, "yells of triumph, or groans of agony" on the battlefield replaced celebration, as "stalwart hands" with "unshrinking hearts" carried implements that had been tested under fire. "All frippery and decoration had long been stripped from the army" by the war's midpoint. As colors themselves dulled, passions toward flags grew more long lasting. Every "old tattered, ball-pierced flag" became a "sacred ensign" of the fight for cause and country.[11]

If war became a sport with its own rules, scorekeeping conventions, and specially marked tools, this competition had uniquely high stakes. Early in 1864, an article in the Confederate press, "What Subjugation Means," reminded readers of what was involved, detailing the anger, pain, and despair that a "maimed and battle-worn" veteran would experience at the moment of defeat. Giving up his flag would be the hardest part, this article claimed, since the moment would recall "a hundred times he has stood in the line of battle under that Southern Cross," when he had "seen its fiery folds flashing almost with a living passion." It would be impossible to forget this flag's "fierce, incarnate glow, as it flashed deep into the enemy lines," nor would memories ever fade of having "followed it throughout, mayhap with naked feet, but with love and devotion in his heart." Though this fictive soldier associated his banner "with a secure and peaceful home and an honorable future for his country," the most concrete images he could summon up about it all had to do with the life of a soldier.[12]

As long as the war continued, there was hope that final surrender and subjugation might never come. In a range of poetic efforts, the image of a beloved battle flag helped to keep soldiers on the field fighting for Confederate victory. One such poem implied that symbols themselves had become an inheritance equal to the land itself: "Our heroes have died, and bequeathed to our care," it began. "Not the soil of our country alone, / But the banner whose loveliness hallowed the air / On the field where our glory has won." More common was a poetic emphasis on the human actions that flags inspired. "I die for thee," one poetic martyr told the flag in his imagined last moment, valuing a piece of cloth and the nation it represented over his own body. Conflating the future of the homeland with the defense of its most cherished object, he declared:

I die for thee—proud banner of the South!
Freely I pour the red tide of my heart
Upon my country's altar. Be she free
And I will die that she may live in light.[13]

By the end of 1864, war had taken a decisive turn, as the reelection of Abraham Lincoln and the march of General William T. Sherman across Georgia put the Confederacy in a death spiral it could not escape. As Confederate armies collapsed one by one, the question of giving up the colors assumed far greater significance than ever before. During negotiations that preceded the surrender of each army, there was never a possibility that Confederate units would be allowed to keep their battle flags. Knowing this, some soldiers chose to hide their regiment's most valuable possession. In at least one case, a company instructed its commander to keep its standard "until such time as our independence shall have been gained." Even more common was the practice of tearing up the colors so that soldiers might be saved from the humiliation of handing over a flag they had vowed to keep from the enemy. This practice also gave each member of the unit a special memento that would help him to remember the flag for which he had fought and which he now saved from capture.[14]

One of the most famous legends of the fate of a battle flag concerned Joseph Shelby's cavalry division, who had spent most of the war in the Trans-Mississippi region. Judging organized resistance to federal power to be futile, Shelby became one of a handful of commanders to flee to Mexico, where he hoped to fight in the service of the Emperor Maximillian before returning to the South in force. According to a contemporary account, his men chose July 4 to say good-bye to their battle flag. After silent prayers to "the dear old banner," five hundred soldiers "with not a dry eye among them" witnessed the burial of this emblem in the Rio Grande, seeing how it sank "slowly and sadly beneath the water." The river was not the only boundary that was crossed in this impromptu ceremony. This flag, and all other war banners, had entered the past for good. A poetic soldier who witnessed this watery burial recorded how these pieces of cloth were no longer subject to being conquered. He declared, with a mixture of relief and sorrow, that

> no foe shall dare
> To lay his hand on our standard there.
> Its folds were braided by fingers fair
> 'Tis the emblem now of their deep despair.[15]

After having waved flags and defied enemies for four years, Confederates in 1865 went about furling banners, mourning their dead, and returning once more to life under the Stars and Stripes. The process of accepting their utter and complete defeat was given a powerful vocabulary by Father Abraham Ryan, a Catholic priest with no record of involvement in wartime flag culture. When Ryan's "Conquered Banner" appeared in the summer of 1865, it captured the prevailing mood of mournful resignation that would continue to dominate the subsequent Lost Cause movement. In the years to come, its opening instructions would set the funereal tone of postwar efforts to present a fight nobly lost. Its opening lines called for yet one more flag ritual, instructing Confederates:

> Furl that Banner, for 'tis weary;
> Round its staff 'tis drooping dreary;
> Furl it, fold it, it is best.

31. As the most influential expression of the Lost Cause, Father Ryan counseled a mournful furling of rebel flags in "The Conquered Banner." Courtesy, Historic New Orleans Collection.

This poem's range of melodramatic images provided an overview of how symbols had mattered over the course of the war. It recalled the opening days of the conflict, when "ten thousand, wildly madly / Swore it should forever wave . . . O'er their freedom or their grave!" It also evoked "the blood that heroes gave" to the Southern Cross as well as the "hands that grasped it" and "the hearts that fondly clasped it." It even looked to the future, assuring Confederates that the flag's "fame on brightest pages . . . / Shall go sounding down the ages," living on in "song and story."

Most of Ryan's poem, and of the Lost Cause understanding of noble defeat that it helped to forge, concerned the painful necessities of 1865, when patriots lay "cold and dead" and unable to keep up the fight. The physical condition of the flag showed the impossibility of continued resistance, since "Broken is its shaft and shattered." With neither men nor symbols equipped for further resistance, Ryan argued that the primary challenge was to contemplate death. The flag could help soldiers do this since it itself had become a sacred marker of their commitment. "Treat it gently, it is holy," Ryan asked on behalf of the conquered banner, "for it droops above the dead."[16]

The early Lost Cause was a death culture rather than a flag culture, though in a range of forms, defeated banners contributed to the overall melancholy. Ryan's own poetry dealt as much with cemeteries as with flags, calling out, as he put it in "The City of the Dead," to

give me the land
Of the wreck and the tomb;
There's grandeur in graves—
There's glory in gloom.[17]

Within this pervasive atmosphere of mortality, Ryan's "Conquered Banner" inspired other poets to consider how flags moved from totems of nationalism to mystical relics of earlier sacrifice. A. J. Requier provided one of the most lasting images with his oft-repeated line of how the "warrior's Banner takes its flight, / To greet the warrior's soul!" Another poet placed these colors in a heavenly afterworld, imagining them being "furled upon the 'silent shore'" as dead heroes stood around them, listening to drums "echoing in eternity." A more explicitly Christian understanding of death and life was offered by a verse that asserted that "you cannot tomb the story / Burned on [the flag's] stainless white!"[18]

In the postwar imperative to mourn dead soldiers and their banners, women became the preeminent guardians of the Confederate heritage. Marginalized by the masculine world of battle flags and martial honor, female patriots spearheaded the "ceremonial bereavement" that defined Reconstruction efforts to honor a defeated stand for principle. In the South's Ladies' Memorial Association movement, mourning became a cultural imperative and graveyards became a primary site for commemorating the late war. While similar activity was undertaken by black southerners and women in the North, former Confederates elevated these practices to a regional ideal. Praying and crying became patriotic acts for women to lead, just as fighting and bleeding during war had been taken care of by men. Since Confederate symbols were primarily used in the context of cemeteries and memorial services, these banners naturally became "sanctified by tears" that were shed primarily by mourning mothers, widows, and sisters. Having already been blessed by blood and fire, the defeated Southern Cross became doused once more by weeping women.[19]

Some hoped that southern white women would also play a role in nurturing renewed affection for the American flag. During wartime, tributes to the Star Spangled Banner showed how female influence could sway the consciences of rebel men, whether it came from a gray-haired Barbara Freitchie or from Julia Ward Howe's narrative voice in her poem "The Flag." Howe's lyric, which she considered a greater accomplishment than her "Battle Hymn of the Republic," called out to rebels to "Come hither, thou son of my mother! / we were reared in the self-same arms." As the American flag gained more domestic associations in the wartime North, some were optimistic that the "old flag" could also transform the private affections of defeated Confederates. The *Richmond New Nation* maintained in 1866 that "the way to sustain a nation, is, first, to base it upon righteousness; and second, to impress its value upon the heart of childhood." To accomplish this, the paper went on to say, all guardians of youth should buy an American flag and "place it in a conspicuous part of the house, where the children may see it daily." As part of the lessons of hearth and home, such a shrine to Union might "speak to the heart of noble aims and patriotic deeds."[20]

Despite hopes that American patriotism would be rekindled by feminine influences, Confederate women showed considerable hostility toward the American flag after their men stopped fighting. They continued to express their bitterness toward federal soldiers, just as they had done in occupied cities during wartime. The mythic recalcitrance of the unreconstructed southern woman became a stock theme of postwar writing, bolstered by actual incidents of young women tearing down and trampling the Stars and Stripes. How much of this image was contrived is hard to say, yet it is clear that women who continued to resist faced fewer risks than did men, who possessed a greater range of rights that could be imperiled by disloyalty. Stories of women who crossed the street or exited through back doors rather than humiliate themselves in walking beneath the American flag strengthened their reputation for spitefulness among northerners. As late as 1899, a prominent member of the United Daughters of the Confederacy argued that the Star Spangled Banner should not be flown at a veterans' reunion in Nashville, even though local troops were returning at the same moment from the American war with Spain.[21]

Southern women acted out their misgivings with Confederate symbols as well as with American flags. The Texas patriot who wore a rebel-flag dress in 1876, for instance, added several provocative accessories, including a set of manacles and chains on her arms and a black veil of doom that she fastened with "the dagger of oppression." Such defiant gestures would fade through the 1880s, as expressions of pride displaced earlier anger. In later manifestations of the Lost Cause, female involvement with flags remained a major theme, however, as the United Daughters of the Confederacy cooperated with male veterans' groups to restore widespread public use of the Southern Cross. As memories of female war stories waned in the North, Confederate women played a crucial part in reinvigorating a tradition of flag poetry, paying particular attention to their own contributions in sewing, crying, and giving up the men who would fight and die for their flag. Louisa Wigfall Wright's praise in her poem "The Confederate Flag," published in 1905, highlighted these themes in its opening stanza:

The hands of our women made it!
'Twas baptized in our mother's tears!
. . . Across vale and plains we watched it,
Where the red tide of battle rolled
And with tear-dimmed eyes we followed
The wave of each silken fold.[22]

Southern men were not immune from the power of Confederate symbols, even if they were more cautious than women were in embracing them publicly. Soon after Reconstruction ended, Carlton McCarthy began the work of rehabilitating the Southern Cross in terms that would echo for years. He hoped to rebut charges of treason that still clung to this symbol by claiming that it was "not the flag of the Confederacy but simply the banner—the battle flag—of the Confederate soldier." McCarthy argued that as a result, this flag "should not share in the condemnation which our case received," nor should it "suffer from its downfall." Indeed, given what he saw as the banner's association with common people in the simple act of defending home and hearth, he expected that "the whole world can unite in a chorus of praise" in its behalf. He hoped to separate this emblem from "all the political significance which attaches to the Confederate flag," by which he presumably meant the Stars and Bars, and not the later national flags that incorporated the Southern Cross. By taking this most familiar of all Confederate symbols out of the political arena, McCarthy expected that its place in history would depend "solely upon the deeds of the armies which bore it amid hardships untold to many victories."[23]

Southern Crosses could become nonpolitical only after Confederate veterans made their loyalties to the Stars and Stripes evident. Men pledged themselves to the American flag with far greater regularity than did women, often vowing to return the symbol to its pre-war meanings. There were a few exceptions. Edward Pollard of Virginia hit a particularly discordant note in 1868 after Sergeant Gilbert H. Bates of Wisconsin marched through Georgia behind an American flag to dramatize the South's new allegiance to a common country. Pollard warned former Confederates not to "crucify your own sentiments, and sin against your own souls" by shifting their loyalties in defeat. He insisted that the American flag had "covered and sanctioned every known crime" during the war, and, as a result, its folds were "crimson with blood, and stained with murder, and rape, and arson, and robbery." "Though it float a thousand years longer," Pollard asserted, this emblem could never "become in the South anything more or less than an object of shuddering hatred and stinging scorn."[24]

Pragmatism won out over emotional intensity for most former soldiers, however, who expressed their resolve to honor the American flag, even if they often stopped short of loving it. During the war, Unionists had held out the national flag as an emblem that could save white southerners from the chaos of secession. During Reconstruction, traditional white leaders saw that embracing the old symbol might restore their legitimacy and bring them back to national power. Patriotic display opened the possibility of new political alliances, even if professions of a fundamental shift in allegiance or a repudiation of their rebellion were rare. A Massachusetts regiment acknowledged the importance of southern initiative when it sent an American flag to the Washington Light Infantry of Charleston, which this unit exhibited prominently at its fair in 1875. Patriotism and political calculation were all but indistinguishable the next year, as the nation's centennial coincided with a pivotal presidential election. Just weeks before the campaign concluded, the former Confederate Senator Benjamin H. Hill accepted an American flag given by Ohio citizens to the city of Atlanta. His praise for this symbol reprised many of the themes that Jefferson Davis had announced before Congress in 1861, using the same image of the flag's separate stars to argue for a federal Union of coequal states. But having fought against this flag, rather than under it, Hill's emotional tone was more far more restrained than that of Davis. His tribute to the flag managed little more than a tepid denunciation of "unmanly concessions on the one side" and "unmanly exaction on the other."[25]

Reunion under the Star Spangled Banner was finally achieved by that supreme duty of men—enlisting in the army and spilling blood for the old red, white, and blue. As many historians have shown, the reconciliation of whites from North and South culminated with the American war with Spain in 1898. As that conflict loomed, a continuing aversion to Yankee blue led some Confederates to suggest the uniforms of the United States army be changed to brown. Yet former Confederate General John Brown Gordon declared that even if forced to wear a disagreeable color, his comrades would still valiantly march to battle "wrapped in the folds of the American flag." This Georgia hero, who served as the commander of the United Confederate Veterans, took pride in extending "the boon of Republican liberty" to Cuban patriots whose struggle

32. Unionists made the Stars and Stripes a part of their appeal to rebels, even during the war. In the end, the appeal to manly self-interest, the theme of the top envelope, was more influential than the hope that reunion of fighting brothers might occur under domestic influences. Courtesy, American Antiquarian Society.

he and other rebel veterans respected. The Cuban cause—to escape from the clutches of a despotic empire—deserved the help of those who remembered their own fight in similar terms. An American army composed of men from both North and South defeated the Spaniards in short order, allowing Cubans to raise their new tricolor flag of independence, which bore a single star.[26]

As a new generation went to war with Spain, the ranks of Civil War veterans thinned considerably. The "living monuments" of elderly soldiers became more decrepit, coming to resemble the tattered flags they waved at the reunions and parades that proliferated between 1890 and 1920. Poets were quick to draw parallels between frazzled veterans and the frayed banners that were ever more apparent at the Lost Cause spectacles that peaked at the turn of the century. There was a widespread awareness that the flags, like the monuments and battlefield parks that were undertaken at this same period, would remain after "the last Confederate soldier / Has gone the way of the world." In striving to perpetuate their wartime heritage, organizations such as Sons of Confederate Veterans and United Daughters of the Confederacy guided Confederate commemoration that might extend indefinitely into the future.[27]

Confederate heritage groups put an enormous effort into flag-related activities. Women of the UDC showed how wartime symbols could evoke loyalty to heroes and the values they had defended with their lives. Unfurling flags, as well as placing them in shrines and endowing them with official histories, was their way of transmitting a distinct view of the past to subsequent generations. These initiatives resembled efforts underway at the same time to develop flag rituals and stories for all American schoolchildren to learn. The Confederate equivalent of a flag cult of civic devotion and respect would be long lasting, assuming a form in the early-twentieth century that still inspires defenders of these colors one hundred years later. A poet from 1915 framed the issue of ancestral pride by responding to Ryan's "Conquered Banner":

Take [the flag] out some time and show it,
Let your children early know it,
Know its glory—not its shame.
Teach them early to adore it,
Scorn forever those who tore it,
Tell them how it won a name.[28]

Confederate flags continued to spark negative passions long after they had been surrendered. For many Unionists, these emblems retained their wartime associations with bloody, treasonous, and diabolical rebellion. Over several decades, the Southern Cross became more acceptable in the North, especially among those veterans personally invested in the shared martial flag culture to which white southerners appealed. Southern flags marked the road of a manly reconciliation, serving to give recognizable form to a "soldiers' faith" in martial virtue.[29]

Northern tributes to Confederate flags began even while active rebellion against the Union was underway. In a series of scattered incidents, tokens of rebellion were not only treated with the respect accorded a worthy foe; they were valued as a way to monumentalize Union heroism. After Elmer Ellsworth was killed by James Jackson in Alexandria, the *New York Tribune* urged patriots to "cherish sacredly the traitor's flag," which had been "purified by this contact from the baseness of its former meaning." In later wartime ceremonies, both the U.S. Congress and the War Department received captured Confederate banners to glorify the exploits of their own soldiers. One congressman inadvertently signaled the contradictions involved here, explaining how "every memento of the rebellion" would be transmitted to "the deep damnation of all future time," but only by having these rebel flags "treasured up as if they were sacred relics, in some depository." At war's end, the five hundred captured banners were placed not in a reliquary, but were tagged and boxed in the archives of the War Department. The status of rebel banners as trophies did cause Union Sanitary Fairs to display them, and at least one federal commander hoisted captured rebel flags on a pole over his military fort, albeit beneath a much larger Stars and Stripes. In each of these instances, treasonous colors testified to the heroism of northern soldiers in bringing the Union one step closer to victory.[30]

General Joshua Chamberlain's famous account of Confederate surrender at Appomattox showed how furling the flags at war's end became a collaborative act between conquerors and conquered. In *The Passing of the Armies*, the Maine general placed the "battle-worn and torn, blood-stained, heart-holding colors" of rebel troops at the center of the scene. Remembering the episode many years later, Chamberlain evoked the pathos of the moment, as beaten men disposed of their flags with "an agony of expression" while some lost all control in "rushing from the ranks, kneeling over them, clinging to them, pressing them to their lips with burning tears." Chamberlain struggled for the best gesture on his part to mark the solemn occasion, wanting to register what he saw as the "proud humiliation" and "the embodiment of manhood" that stood before him. This was important if for nothing else than that their sorrow rekindled "memories that bound us together as no other bond." His decision was to order a marching salute to each regiment who surrendered their flags and to instruct his own troops to remain silent before symbols whose entire existence had been propelled forward through patriotic words and music. As he explained, there was a funereal drama in the stillness: "On our part not a sound of trumpet more, nor roll of drum; not a cheer, nor word, nor whisper of vain-glorying, nor motion of man standing again at the order, but an awed stillness rather, and breath-holding, as if it were the passing of the dead!"[31]

Chamberlain's recollections of the surrender were filtered through his own experience. He displaced the bitterness of the moment onto a single Confederate official who defiantly explained to the commander that "we hate you, sir." On the day itself, there were probably a good many more hard feelings. Some Confederate soldiers looking back on the occasion did seem to recognize the gesture of respect and to appreciate how the "feelings of the southern troops were spared," as John Esten Cooke later put it. But a Confederate from South

33. Captured Confederate flags marked the victory of Union arms, as was clear
in the ceremony illustrated here, in which General George Custer presented
trophies to the United States War Department. *Harper's Weekly*, November
12, 1864. Courtesy, Michigan State University Libraries.

Carolina mainly remembered the insult of having to lay down his banner before
the "lowest and filthiest" regiment of Yankees he had ever seen. Another expressed fear, deciding not to comfort a woman crying in the background because of uncertainty of how the Yankee soldiers might react. Lingering uncertainty about the future also shaped the prevailing mood. As one Confederate
officer put it: "We have no money, we have no niggers, and we have no credit.
What we are to do, God only knows."[32]

When Chamberlain first published his account in a 1901 newspaper article,
he was still thoroughly convinced that Confederates had been "fatally wrong in
striking at the old flag" and accused them of "misreading its deeper meaning
and the innermost law of the people's life." But even though they were "blind
to the signs of the times in the march of man," these soldiers nonetheless "fought
as they were taught, true to such ideals as they saw, and put into their cause
their best." This understanding, and the salute of "honor to honor" that enacted
it, was more in keeping with the memories of the early-twentieth century than
of 1865, when the flight of armies, the burning of cities, and the toppling of

presidents captivated the public imagination. For later generations safely removed from this political cataclysm, the solemn surrender of troops showed
how a fierce Civil War had ended with amity. The scene would provide later
writers an irresistible means of bringing the story of a noble war to a close.[33]

During Reconstruction, northern respect toward former enemies and their
flag heroism was more halting and provisional. In 1866, Herman Melville's
"Rebel Color-Bearers at Shiloh" recalled a moment from four years earlier,
when Yankee commanders expressed a shared martial flag culture. "Perish their
Cause! but mark the men" they spoke through Melville's voice. After lecturing
readers that "the life in the veins of Treason lags, / Her daring color-bearers
drop their flags / And yield," Melville then asked:

> *Now* shall we fire?
> Can poor spite be?
> Shall nobleness in victory less aspire
> Than in reverse? Spare Spleen her ire,
> And think how Grant met Lee.[34]

After a flag-draped four years, Confederate battle colors gave way to other
visual images during the first years of peace. Northerners illustrated the end
of the war by depicting Jefferson Davis in petticoats to undermine his manliness
and by metaphorically waving the "bloody shirt" to keep the memory of rebel
atrocities alive. Northerners who counseled quick reunion also relied on cloth
metaphors, introducing visions of the "Blue and the Gray" achieving mutual
understanding and comradeship in a reunited country. The sword supposedly
offered by Lee to Grant also became a motif, not only in Melville's poem, but
in the mass-produced prints that made the last meeting at Appomattox almost
immediately available to the American public. Horace Greeley added yet another powerful image in calling North and South to "grasp hands" with one
another during his campaign for president in 1872. In admitting that former
enemies had to do so across a "bloody chasm" of recent history, he tacitly
admitted how difficult this task might be.[35]

While former Confederates buried their dead and mourned their conquered
banners, they scrupulously avoided any overt signal that armed rebellion might
again be attempted. There were frequent laments about the "passing of the
gray," and several poets responded to federal orders that Confederate uniforms
could be worn only after their buttons had been removed or covered.[36] Yet
when it came to cloth, neither uniforms nor battle flags were as effective in
bringing Reconstruction to an end as were the hoods and masks that helped
the Ku Klux Klan wage a campaign of terror against black civilians, rather than
take up war against enemy soldiers that had beaten them so decisively. Former
rebels knew that openly waving battle flags would discredit their claims to
loyalty and delay their resumption of political power. So while Confederate
emblems were treasured in private, there were very few instances of their public

display outside of memorial services. Federal troops spent little time punishing flag wavers, though there were scattered instances when this occurred, as the humorist "Bill Arp" related near the end of Reconstruction. Despite later myths about the widespread suppression of flags by occupying troops, the postwar South witnessed nothing like the programmatic burning of flags and banning of tartans that followed the Jacobite uprising in Scotland in 1745. Nor was there any serious attempt to pass postwar legislation against enemy symbols, as would the case in the de-Nazification efforts against the swastika following World War II.[37]

Prudence governed southern use of Confederate symbols even after white rule was reestablished there. Rebel emblems still connoted treason in the North, where they appeared as the symbolic villains in the flurry of patriotic stage plays that honored the Stars and Stripes in the 1870s and 1880s. Knowing the sensitivity of northern opinion, Governor James Kemper of Virginia warned his fellow Confederate veterans against excessive use of the Southern Cross when they dedicated a monument to Stonewall Jackson in 1875. Though sectional tensions eased in the 1880s, rebel flags still provoked angry responses from the Grand Army of the Republic, the primary group of Union veterans. This organization successfully defeated a proposal from Grover Cleveland's War Department to return captured Confederate standards to southern governors in 1887. Even though the initiative was quickly reversed, it became part of the GAR campaign against Cleveland the following year. The angry feelings expressed by this group showed that not all Union soldiers were ready to accept that fidelity of Confederates to martial honor should excuse them for treason. The GAR commander in chief went so far as to call for passing a federal law against Confederate flags in 1890, and, two years, later, he charged that the "display of that flag" was little more than an attempt to "fire the hearts of the young generation of the south to rebellion."[38]

Returning captured battle colors to the South generated more controversy than any other Confederate flag issue between the Civil War and the Civil Rights movement. Notably, there was little defiant anger among white southerners on this issue, as many spoke out against the needless friction this episode caused. "Appomattox meant 'forever,' " wrote one southern poet, urging Confederates to have "No repinings for the past / Symbols of a grand oblation, / Keep those flags forever furled." A correspondent of Jefferson Davis likewise complained that "the work of restoring fraternal feelings among the true soldiers" had been "going on quietly and effectively" until this "mortifying blunder" stirred up trouble. After this flareup subsided, southerners continued to respect the finality of Union victory, even if meant relinquishing claims to surrendered flags. A poem printed in *Confederate Veteran* in 1893 urged southerners to "bow to the will of God not man" and recognize "our struggle was o'er" and that the Southern Cross should remain "the silent epitaph of a cause that is dead."[39]

Accepting defeat in both political and symbolic terms helped former rebels to present themselves as stalwart defenders of national authority. The Confederate battle flag was "emblematic of the strongest patriotism and the highest type of chivalry the human race has ever known," one writer in the *Confederate Veteran* summed up. As long as this banner testified to the predominance of the "Confederate soldier element," then "anarchy will never get hold." Making this case was important in the 1890s, when the pledge of allegiance to the Stars and Stripes and the move for schoolhouse banners framed questions of mixed loyalties in terms of vows toward cloth banners. Just as Unionists in wartime had been willing to concede that Confederate battle colors were preferable to the black flag of guerillas, so in an age threatened by the red flag of revolution, the Southern Cross did not seem nearly so ominous. With their tattered banner purged "now from hate and malice," Confederate Americans became the only group within the United States whose dual allegiances were widely seen as a stabilizing force rather than a subversive one.[40]

The fate of the captured battle flags was revisited early in the twentieth century, after the passage of another twenty years had changed circumstances considerably. One northern poet wondered:

Why cling to those moth-eaten banners?
What glory or honor to gain
While the nation is shouting hosannas
Uniting her sons to fight Spain?

The clear lesson to be drawn was to "send back the Johnnies their bunting / With greetings from the Blue to the Gray." Taking a stance that exuded confidence and self-conscious generosity, Congress did just this, voting to return hundreds of captured flags in 1905 and again in 1906.[41]

By the time battle flags were shipped back to the South, these relics of a past war had ceased to challenge the authority of the Stars and Stripes. Some commentators even suggested that the Southern Cross had been responsible for the salvation of the country at large, since men had crucified themselves for this piece of cloth so that the Union could achieve immortality.[42] Northern veterans were unlikely to go this far, but they could appreciate the "subtle battle brotherhood" that Stephen Crane described in 1895, in which rules of combat became "more potent than the cause for which [men] were fighting." In the world of manly bravery that *The Red Badge of Courage* popularized, political differences faded in importance, as a new generation looked back in awe on a "mysterious fraternity born of the smoke and danger of death." In this rendering of what the war had meant, flags held a special place, since heroism on their behalf provided what many veterans recognized as "the brightest pictures of the war," whether performed by ally or by enemy.[43]

The central pageant of white reunion was the fiftieth anniversary celebration at Gettysburg, the largest of the joint "Blue-Gray" gatherings. There was an

34. This ceremony, greeting the return of Florida banners to Tallahassee in 1905, demonstrated how rebel emblems of the Lost Cause were framed within icons of American patriotism, like the oversized Stars and Stripes and the portrait of George Washington. Courtesy, Museum of the Confederacy.

abundance of flag symbolism on this occasion, which began with President Woodrow Wilson standing between a gray-haired soldier holding the Stars and Stripes and another waving the Stainless Banner. As with any good melodrama, this self-consciously happy ending was made even better with an unexpected and seemingly contrived twist of the plot. In the midst of the festivities, the *New York Times* reported, a southern sergeant had brought to the reunion half of a Confederate battle flag, which he himself had torn during heavy fighting and then saved as a souvenir. As a much older man, he had successfully located the very color-bearer who had kept the other half of this banner in 1863. This reunion caused both men to rejoice. They seemed to sense, as would those who read of this incident, that there was larger significance in a pledge to sew back together pieces of a Southern Cross that no longer threatened treason.[44]

Less than fifty years after Confederates had surrendered their banners, relics of a defeated cause were unfurled once more. Flags that had been carefully saved from the war were joined by a flood of new mass-produced rebel colors, which flag companies helped to make more prominent in the New South than they had been in the Confederacy. Once-conquered banners achieved an undeniable moment of triumph. The Confederate view of the Civil War had been largely accepted as a national consensus; as a result, white southerners could honor their dying veterans without antagonizing former enemies in the North.

Reclaiming national power also allowed white southerners to order racial issues that had provoked their rebellion in the first place. In this way, the fate of black southerners was bound up with the reemergence of rebel flags. To appreciate the connections between unfurled banners and resurgent white supremacy requires considering the historical moment of the 1890s in the broad perspective of American culture and politics. As David Blight has recently shown, this was the period when a martial strain of national reconciliation displaced emancipationist meanings of the Civil War, ending a long contest that had tragically pitted the "imperative of healing" between former enemies against the war's "imperative of justice."[45]

White reconciliation in the late-nineteenth century held tremendous consequences for African Americans. In 1875, Frederick Douglass feared a future in which "this great white race has renewed its vows of patriotism," and he was uneasy about what would happen when collective commitment "flowed back into its accustomed channels." "If war among the whites brought peace and liberty to the blacks," he asked, "what will peace among the whites bring?" Benjamin H. Hill of Georgia suggested an answer the next year when he received an American flag from Ohioans, remarking on that occasion that "the dear noble boys of the white race, North or South" were "worth more to civilization and human happiness than the whole African race of the world." If reunion were to succeed, chastened rebels had to assume control of racial issues, Hill declared, and whites had to put past quarrels behind them. To the regret of some and the delight of others, the Compromise of 1877 that settled the disputed presidential election meant to contemporaries that "the negro will disappear from the field of national politics" and that thereafter "the nation as a nation, will have nothing more to do with him."[46]

Local control did return to southern whites by the turn of the century, and legal segregation and massive violence against former slaves was the main result. By 1915, what had begun as a question of regional autonomy became nationalized, as a new southern president brought Jim Crow institutions into the workings of the federal government. The white South that had suffered defeat in 1865 earned a new dispensation, gaining confidence that it would thereafter write its own history, build its own monuments, fly its own flags, and remain first and foremost a white man's country.[47]

As a truly national phenomenon, the "blood brotherhood" achieved by whites involved the Stars and Stripes as much as the Southern Cross. Frederick Douglass had sensed this during the war, warning listeners that slaveholders had embraced the "Confederate rag" only after failing to get their way under the "glorious Star Spangled Banner." White reconciliation that culminated at the turn of the century returned both these flags to white control and ended a long postwar battle over the meaning of American nationalism that had survived its greatest challenge. In 1865, the future of national ideas and symbols remained an open question. White southerners fantasized about returning the Stars and Stripes to its pre-war associations, imagining how, as one poet put it, the old flag's "benignant gleam" would invoke past glories until "each bitter memory dies" and the "Anglo-Saxon race" would "unite beneath that fold." The former Confederate hero Raphael Semmes received an American flag in Memphis in 1867 with the explanation that he had warred on the Stars and Stripes only when it had "ceased to represent the Constitution" and had become a "new and strange emblem." He vowed in this ceremony to strip the flag he had once loved of all associations with Republican zealotry and imbue it once more with the glories of the Revolution and the War of 1812.[48]

African Americans used the same sort of patriotic conventions to meld the causes of Union and of black freedom. Shortly after the surrender of rebel armies, one black poet linked past sacrifice with future agendas. "Our blood beneath this banner / Has mingled with the whites," he sang, and "'neath its folds we now demand / Our just and equal rights." Pioneering their own celebrations and memorial rituals, African American men and women asked for equal justice in return for the aid they had given the Union in war. In Charleston, Reverend E. J. Adams contrasted the past with the probable future. "The bloody crimson stripes" on the American flag had been transformed, he argued before a crowd of former slaves. "Once emblematic of the bloody furrows ploughed upon the quivering flesh of four million slaves," these stripes had become "emblematic of the bloody sacrifice offered upon the altars of American liberty." As his remarks indicated, both races in the South saw their future wrapped up the meanings of an ever-fluctuating American flag.[49]

Initial black attempts to build upon the emancipationist meanings of the Stars and Stripes rang hollow by the end of the nineteenth century. Those who felt this betrayal most deeply returned to earlier levels of cynicism about American patriotism. Bishop Henry McNeal Turner of the A.M.E. church had rejoiced in 1866 that "the nation's great emblem is no longer against us, for we claim the protection of the Stars and Stripes." Yet despite his prediction that "the glories of its fadeless escutcheon will ever bid us go free," less than twenty years later he realized that such predictions had been premature. The decision of the Supreme Court in 1883 to strike down the Civil Rights laws "absolves the negro's allegiance to the general government," Turner lashed out, angrily exclaiming that this would be the beginning of a steady erosion of black rights, and that this made the Stars and Stripes into "a rag of contempt instead of a symbol of liberty." His unusually bitter language expressed frustration at a fickle federal government that would alone decide whether those who had defended the American flag would be worthy of its protection.[50]

Up through the Civil Rights movement of the 1960s, black Americans focused a great deal more energy on redeeming the Stars and Stripes than on attacking Confederate colors. Disillusionment like that expressed by Turner was accompanied by attempts to nurture memories of how Union, emancipation, and African American sacrifice had been stitched together under a common flag during the 1860s. The unveiling of the monument to the Fifty-fourth Massachusetts Regiment in 1897 was a special moment; Booker T. Washington, who had traveled to Boston to take part, remembered how the crowd "seemed to lose entirely control of itself" when Sergeant Carney unveiled the very flag that he had carried back to the lines without allowing it to touch the ground. In 1913, the "Star of Ethiopia" pageant staged by W.E.B. Du Bois similarly featured a black soldier who told onlookers, in the theatrical language of an earlier flag culture: "when the stars were falling in quick succession from our flag, I and my black comrades stepped beneath them, caught them upon the points of our bayonets and pinned them back to Old Glory!" Such tributes to black patriotism of the 1860s were increasingly drowned out, however, by memories of a war in which valor had become far more important than root causes or unresolved consequences.[51]

Black activists kept waving the flag, though they changed what this was meant to accomplish. During the Second Reconstruction of the mid-twentieth century, Civil Rights demonstrators appealed to a set of abstract constitutional principles in their use of the red, white, and blue. Memories of the earlier war for the Union was largely ceded to whites, as the conflict was interpreted as a war of sections rather than a struggle over slavery. Rallying to the flag in the Civil Rights era announced a new alliance between nonviolent protesters and a federal government willing to make a stand for black rights for the first time since Reconstruction. Black southerners achieved their region's second heroic period, which matched the drama and idealism of the Civil War, even if it required far less bloodshed.

If participants in today's debates often seem to talk past one another, it is because they have come to the controversy by very different paths and seek different goals in the fight. Throughout the twentieth century white southerners have been a great deal more invested in the Southern Cross than have African Americans, who have set their sights mainly on the Star Spangled Banner. Confederate heritage groups have been involved with Civil War flags for the longest period and with the most consistency, transmitting to posterity a solemn flag cult that focuses on soldiers' martial honor, which was supposedly divorced from proslavery politics. Their formulation of the Confederate flag's meaning, which had been codified by at least the 1890s, has coexisted with other, less commemorative, uses of this emblem in more recent years. As rebel banners have been commercialized as regional markers, they have become as likely to appear on bumper stickers, shot glasses, and beach towels as in military parks or cemeteries. This proliferation has been lamented by those most committed to the quasi-religious cult of the Lost Cause, as have the frequent attempts to inject the rebel battle flag into the political arena. Heritage groups that are committed to the purity of the Confederate flag's original defenders have tried to minimize the explicitly racist ways this banner has been used in modern American culture. Despite their efforts to obscure the fact, rebel colors have defied federal enforcement of civil rights at least since the Dixiecrat movement of 1948. In challenging the American flag once more, white supremacists returned the Confederate emblem to an oppositional message that the Lost Cause had tried to remove from its meaning.[52]

Black southerners have come to devote energy toward Confederate symbols even more recently, and these efforts have had a tremendous impact on how Americans now think about rebel emblems. Once a national commitment to Civil Rights had been won under a redeemed American flag, southern blacks slowly shifted their attention toward the Southern Cross. Individual black southerners spoke out earliest, complaining about an icon of the Confederacy that was oblivious to black perspectives in its representation of region. Nearly twenty years ago, the first African American cheerleader at the University of Mississippi publicly expressed her unwillingness to wave a banner that she associated with the worst of her state's past. In the 1990s, more organized efforts against Confederate symbols began to take shape and soon developed their own momentum. Using symbols to protest historical injustices was part of a global trend. At the same time that black southerners were discrediting Confederate colors, aboriginal rights' groups in Australia rallied against another Southern Cross flag, claiming that the country's national banner perpetuated a white settler nationalism and shamefully denied the violence of British imperialism. In both these cases, complaints about symbols have forced a reckoning with legacies from the past that had festered unresolved for generations.[53]

Black southerners who rally against Confederate emblems often claim their right to shape the region's sense of itself. This has involved not just protesting explicit racism, but the still more ambitious goal of achieving a biracial vision of the past. An unusually subversive plea for black inclusion in southern culture has been offered by the designers of NuSouth clothing. Aimed primarily at southern African Americans, this company's apparel features a recognizable rebel flag in the colors of African national liberation. In their logo, green replaces white in the stars, black replaces the blue in the cross, while the predominate red remains the same. "We were claiming our territory," one of the designers has said in explaining this striking design. "The South—that's our Ellis Island; that's how we came into this country." This notably successful marketing strategy began with a determination to "take the opposition's worst image and wear it with pride." NuSouth founders promise other African Americans that "by wearing [the flag], you look at it, you pronounce it, taste it, chew it, digest it. You embrace it and make it mean something else."[54]

Current debates about the Southern Cross have generated, for the first time in a very long time, some of the intensity that flags achieved during the Civil War, when pieces of colored cloth first became soaked in gore and defined by conflict. Criticism of Confederate flags has changed considerably from the days of the war, not least in the fact that it is now slavery rather than treason that has become the most controversial associations of these symbols. This shift is to be expected, since racial slavery unleashes current passions in a way that secession simply does not. Among the raw emotions that Confederate symbols touch today are pride and anger, bitterness and denial, and nostalgia and cynicism. Rarely do they summon up a renewed spirit of political independence or the willingness to pledge future deaths fighting against threats to dissolve the United States.

The heart of the matter in current commemorative struggles is how best to understand a southern past marked by bloodshed. Defenders of the flag continue to monumentalize the blood of soldiers who sacrificed during four of the most dramatic years of American history. Opponents of the Southern Cross have made this emblem into a countermonument that recalls blood wrung from slaves over a much longer period of time. Both sides share a common concern about the suffering of ancestors, even if they are bitterly divided about which deaths should be publicly recognized. The basic dispute concerns how blood shaped the meaning of colored cloth and whether a flag that still generates strong emotions was purified with glory or stained with guilt.

NOTES

Abbreviations

HEH	Henry E. Huntington Library, San Marino, California
MOC	Museum of the Confederacy, Richmond, Virginia
NA-CFD	National Archives, Confederate Flag Designs, Record Group 109
O.R.	*The War of the Rebellion: A Compilation of the Official Records of the Union and Confederate Armies*, 128 vols. (Washington, D.C.: GPO, 1880–1901)
O.R. Navy	*Official Records of the Union and Confederate Navies in the War of the Rebellion*, 30 vols. (Washington, D.C.: GPO, 1922). References are to series, volume, part, and page.
SHSP	*Southern Historical Society Papers*
VHS	Virginia Historical Society, Richmond, Virginia

Introduction
WAVING COLORS AND BOILING BLOOD

1. Tony Horwitz, *Confederates in the Attic: Dispatches from the Unfinished Civil War* (New York: Pantheon, 1998); J. Michael Martinez, William D. Richardson, and Ron McNinch-Su, eds., *Confederate Symbols in the Contemporary South* (Gainesville: University of Florida Press, 2000).

2. The sacred importance of flags in American culture is the main theme of Caroline Marvin and David W. Ingle, *Blood Sacrifice and the Nation: Totem Rituals and the American Flag* (New York: Cambridge University Press, 1999). Two other valuable perspectives are provided in Robert Justin Goldstein, *Saving Old Glory: The History of the American Flag Desecration Controversy* (Boulder, Colo.: Westview Press, 1995); and Albert Boime, *The Unveiling of National Icons: A Plea for Patriotic Iconoclasm in a Nationalist Era* (New York: Cambridge University Press, 1998), 18–81.

3. Quotation from Edward Pollard, *The Two Nations; A Key to the History of the American War* (Richmond, Va.: Ayres and Wade, 1864), 8. Among the most influential formulations are Kenneth Stampp, "The Southern Road to Appomattox," in *The Imperiled Union: Essays on the Background of the Civil War* (Oxford: Oxford University Press, 1980), 246–70; David Potter, "The Historian's Use of Nationalism and Vice Versa," in *The South and the Sectional Conflict* (Baton Rouge: Louisiana University Press, 1968), 34–83; and Richard E. Beringer, Herman Hattaway, Archer Jones, and William N. Still, Jr., *Why the South Lost the Civil War* (Athens: University of Georgia Press, 1986).

4. Drew Gilpin Faust, *The Creation of Confederate Nationalism: Ideology and Identity in the Civil War South* (Baton Rouge: Louisiana State University Press, 1988). The classic works on nationalism that informed Faust's book included Benedict Anderson, *Imagined Communities: Reflections on the Origin and Spread of Nationalism* (London: Verso, 1983); and Clifford Geertz, "Ideology as a Cultural System" in *The Interpretation of Cultures* (New York: Basic Books, 1973), 193–233. Pioneer attempts by European historians to study ritual and symbols have included George Mosse, *The Nationalization of the Masses: Political Symbolism and Mass Movements in Germany from the Napoleonic Wars through*

the Third Reich (New York: H. Fertig, 1975); Lynn Hunt, *Politics, Culture, and Class in the French Revolution* (Berkeley and Los Angeles: University of California Press, 1984); and Sean Wilentz, ed., *Rites of Power: Symbolism, Ritual, and Politics since the Middle Ages* (Philadelphia: University of Pennsylvania Press, 1985). Confederate scholarship that influenced by Faust's approach include Reid Mitchell, "Nationalism," in *The Encyclopedia of the Confederacy* (New York: Simon and Schuster, 1995): 1111–16; George Rable, *The Confederate Republic: A Revolution against Politics* (Chapel Hill: University of North Carolina Press, 1994); Harry S. Stout, "The Life and Death of the Confederate Jeremiad" (lectures at Duke University, 1992); and Gary Gallagher, *The Confederate War: How Nationalism, Will, and Strategy Could Not Stave off Defeat* (Cambridge: Harvard University Press, 1997).

5. There is no scholarly consensus about the distinction between nationalism and patriotism, two concepts that are more often than not blurred together. This book considers those efforts to express or instill emotional loyalty to a government-led collective effort as *patriotic* and reserves the term *nationalist* for those projects, which need not be emotional in nature, aimed at establishing an independent, indivisible, and fully sovereign nation-state. Approaches to emotive patriotism that have informed this distinction include Maurizo Viroli, *For Love of Country* (New York: Oxford University Press, 1995); John Bodnar, ed., *Bonds of Affection: Americans Define Their Patriotism* (Princeton: Princeton University Press, 1996); Lauren Berlant, *The Anatomy of National Fantasy: Hawthorne, Utopia, and Everyday Life* (Chicago: University of Chicago Press, 1991); Julia Adams, "Culture in Rational-Choice Theories of State Formation" and Mabel Berezin, "Political Belonging: Emotion, Nation, and Identity in Fascist Italy," both in George Steinmetz, *State/Culture: State-Formation after the Cultural Turn* (Ithaca: Cornell University Press, 1999), 98–122, 355–77.

6. Charles Royster, *The Destructive War: William Tecumseh Sherman, Stonewall Jackson, and the Americans* (New York: Knopf, 1991), 148. While there is an enormous amount of material on flags, much of it is focused on military aspects. The most helpful of these popular histories is Devereaux D. Cannon, Jr., *The Flags of the Confederacy: An Illustrated History* (Memphis, Tenn.: St. Luke's Press, 1988); two very informative works that attend to the historical context are John Coski, "The Confederate Battle Flag in Historical Perspective," in Martinez et al., *Confederate Symbols in the Contemporary South*, 89–129; and Kevin Thornton, "The Confederate Flag and the Meaning of Southern History," *Southern Cultures* 2 (Winter 1996): 233–45.

7. Scot M. Guenter uses the notion of "flag culture" in *The American Flag, 1777–1924: Cultural Shifts from Creation to Codification* (Rutherford, N.J.: Farleigh Dickinson University Press, 1990), 44–65; Raymond Firth notes how the meanings of flags depend on their uses in *Symbols Public and Private* (Ithaca: Cornell University Press, 1973), 328–67.

8. Edmund Wilson, *Patriotic Gore: Studies in the Literature of the American Civil War* (New York: Oxford University Press, 1962), 460–61. Ann Douglas makes an even more withering critique of sentimentalism in *The Feminization of American Culture* (New York: Knopf, 1977); while Alice Fahs provides a needed corrective in *The Imagined Civil War: Popular Literature of the North and South* (Chapel Hill: University of North Carolina Press, 2001). The notion of "felt history" was coined by Robert Penn Warren in *The Legacy of the Civil War: Meditations on the Centennial* (New York: Random House, 1961).

9. Anne C. Rose, *Victorian America and the Civil War* (New York: Cambridge University Press, 1992), 8. My understanding of emotional history is informed by Peter K. Stearns, *American Cool: Creating a Twentieth-Century Emotional Style* (New York: New York University Press, 1994); Peter N. Stearns and Jan Lewis, eds., *An Emotional History of the United States* (New York: New York University Press, 1998); Andrew Burstein, *Sentimental Democracy: The Evolution of America's Romantic Self-Image* (New York: Hill and Wang, 1999); Mary Chapman and Glenn Hendler, eds., *Sentimental Men: Masculinity and the Politics of Affect in American Culture* (Berkeley and Los Angeles: University of California Press, 1999); and Glenn Hendler, *Public Sentiments: Structures of Feeling in Nineteenth-Century American Literature* (Chapel Hill: University of North Carolina Press, 2001).

10. Sidney Lanier in *The Centennial Edition of Sidney Lanier* (Baltimore: Johns Hopkins University Press, 1945), 7:33, 5:197–200.

11. Fahs, *The Imagined Civil War*, 28. For the context of melodramatic performances in American culture, I have relied on David Grimsted, *Melodrama Unveiled: American Theater and Culture, 1800–1850* (Chicago: University of Chicago Press, 1968); James H. Dormon, Jr., *Theater in the Antebellum South, 1815–1861* (Chapel Hill: University of North Carolina Press, 1967); Bruce A. McConachie, *Melodramatic Formations: American Theatre and Society, 1820–1870* (Iowa City: University of Iowa Press, 1992); and for broader concepts of the relation of theatricality to public life, Rosemarie K. Bank, *Theatre Culture in America, 1825–1860* (New York: Cambridge University Press, 1997).

12. Attention to melodrama as a cultural form, rather than a strictly theatrical genre, has been spurred by Peter Brooks, *The Melodramatic Imagination: Balzac, Henry James, Melodrama, and the Mode of Excess* (New Haven: Yale University Press, 1976). Among those who have applied his insights to cultural history are Lynn Hunt, *The Family Romance of the French Revolution* (Berkeley and Los Angeles: University of California Press, 1992); Judith Walkowitz, *City of Dreadful Delights: Narratives of Sexual Danger in Late-Victorian London* (Chicago: University of Chicago Press, 1992); Patrick Joyce, *Democratic Subjects: The Self and the Social in Nineteenth-Century England* (New York: Cambridge University Press, 1994); and Elaine Hadley, *Melodramatic Tactics: Theatricalized Dissent in the English Marketplace, 1800–1885* (Stanford, Calif.: Stanford University Press, 1995).

13. This conflicted Victorian attitude toward feeling is cogently addressed in Stearns, *American Cool*, 16–57; while its relevance in soldiers' lives is explored in Michael Barton, *Goodmen: The Character of Civil War Soldiers* (University Park: Pennsylvania State University Press, 1981). The dehumanizing potential of war violence is a main theme in Barbara Ehrenreich, *Blood Rites: Origins and History of the Passions of War* (New York: Metropolitan Books, 1997); and Joanna Bourke, *An Intimate History of Killing: Face-to-Face Killing in Twentieth-Century Warfare* (London: Granta Books, 1999).

Chapter One
THE STARS AND STRIPES OF SENATOR DAVIS

1. See Davis's library card as reproduced in Lynda Lasswell Criss et al., eds., *The Papers of Jefferson Davis* (Baton Rouge: Louisiana State University Press, 1985–), 7:31. These records have been utilized in the latest and most complete biography of Davis,

William J. Cooper, *Jefferson Davis, American* (Baton Rouge: Louisiana State University Press, 2000).

2. Schuyler Hamilton, *History of the National Flag of the United States of America* (Philadelphia: Lippincott, Grambo, and Co, 1852).

3. Scot M. Guenter, *The American Flag, 1777–1924: Cultural Shifts from Creation to Codification* (Rutherford, N.J.: Farleigh Dickinson University Press, 1990); George Henry Preble, *The History of the Flag of the United States* (Boston: A. Williams and Co., 1880).

4. Cynthia M. Koch, "Teaching Patriotism: Private Virtue for the Public Good in the Early Republic," in John Bodnar, ed., *Bonds of Affection: Americans Define their Patriotism* (Princeton: Princeton University Press, 1996), 19–52; Wilbur Zelinsky, *Nation into State: The Shifting Symbolic Foundations of American Nationalism* (Chapel Hill: University of North Carolina Press, 1988).

5. David Waldstreicher, *In the Midst of Perpetual Fetes: The Making of American Nationalism, 1776–1820* (Chapel Hill: University of North Carolina Press, 1997); Susan G. Davis, *Parades and Power: Street Theater in Nineteenth-Century Philadelphia* (Berkeley and Los Angeles: University of California Press, 1986).

6. Charles Royster, "A Nation Forged in Blood," in Ronald Hoffman and Peter J. Albert, eds., *Arms and Independence: The Military Character of the American Revolution* (Charlottesville: University Press of Virginia, 1984), 25–49.

7. John A. Quitman, *History of the Raising of the National Flag* (Washington, D.C.: GPO, 1855); Robert E. May, *John A. Quitman: Old South Crusader* (Baton Rouge: Louisiana State University Press, 1985); Robert W. Johannsen, *To the Halls of Montezuma: The Mexican War in the American Imagination* (New York: Oxford University Press, 1985), 52–55, 132–33. Quotation from Hamilton, *History of the National Flag,* 115.

8. *Speeches of Hon. Jefferson Davis of Mississippi, Delivered during the Summer of 1858* (Baltimore: J. Murphy and Co., 1859), 50–55; "A Southerner," no. 69 in NA-CFD.

9. Dunbar Rowland, ed., *Jefferson Davis, Constitutionalist* (Jackson: Mississippi Department of Archives and History, 1923), 3:358.

10. Jefferson Davis, "Address to the Senate on South Carolina Affairs," in Jon Wakelyn, ed., *Southern Editorials on Secession* (Chapel Hill: University of North Carolina Press, 1996), 135. The following paragraphs all draw from this speech.

11. David Detzer, *Allegiance: Fort Sumter, Charleston, and the Beginning of the Civil War* (New York: Harcourt, 2001), 116, 127–29.

12. Davis, "Address to the Senate," 124–25.

13. For the development of Davis as an orator, see Cooper, *Jefferson Davis, American,* 101–2, 180, 209–14, 290–93.

14. *Atlanta Gate City Guardian,* February 21, 1861; Varina Davis, *Jefferson Davis, Ex-President of the Confederate States of America: A Memoir by His Wife* (New York: Belford Co., 1890), 2:36.

15. Criss et al., eds., *The Papers of Jefferson Davis* 7:185; *Charleston Mercury,* June 15, 1861.

16. Mark E. Neely, Jr., Harold Holzer, and Gabor S. Boritt, *The Confederate Image: Prints of the Lost Cause* (Chapel Hill: University of North Carolina Press, 1987); Stephen W. Berry, "When Mail Was Armor: Envelopes of the Great Rebellion, 1861–1865," *Southern Cultures* 4 (Fall 1998): 63–83.

17. Rowland, *Jefferson Davis,* 1:46; Joseph E. Chance, *Jefferson Davis's Mexican War Regiment* (Jackson: University Press of Mississippi, 1991), 132–33.

Chapter Two
THE STANDARDS OF STATE RESISTANCE

1. For recent historical studies of symbolic actions during transitional moments, see David Waldstreicher, *In the Midst of Perpetual Fetes: The Making of American Nationalism* (Chapel Hill: University of North Carolina Press, 1997); Sean Kelsey, *Imagining a Republic: The Political Culture of the English Commonwealth, 1649–1653* (Stanford, Calif.: Stanford University Press, 1997); Mabel Berezin, *Making the Fascist Self: The Political Culture of Interwar Italy* (Ithaca: Cornell University Press, 1997); Matthew Truesdell, *Spectacular Politics: Louis-Napoleon Bonaparte and the Fete Imperiale, 1849–1870* (New York: Oxford University Press, 1997); and Orlando Figes and Boris Kolonitskii, *Interpreting the Russian Revolution: The Language and Symbols of 1917* (New Haven: Yale University Press, 1999).

2. *Charleston Courier,* November 16, 1860; *New Orleans Delta,* December 1, 1860; *Richmond Enquirer,* December 10, 1860. Though a resistance flag was unfurled in Savannah the night Lincoln's election was confirmed, the Georgia port subsequently lagged behind the Carolina cities in the volume of reported banners.

3. William C. Davis, ed., *A Fire-Eater Remembers: The Confederate Memoir of Robert Barnwell Rhett* (Columbia: University of South Carolina Press, 2000), 7; Steven Channing, *Crisis of Fear: Secession in South Carolina* (New York: W. W. Norton, 1970), 249; Manisha Sinha, *The Counterrevolution of Slavery: Politics and Ideology in Antebellum South Carolina* (Chapel Hill: University of North Carolina Press, 2000).

4. *Charleston Courier,* November 11, 1860; *New Orleans Daily Delta,* November 8, December 1, 12, 1860; *Mobile Advertiser,* December 19, 1860; *Journal of the Convention of the People of South Carolina* (Charleston, S.C.: Evans and Cogswell, 1861), 5.

5. *Charleston Courier,* November 17, 1860, *Cincinnati Enquirer,* November 14, 1860.

6. Benedict Anderson, *Imagined Communities: Reflections on the Origin and Spread of Nationalism* (London: Verso, 1983); Karl Wolfgang Deutsch, *Nationalism and Social Communication: An Inquiry into the Foundations of Nationality* (Cambridge: M.I.T. Press, 1952); Waldstreicher, *In the Midst of Perpetual Fetes;* David M. Henkin, *City Reading: Written Words and Public Spaces* (New York: Columbia University Press, 1998), 101–36.

7. Richard Johns, *Spreading the News: The American Postal System from Franklin to Morse* (Cambridge: Harvard University Press, 1995); Menaheim Blondheim, *News over the Wires: The Telegraph and the Flow of Public Information in America, 1844–1897* (Cambridge: Harvard University Press, 1994); *Sandusky (Ohio) Daily Commercial Register,* December 5, 1860, in Howard Cecil Perkins, ed., *Northern Editorials on Secession* (New York: D. Appleton, 1942), 1039.

8. Examples of flag-related dispatches that appeared throughout the northern press can be seen in the *New York Times,* November 10, 1860; *Springfield (Mass.) Daily Republican,* November 19, 27, 1860; *Cincinnati Enquirer,* November 11, 14, 1860, March 6, 1861; *Detroit Free Press,* November 17, 1860; and *Chicago Tribune,* November 16, December 1, 1860.

9. *Jersey City American Standard,* May 4, 1861, in Perkins, *Northern Editorials,* 1056.

10. *Montgomery Mail*, January 11, 1861; *Columbia South Carolinian*, November 10, 1860. For more on the role of the press during secession, see David Reynold, *Editors Make War: Southern Newspapers in the Secession Crisis* (Nashville, Tenn.: Vanderbilt University Press, 1970).

11. Augusta Jane Evans, *Macaria; or, Altars of Sacrifice* (1864; reprint, Baton Rouge: Louisiana State University Press, 1992), 307. The generalizations of this paragraph rest on the increasing reports in the major southern dailies of flags beyond the streets of southern cities, especially during December of 1860.

12. *Charleston Courier*, November 16, 1860. Similar representations of slave-produced wealth had been featured on nullification-era flags, described in Wylma Anne Wates, "'A Flag Worthy of Your State and People': The South Carolina State Flag," *South Carolina Historical Magazine* 86 (1985): 323.

13. *Charleston Courier*, December 17, 18, 21, 1860, January 9, 1861; Lucius Cuthbert, *The Scriptural Grounds for Secession from the Union* (Charleston, S.C., 1860), 3; Stephanie McCurry explores the evangelical context of Carolina secession in *Masters of Small Worlds: Yeoman Households, Gender Relations, and the Political Culture of the Antebellum South Carolina Low Country* (New York: Oxford University Press, 1995), 277–304.

14. Quotes here are from the *Boston Traveler* article about the battle of Fort Sullivan, as excerpted in the *Charleston Courier*, November 21, 1860. See also Wates, "'A Flag Worthy of Your State and People'"; and Jack Allen Myer, *South Carolina in the Mexican War: A History of the Palmetto Regiment of Volunteers, 1846–1917* (Columbia: University of South Carolina Press, 1997). Stephanie McCurry provides an interesting reading of the entwined palmetto and snake as phallic images in *Masters of Small Worlds*, 302–3. For more on the rattlesnake see chapter 6 below.

15. Charles C. Jones distills the array of antebellum sources in *Sergeant William Jasper: An Address before the Georgia Historical Society in Savannah, Ga.* (Albany, Ga.: J. Munsell, 1876); a briefer account contemporary with secession appears in William Gilmore Simms, *The History of South Carolina from Its First European Discovery to Its Erection into a Republic* (New York: D. Appleton, 1860), 201–11. For the portrayal of Jasper in local dramatic productions, see Len Travers, *Celebrating the Fourth: Independence Day and the Rites of Nationalism in the Early Republic* (Amherst: University of Massachusetts Press, 1997), 126. George Fenwick Jones argues that Jasper was from Germany, rather than Ireland, as most in the nineteenth century claimed. See "Sergeant Johann Wilhelm Jasper," *Georgia Historical Quarterly* 65 (Spring 1981): 7–15. The artist Jasper Johns was named for this patriot hero and has himself suggested intriguing connections between the Palmetto Fort legend and his depiction of flag icons in paintings. See Albert Boime, *The Unveiling of National Icons: A Plea for Iconoclasm in a Nationalist Era* (New York: Cambridge University Press, 1998), 44–48.

16. For the flying of palmetto flags beyond Carolina, see *Charleston Courier*, November 17, December 1, 6, 1860; *Savannah Morning News*, January 14, 1861; *Memphis Daily Avalanche*, February 22, 1861; *Frank Leslie's Illustrated Weekly*, February 2, 1861; and George Henry Preble, *History of the Flag of the United States of America* (Boston: A. Williams and Co., 1880), 404. DeBow quotation appears, along with news of a palmetto flag in New Orleans, in *DeBow's Review* 30 (February 1861): 251–53.

17. Edward W. Richardson, *Standards and Colors of the American Revolution* (Philadelphia: University of Pennsylvania Press, 1982). For the cultural context of the Betsy Ross legend, see Scot M. Guenter, *The American Flag, 1777–1924: Cultural Shifts from*

Creation to Codification (Rutherford, N.J.: Farleigh Dickinson University Press, 1990), 101–3; and Joanne Menezes, "The Birthing of the American Flag and the Invention of an American Founding Mother in the Image of Betsy Ross," in Jean Pickering and Suzanne Kehde, eds., *Narratives of Nostalgia* (New York: New York University Press, 1997), 74–87. Edmund Ruffin urged adoption of the colonial crescent flag by South Carolina, as reported in the *Charleston Courier*, November 13, 1861, and as he recorded in William K. Scarborough, ed., *The Diary of Edmund Ruffin* (Baton Rouge: Louisiana State University Press, 1966), 2:488.

18. Lynn Hunt, *Culture, Politics, and Class in the French Revolution* (Berkeley and Los Angeles: University of California Press, 1984), 29; Raoul Giradet, "The Three Colors: Neither White nor Red," and Michel Vovell, "La Marseillaise: War or Peace," both in Pierre Nora, ed., *Realms of Memory: The Construction of the French Past*, vol. 3, *Symbols* (New York: Columbia University Press, 1996), 3–74. The appeal of symbols and patriotic pageantry among English radicals is explored in James A. Epstein, *Radical Expression: Political Language, Ritual, and Symbol in England, 1790–1850* (New York: Oxford University Press, 1994); and Margot C. Finn, *After Chartism: Class and Nation in English Radical Politics, 1848–1874* (New York: Cambridge University Press, 1993).

19. Simms, *The History of South Carolina*, 210–11. For the debate over the proper colors for the South Carolina flag, see *Charleston Courier*, January 21–31, 1861.

20. G. Ward Hubbs, "Lone Star Flags and Nameless Rags," *Alabama Review* 39 (October 1986): 271–301; L. W. Kemp, "Official Flags of the Republic of Texas," *Southwestern Historical Quarterly* 65 (April 1956): 486–90; Frank Wilson Kiel, "A Fifteen Star Texas Flag: A Banner Used at the Time of Secession—February 1861 and March 1861," *Southwestern Historical Quarterly* 103 (January 2000): 357–65.

21. O.R., ser. 1, vol. 1, 252 (South Carolina), 329 (Mississippi), 480 (North Carolina), 491 (Louisiana); *Savannah Daily Morning News*, November 15, 1860; *Charleston Courier*, January 19, 1861; *Savannah Republican* February 2, 1861; "Georgia's Flag," *SHSP* 31 (1903): 236–37.

22. *Charleston Courier*, January 28, 1861. In the 1830s, the flying of a separate Virginia flag was condemned as a disunionist gesture, as is explained in Preble, *The History of the Flag*, 623–24. Each of the state flags from 1861 is listed, with helpful illustrations, in Devereaux D. Cannon, Jr., *The Flags of the Confederacy: An Illustrated History* (Memphis, Tenn.: St. Luke's Press, 1988), 34–48.

23. The "moistening" is reported in the *Charleston Courier*, November 17, 1860.

24. *Charleston Courier*, December 1, 1860, January 19, 1861; *New Orleans Delta* December 22, 1860; *Savannah Morning News*, January 5, 1861; and the reporting of such a scene in Scarborough, *The Diary of Edmund Ruffin* 2:496–97. The leading scholarly accounts of Confederate music are Richard Harwell, *Confederate Music* (Chapel Hill: University of North Carolina Press, 1950); and E. Lawrence Abel, *Singing the New Nation: How Music Shaped the Confederacy, 1861–1865* (Mechanicsburg, Pa.: Stackpole Press, 2000), which devotes more attention to the secession crisis and, especially, to the "Bonnie Blue Flag." See also the brief but informative comments about music in Drew Gilpin Faust, *The Creation of Confederate Nationalism: Identity and Ideology in the Civil War South* (Baton Rouge: Louisiana State University Press, 1988), 18–21, 65–69.

25. Richard Harwell, "The Star of the Bonnie Blue Flag," *Civil War History* 4 (September 1958): 285–90; Abel, *Singing the New Nation*, 52–66.

26. Edward Young McMorries, *History of the First Regiment, Alabama Volunteer Infantry, C.S.A.* (Montgomery, Ala.: Brown Printers, 1904), 21–22.

27. Information about Mitchell's performances originally appeared in the *Montgomery Mail*, December 21, 1860; the scene is discussed in William C. Davis, *"A Government of Our Own": The Making of the Confederacy* (New York: Free Press, 1994), 42; and Hubbs, "Lone Star Flags and Nameless Rags," 288. On Christy's Minstrels, see David Detzer, *Allegiance: Fort Sumter, Charleston, and the Beginning of the Civil War* (New York: Harcourt, 2001), 108. John Smith Kendall, *The Golden Age of New Orleans Theater* (Baton Rouge: Louisiana State University Press, 1952), 374–402; Hewitt's various productions will be considered below.

28. *Charleston Courier*, November 14, 1861; *Savannah Republican*, January 17, 1861, Hubbs, "Lone Star Flags and Nameless Rags," 279–81; W. Stanley Hoole, "The Alabama Secession Flag," *Alabama Historical Quarterly* 3 (Fall–Winter 1941): 364–67; William R. Smith, *History and Debates of the Convention of the People of Alabama* (Montgomery: White, Pfister, and Co., 1861), 119–20.

29. Caroline Marvin and David W. Ingle explore the fertility aspects of American flag rituals in *Blood Sacrifice and the Nation: Totem Rituals and the American Flag* (New York: Cambridge University Press, 1999), 250–54, 271–75.

30. Curtis Carroll Davis, ed., *"The End of an Era," by John Sergeant Wise* (New York: Thomas Yoseloff, 1965), 160; two similarly sad reflections are made by Lucy Muse Walton Fletcher and Emma Mordecai, in Joan Cashin, ed., *Our Common Affairs: Texts from Women in the Old South* (Baltimore: Johns Hopkins University Press, 1996), 264, 293; while a far angrier response appears in David D. Ryan, ed., *A Yankee Spy in Richmond: The Civil War Diary of "Crazy Bet" Van Lew* (Mechanicsburg, Pa.: Stackpole Books, 1996), 31.

31. Henry Timrod, "Ode on the Meeting of the Southern Congress" (undated broadside at HEH). The quasi-sacred aura of central power is established by Clifford Geertz, "Centers, Kings, and Charisma: Reflections on the Symbolics of Power," in *Local Knowledge: Further Essays in Interpretive Anthropology* (New York: Basic Books, 1983); and elaborated in many of the selections in Sean Wilentz, ed., *Rites of Power: Symbolism, Ritual, and Politics since the Middle Ages* (Philadelphia: University of Pennsylvania Press, 1985).

32. Preble, *History of the Flag*, 36–43.

33. *Charleston Courier*, November 9, 1860; *Detroit Free Press*, November 10, 1860; Foreign Office, Great Britain, *Correspondence Relative to the Civil War in the United States*, pt. 1, November 1860 to January 1862 (F.O. 414/17). Nicholas Kessler brought this material to my attention in research that he conducted at Yale University in 1995.

34. See, for instance, the reports in the *Charleston Mercury*, August 28, December 21, 1861; "Lines to the Southern Banner," in Frank Moore, *Rebel Rhymes and Rhapsodies* (New York: G. P. Putnam, 1864), 279; "The Flag of the South" in *Richmond Daily Dispatch*, April 16, 1861; A. C. H. Beale, "The First Confederate Flag on the Atlantic," *SHSP* 15 (1907): 227–28.

35. O.R., ser. 1, vol. 50, part 1, 478, 510; Elijah Robinson Kennedy, *The Contest for California in 1861: How Colonel E. D. Baker Saved the Pacific States for the Union* (New York: Houghton Mifflin, 1912), 209–29. Notably, it was the young Bret Harte who waved the American banner at the San Francisco "monster meeting."

36. Rutherford B. Hayes, "The Loyal Legion Address of October 7, 1891," in James Grant Wilson and Titus Munson Coan, eds., *Personal Recollections of the War of the Rebellion* (New York: Published by the Commandery, 1891), 380.

37. DeBow quoted in Channing, *Crisis of Fear*, 260; Carol Bleser, ed., *The Hammonds of Redcliffe* (New York: Oxford, 1981), 88–89. For Hammond's earlier anxieties about the French Revolution, see Eugene Genovese, *The Slaveholders' Dilemma: Freedom and Progress in Southern Conservative Thought, 1820–1860* (Columbia: University of South Carolina Press, 1992), 85–107. The classic work on crowd actions in revolutionary Europe remains George F. E. Rude, *The Crowd in History: A Study of Popular Disturbances in France and England, 1730–1848* (New York: Wiley, 1964).

38. Rev. James Henley Thornwell, *The State of the Country: An Article Republished from the Southern Presbyterian Review* (New Orleans: True Sentinel Office, 1861), 4–5; Faust, *The Creation of Confederate Nationalism*, 21. The emphasis on legitimacy during the secession conventions is a major theme of Mark E. Brandon, *Free in the World: American Slavery and Constitutional Failure* (Princeton: Princeton University Press, 1998).

39. "The Pelican Flag," from *New Orleans Delta*, reprinted in *Charleston Courier*, February 13, 1861; *New Orleans Daily Picayune*, February 12, 1861. An earlier telegraph dispatch reported the opening of the Louisiana convention beneath a flag with fifteen stars, for each of the slave states; see *Memphis Avalanche*, January 24, 1861. Both the popular and official Louisiana emblem is featured in Cannon, *The Flags of the Confederacy*.

40. *The Southern Marseillaise; As Sung by Miss Maggie Mitchell, at the New Montgomery Theatre, on Friday Evening, December 14, 1860* (undated broadside in Nicholson Collection, HEH). The closing reference in this quotation conveys the widespread suspicions that abolitionists were responsible for a spate of arsons in Texas. Another suggestive revisions to this French song was made in A.E. Blackmar, *The Southern Marseillaise* (New Orleans, 1861). *Mobile Tribune* quoted in *New Orleans Delta*, November 8, 1860. Various state cockades are described in the *Charleston Courier*, December 22, 1860.

Chapter Three
SELECTING AND SINGING A NEW CONSTELLATION

1. William Howard Russell, *My Diary North and South* (New York: O. S. Felt, 1863), 91–95.

2. The following discussion relies on William C. Davis, "*A Government of Our Own*": *The Making of the Confederacy* (New York: Free Press, 1994); George C. Rable, *The Confederate Republic: A Revolution against Politics* (Chapel Hill: University of North Carolina Press, 1994); Drew Gilpin Faust, *The Creation of Confederate Nationalism: Ideology and Identity in the Civil War South* (Baton Rouge: Louisiana State University Press, 1988), 9; and, especially, coverage of the convention in the *Charleston Courier*, the *Savannah Daily News*, and the *New Orleans Picayune*; and on the material found in *Journal of the Congress of the Confederate States* (Washington, D.C., 1903). The importance of slavery to Confederate leaders is shown in Charles Dew, *Apostles of Disunion: Southern Secession Commissioners and the Causes of the Civil War* (Charlottesville: University Press of Virginia, 2001), while the tensions over how explicitly slavery should be defended by the

new government is a theme of Robert E. Bonner, *Southern Slaveholders and the Crisis of American Nationhood* (forthcoming).

3. *Charleston Courier*, February 14, 16, 1861.

4. *New Orleans Picayune*, December 7, 1860; *New Orleans Bulletin*, February 20, 1861; *New Orleans Crescent* quoted in *Augusta Chronicle and Sentinel*, January 3, 1861; *Atlanta Gate City Guardian*, February 12, 1861; *Charleston Courier*, January 30, 1861; *Memphis Daily Avalanche*, February 1, 1861.

5. *Charleston Courier*, February 16, 1861; Brooke's plea for more openness is reported in the *Savannah Daily Morning News*, February 19, 21, 1861; his votes during secret session are included in *Journal of the Congress of the Confederate State*, vol. 1.

6. David M. Potter, *The Impending Crisis, 1848–1861* (New York: Harper and Row, 1976), 484. See also Potter's seminal essay "The Historian's Use of Nationalism, and Vice Versa," in *The South and the Sectional Conflict* (Baton Rouge: Louisiana State University Press, 1968), 34–83; as well as Anne Norton, *Alternative America: A Reading of Antebellum Political Culture* (Chicago: University of Chicago Press, 1986); Liah Greenfeld, *Nationalism: Five Roads to Modernity* (Cambridge: Harvard University Press, 1992); and Michael Morrison, *Slavery and the American West: The Eclipse of Manifest Destiny and the Coming of the Civil War* (Chapel Hill: University of North Carolina Press, 1997). Southern attempts to articulate American nationalism are discussed in Ann Sarah Rubin, "Seventy-six and Sixty-one: Confederates Remember the American Revolution," in W. Fitzhugh Brundage, *Where These Memories Grow: History, Memory, and Southern Identity* (Chapel Hill: University of North Carolina Press), 85–106; and Bonner, *Southern Slaveholders and the Crisis of American Nationhood*. Distinct versions of northern nationalism (which tended to coincide more strongly with Unionism than did its southern variant) have received fresh attention in Harlow Shiedley, *Sectional Nationalism: Massachusetts Conservative Leaders and the Transformation of America, 1815–1836* (Boston: Northeastern University Press, 1998); and Susan-Mary Grant, *North over South: Northern Nationalism and American Identity in the Antebellum Era* (Lawrence: University Press of Kansas, 2000).

7. *Charleston Courier*, February 16, 1861. For more on Miles, and his tendency to be drawn to symbolic issues, see Eric Walther, *The Fire-Eaters* (Baton Rouge: Louisiana State University Press, 1992), 270–96. A writer in the *Savannah Daily Morning News* of February 16, 1861, claimed that efforts to retain patriotic symbols were merely a pretext for reconstructing the Union with the free states, a widespread fear of many witnessing the convention's actions.

8. *Charleston Courier*, February 16, 19, 1861; no. 119 in NA-CFD.

9. *Charleston Courier*, February 16, 1861; *DeBow's Review* 30 (March 1861): 381; Davis, *A Government of Our Own*, 119–20, 124.

10. Miles, "Report of the Flag Committee," in *Charleston Courier*, March 8, 1861; and *New Orleans Picayune*, March 9, 1961. The Miles report was widely reprinted in the newspaper press and even on the back of a piece of sheet music, James H. Huber, *The Song of the South* (New Orleans, 1861). It can also be found *DeBow's Review* 30 (April 1861): 486; and in the *Journal of the Congress of the Confederate States* 1:101–2. For the coining of "Bars" see *Montgomery Mail*, quoted in *Savannah Morning News*, March 28, 1861.

11. *Athens (Ga.) Watchman*, March 13, 1861; *Augusta Chronicle and Sentinel*, March 9, 1861; *Charleston Courier*, February 16, 1861.

12. Gilchrist, no. 16; NA-CFD; in no. 63 of these designs, Thomas Butler King combined a flag suggestion with a request that his son be given a patronage position in the new government.

13. Gilchrist, no. 16; Platt, no. 106; Sell no. 122; Anonymous, no. 71; Shellman no. 85, all in NA-CFD.

14. Boutheneau, no. 97 and no. 128; Lady of Georgia, no. 78; Ladd no. 64, all in NA-CFD. The classic treatment of sacrificial female patriotism is Drew Gilpin Faust, "Altars of Sacrifice: Confederate Women and the Narratives of War," *Journal of American History* 76 (March 1990): 1200–1228.

15. Boyce quoted in *Charleston Courier*, February 16, 1861. The *Charleston Courier* recorded designs from seven women and three men while printing in full the letters relating to two female-designed flags and none of those offered by men. The preponderance of men seen in table 4.1 provides a striking contrast to later claims of female influence, as reported in Faust, *Creation of Confederate Nationalism*, 8.

16. Boutheneau, no. 97 and no. 128, sent her suggestions on palmetto flag stationery, as did no. 47, no. 53, no. 75, and no. 113 in NA-CFD. For more on the Southern Cross, see chapter 5, below.

17. Kirk Savage, *Standing Soldiers, Kneeling Slaves: Race, War, and Monument in Nineteenth-Century America* (Princeton: Princeton University Press, 1997), 31–51.

18. Gaston, no. 102 and no. 135, in NA-CFD; Francis Lieber to Henry Drisler, October 8, 1865, Francis Lieber Papers, HEH.

19. In addition to Gaston's, flags invoking slavery were sent by "Disunion," no. 76; William M. Brantley, no. 124; and W. Floyd Wigg, no. 132, all in NA-CFD. See also Dew, *Apostles of Disunion*. William Preston Johnston specifically urged Jefferson Davis to choose a derivative flag to lure the border states; see his letter of April 26, 1861, in Lynda Lasswell Criss, et al. eds., *The Papers of Jefferson Davis* (Baton Rouge: Louisiana State University Press, 1985–), 7:129.

20. Miles, "Report of the Flag Committee"; later racial subthemes are explored in greater depth in chapter 5, below.

21. Carpenter, no. 51 in NA-CFD; Wright speech in *Charleston Courier*, February 26, 1861; Miles, "Report of the Flag Committee."

22. Carpenter, no. 59; Augustin L. Tarceau, no. 118; "Lady of South Carolina," no. 67 in NA-CFD. The last urged that this grandeur could be achieved only with an explicit recognition of God.

23. The notion of grammar and syntax in flags is set forth in Karen Cerula, *Identity Designs: The Sights and Sounds of a Nation* (New Brunswick, N.J.: Rutgers University Press, 1995). For the postwar debate, see Orren Randolph Smith, *History of the Stars and Bars* (Raleigh, N.C., 1913); and Sons of Confederate Veterans, *Report of the Stars and Bars Committee* (Washington, D.C., 1917), both at VHS.

24. DeBow, no. 72; "A Citadel Cadet," no. 93; Wightt, no. 67; T. May Thorpe, no. 126, all in NA-CFD.

25. Anonymous, no. 48; Laurens, no. 75; "A Lady of Georgia," no. 78, C. Kirkwood Otey, no. 90, all in NA-CFD.

26. J. D. P., no. 123 in NA-CFD; *Charleston Courier*, March 7, 1861; "Z," no. 23; "A Georgian," no. 78, both in NA-CFD. Similar sentiments are expressed in nos. 3, 15, 16, 20, 69, 106, 116, NA-CFD.

27. H. Augustus Pond, no. 78 and P. J. Anderson, no. 12, both in NA-CFD.

28. Richard E. Beringer, Herman Hattaway, Archer Jones, and William N. Still, Jr., *Why the South Lost the Civil War* (Athens: University of Georgia Press, 1986), 76–81; David Waldstreicher, *In the Midst of Perpetual Fetes: The Making of American Nationalism* (Chapel Hill: University of North Carolina Press, 1997), 51; Maurice Dommanget, *Histoire du Drapeau Rouge: Des Origines à la Guerre de 1939* (Paris: Editions de l'Etoile, 1967). See also Arundhati Virmani, "National Symbols under Colonial Domination: The Nationalization of the Indian Flag, March–August 1923," *Past and Present* 164 (August 1999); and Malcolm Quinn, *The Swastika: Constructing the Symbol* (London: Routledge, 1994).

29. *New York Tribune*, March 5, 1861; *Harper's Weekly*, March 9, 1861.

30. *Montgomery Advertiser*, March 5, 1861; *Charleston Courier*, March 7, 1861.

31. C. Vann Woodward and Elizabeth Muhlenfeld, eds., *The Private Mary Chesnut: The Unpublished Civil War Diaries* (New York: Oxford University Press, 1984), 22; in a later version Chesnut attributed these same sentiments to Captain Duncan Ingraham. See C. Vann Woodward, ed., *Mary Chesnut's Civil War* (New Haven: Yale University Press, 1989), 16.

32. *Memphis Daily Avalanche*, March 30, 1861; *Richmond Enquirer*, March 26, 1861; Edward B. Williams, *Rebel Brothers: The Civil War Letters of the Truehearts* (College Station: Texas A&M University Press, 1995), 15–41; Eliza McHatton Ripley, *From Flag to Flag: A Woman's Adventures and Experiences in the South during the War, in Mexico, and in Cuba* (New York: D. Appleton, 1896), 11. Congress did acquire its own oversized version of the Stars and Bars in late March, which required the reinforcement of the staff above the building to keep it aloft. See W. J. Hooper to Miles, March 30, 1861, in William Porcher Miles Papers, Southern Historical Collection, University of North Carolina at Chapel Hill.

33. *Charleston Courier*, March 27, 1861; *New Orleans Daily Picayune*, March 27, 1861; *Savannah Morning News*, April 12, 1861; *Thomaston (Ga.) Southern Enterprise*, March 13, 1861; Stephen W. Berry, "When Mail Was Armor: Envelopes of the Great Rebellion, 1861–1865," *Southern Cultures* 4 (Fall 1998): 63–83.

34. *Richmond Dispatch*, March 9–April 15, 1861.

35. Russell, *My Diary North and South*; *Charleston Mercury*, April 30, 1861.

36. *New York Herald*, April 21, 1861; Everett quoted in Preble, *History of the Flag*, 459; Mark Wahlgreen Summers, "'Freedom and Law Must Die Ere They Sever': The North," in Gabor S. Borrit, ed., *Why the Civil War Came* (New York: Oxford University Press, 1996); Alice Fahs, *The Imagined Civil War: Popular Literature of the North and South, 1861–1865* (Chapel Hill: University of North Carolina Press, 2001), 68–83.

37. Russell letter of July 8, 1861, quoted in *Savannah Republican*, August 20, 1861; David Detzer, *Allegiance: Fort Sumter, Charleston, and the Beginning of the Civil War* (New York: Harcourt, 2001), 129; Barry O'Neill, *Honor, Symbols, and War* (Ann Arbor: University of Michigan Press, 1999), 142–43. O'Neill explains how the Second China War of 1856–60 was sparked by the "Incident of the Lurcha Arrow," in which the British colors were hauled down from a Chinese ship under British registry.

38. *Harper's Weekly*, May 4, 1861; *New Orleans Picayune*, April 27, 1861.

39. [Edward Pollard], *The Southern Spy: Letters on the Policy and Inauguration of the Lincoln War* (Richmond, Va.: West and Johnson, 1861), 92; Bishop Stephen Elliot, *God's Presence with the Confederate States* (Savannah, Ga.: W. Thorne Williams, 1861), 21; T. V. Moore, *God Our Refuge and Strength in This War* (Richmond, Va.: W. Hargrave,

White, 1861), 22; *Richmond Enquirer*, April 16, May 10, 1861; *Richmond Whig*, July 2, 1861; *Richmond Examiner*, April 13, 1864.

40. "Alexander Stephens's Unionist Speech, Wednesday Evening, November 14," in William Freehling, ed., *Secession Debated: Georgia's Showdown in 1860* (New York: Oxford University Press, 1992), 64. Walter Bagehot introduces the distinction between majestic and efficient government in *The English Constitution* (London: H. S. King, 1872).

41. *New Orleans Picayune*, December 7, 1860; *Charleston Courier*, February 16, 1861, quotes Representative Brooke, who made a similar argument and recited lines from the song in his appeal in Congress for the Stars and Stripes. Ironically, a committee of Northern publicists made a simultaneous attempt to replace "The Star Spangled Banner," which many in the North considered too martial for use as a national song. See Richard Grant White, *National Hymns: How They Are Written and How They Are Not Written* (New York: Rudd and Carleton, 1861).

42. Faust, *The Creation of Confederate Nationalism*, 18–21; Richard Harwell, *Confederate Music* (Chapel Hill: University of North Carolina Press, 1950); E. Lawrence Abel, *Singing the New Nation: How Music Shaped the Confederacy, 1861–1865* (Mechanicsburg, Pa.: Stackpole Books, 2000). For struggles over the regulation of music, see Laura Mason, *Singing the French Revolution: Popular Culture and Politics, 1787–1799* (Ithaca: Cornell University Press, 1996); and George Mosse, *The Nationalization of the Masses: Political Symbolism and Mass Movements in Germany from the Napoleonic Wars through the Third Reich* (New York: H. Fertig, 1975), 137–40.

43. Edwin Heriot, "The Flag of the South," in *Charleston Courier*, March 16, 1861; "The Stars and Bars" and "The Flag of Secession," undated broadsides at HEH; *Our Southern Flag: A National Song Written by Samuel L. Hammond and Respectfully dedicated to the Citadel Cadets of Charleston* (Charleston, S.C., 1861). Among other poems written to the tune of the "Stars Spangled Banner" were St. George Tucker, "The Southern Cross," *Southern Literary Messenger* 32 (March, 1861): 189; and M. B., "The Starry Barred Banner," in *Charleston Courier*, December 18, 1861.

44. J. S. Prevatt, "The Southern Flag—Red, White, and Blue," undated broadside at HEH; M. F. Bigney, "The Battle Field of Manassas," in Frank Moore, *Rebel Rhymes and Rhapsodies* (New York: G. P. Putnam, 1864); see also Theodore Von La Hache, *The New Red, White and Blue* (New Orleans: A. E. Blackmar, 1862); and T. V. Russell, *Hurrah for the Flag!* (Macon, Ga.: J.W. Burke, 1864).

45. P. T. D., *Farewell to the "Star-Spangled Banner"* (Richmond, Va.: J. W. Davies, 1861); Ella D. Clark, *Adieu to the "Star-Spangled Banner" Forever* (New Orleans: A. E. Blackmar, 1861); J. R. Barrick, "The Confederate Flag," in Moore, *Rebel Rhymes*, 183; P. E. Collins, *The Banner of the South* (Mobile, Ala.: J. H. Snow, 1861); A. J. Requier, "The Stars and Bars," in "Bohemian," *War Songs of the South* (Richmond, Va.: West and Johnson, 1863), 100–105; *North Carolina: A Call to Arms!* (Raleigh, N.C.: Thompson and Co., 1861); Tucker, "The Southern Cross"; "A Lady of South Carolina" and "The Flag," in *Baltimore South*, June 6, 8, and 15, 1861.

46. Rev. John Collins McCabe, "The Stars and Stripes," *Southern Illustrated News*, October 4, 1862; Ellen Key Blunt, "An Appeal for the Country," *National Intelligencer*, February 6, 1861; Camden (S.C.) *Confederate*, December 6, 1861 (for a claim that fifteen members of the Key family were "in arms against the tyranny at Washington"); "The Southern Cross," in *Savannah Morning News*, October 6, 1862, and *Charleston Courier*,

October 28, 1862. Details about the Baltimore suppression can be found in Col. J. Thomas Scharf, *The Chronicles of Baltimore* (Baltimore: Turnbull Brothers, 1874), 628. This poem was also printed as an 1862 broadside (held at HEH) entitled *To God and Liberty*, perhaps to distinguish it from St. George Tucker's equally well known poem "The Southern Cross."

47. Harry Macarthy, *Our Flag—The Origin of the Stars and Bars* (New Orleans: A. E. Blackmar, 1861). Similar themes can be seen in Henry Keeling, *The New Constellation—The Confederate Flag* (Richmond, Va., 1861); Dan Townsend "Freedom's New Banner," *Richmond Daily Dispatch*, June 30, 1862; and Robert F. Carlin, *The Southern Constellation* (Macon, Ga.: Schreiner and Sons, 1863).

48. Viola, "The Flag of the South," in *Charleston Courier*, March 3, 1862; *The Confederate Flag. Written by Mrs. C. D. Elder of New Orleans. Music by Sig. G. George, of Norfolk, Va.* (New Orleans: A. E. Blackmar, 1861).

49. J. H. H., "Southern Song of Freedom," first published in the *Richmond Enquirer*, May 14, 1861.

50. "To the Troops of Virginia," *Richmond Daily Dispatch*, July 31, 1861.

Chapter Four
BLOOD SACRIFICE AND THE COLORS OF WAR

1. This paragraph and much of the following chapter have been informed by Caroline Marvin and David W. Ingle, *Blood Sacrifice and the Nation: Totem Rituals and the American Flag* (New York: Cambridge University Press, 1999).

2. Thomas Carlyle, *Sartor Resartus* (1836; reprint New York: Oxford University Press, 1987), 168.

3. "Ellsworth," *Atlantic Monthly* 7 (July 1861): 119; Robert Garth Scott, ed., *Forgotten Valor: The Memoirs and Civil War Letters of Orlando B. Wilcox* (Kent, Ohio: Kent State University Press, 1999); W. Burns Jones, Jr., "The Marshall House Incident," *Northern Virginia Heritage* 10 (February 1988): 3–8.

4. *Charleston Mercury*, May 27, 1861; *Memphis Avalanche*, May 29, 1861; *Savannah Daily Morning News*, May 28, 1861; *Life of James W. Jackson, the Alexandria Hero, the Slayer of Ellsworth, the First Martyr in the Cause of Southern Independence* (Richmond, Va.: West and Johnson, 1862). This anonymous pamphlet appeared in the spring of that year, as shown by a notice in the *Richmond Dispatch*, April 19, 1862.

5. *Life of James W. Jackson*, 9–14.

6. Ibid, 10; Jones, "The Marshall House Incident"; *Charleston Mercury*, May 26, 1861.

7. Jones, "The Marshall House Incident," 8; "Ellsworth," 121; Michael Burlingame, ed., *Lincoln's Journalist: John Hay's Anonymous Writings for the Press, 1860–1864* (Carbondale: Southern Illinois University Press, 1998), 62–63.

8. Jones, "The Marshall House Incident"; Mark E. Neely, Jr. and Harold Holzer, *The Union Image: Popular Prints of the Civil War North* (Chapel Hill: University of North Carolina Press, 2000), 27–30; *Harper's Weekly*, June 8, 1861.

9. *New Orleans Picayune*, June 6, 1861; "Stand by Your Flag," in *Richmond Daily Dispatch*, May 31, 1861; Lena Lyle, "The Fall of Ellsworth," *Memphis Avalanche*, May 30, 1861; *Charleston Courier*, May 27, June 3, 1861; *Savannah Daily Morning News*, July 15, 1861.

10. *Charleston Mercury*, May 26, 1861; T. F., "Jackson, Our First Martyr," *Southern Field and Fireside*, June 1, 1861; "To the Memory of the Lamented Jackson," *Richmond Enquirer*, June 13, 1861; *Charleston Courier*, May 26, 1861.

11. This telegraph dispatch appeared in most papers on May 25, 1861; *New York Tribune*, May 27, 1861; *Charleston Courier*, May 29, 1861; *Richmond Enquirer*, June 11, 1861.

12. Marvin and Ingle, *Blood Sacrifice and the Nation*, 41–62.

13. J. Wright Simmons, "The Martyr of Alexandria," *New Orleans Crescent*, reprinted in Bohemia, *War Songs of the South* (Richmond, Va.: West and Johnson, 1862), 129; William Henry Holcombe, "Jackson, the Alexandria Martyr," *Southern Literary Messenger* (August 1861): 148; T. F., "Jackson, Our First Martyr."

14. "Stand by Your Flag," *Richmond Daily Dispatch*, May 31, 1861; T. F., "Jackson, Our First Martyr"; Andrew Devilbliss, *To the Memory of Jackson of Alexandria* (New Orleans: Hopkins Printers, [1861]).

15. "Stand by Your Flag"; *Franklin (La.) Attakapas Register,* June 20, 1861; Devilbliss, *To the Memory of Jackson*; *Richmond Daily Dispatch*, May 27, 1861; *Savannah Republican*, July 13, 1861; *Richmond Enquirer*, June 18, 1861.

16. *Charleston Courier*, April 3, 1861.

17. Reid Mitchell, *Civil War Soldiers: Their Expectations and Their Experiences* (New York: Vintage Books, 1988), 19–22.

18. *Memphis Avalanche*, July 5, 1861; *Charleston Courier*, June 29, 1861, December 20, 1860.

19. Emile Durkheim, *The Elementary Forms of Religious Life*, ed. and trans. Karen E. Fields (New York: Free Press, 1995), 232–33.

20. The summary of local battle flags in this and the following paragraph is based primarily on contemporary press coverage. A helpful sampling can be found in Rebecca Ansell Rose, *Colours of the Gray: An Illustrated Index of Wartime Flags from the Museum of the Confederacy's Collection* (Richmond, Va.: Museum of the Confederacy, 1998).

21. *Natchez Courier*, May 25, 1861.

22. Quotation from *Savannah Republican*, June 18, 1861. Barbara Ehrenreich notes the gender division of warmaking and clothmaking in ancient societies in *Blood Rites: The Passions of War* (New York: Metropolitan Books, 1997), 125–31. The representational role American women played in patriotic display is addressed in Mary P. Ryan, *Women in Public: Between Banners and Ballots, 1825–1880* (Baltimore: Johns Hopkins University Press, 1990), while the specifically southern dynamic of proslavery domesticity is set forth in Stephanie McCurry, *Masters of Small Worlds: Yeomen Households, Gender Relations, and the Political Culture of the Antebellum South Carolina Low Country* (New York: Oxford University Press, 1995).

23. *Augusta Sentinel and Chronicle*, May 19, 1861; *Atlanta Commonwealth*, in Thomas Dyer, *Secret Yankees: The Union Circle in Confederate Atlanta* (Baltimore: Johns Hopkins University Press, 1999), 55; *New Orleans Picayune*, April 21, 1861.

24. *Columbus (Ga.) Daily Enquirer*, June 24, 1861; *Savannah Republican,* May 22, 1861; *Natchez Courier*, May 25, 1861; *Savannah Morning News*, April 8, 1861; *Nashville Union and American*, December 22, 1861.

25. *Columbus Daily Enquirer,* June 24, 1861; *Savannah Republican*, July 2, 1861; *Arkansas Gazette*, quoted in Michael B. Douglas, *Confederate Arkansas: The People and Policies of a Frontier State in Wartime* (University: University of Alabama Press, 1976),

72; *Franklin (La.) Attakapas Register*, July 18, 1861; Bartow quoted in Alexander Lawrence, *A Present for Mr. Lincoln: The Story of Savannah from Secession to Sherman* (Macon, Ga.: Ardivan Press, 1961), 28.

26. *Augusta Sentinel and Chronicle*, May 19, 1861; *New Orleans Picayune*, April 19, 1861.

27. Col. D. K. McRae, *On Love of Country: An Address Delivered before the Young Ladies of the Clio Society of Oxford Female College, June 2nd, 1862* (Raleigh, N.C.: Strotham and Marcom, 1862); William Gilmore Simms, "Oh, the Sweet South," *Southern Literary Messenger* 32 (January 1861): 5.

28. Paul Fussell, *The Great War and Modern Memory* (New York: Oxford University Press, 1975); Simms, "Oh, the Sweet South"; *Augusta Chronicle and Sentinel*, May 19, 1861.

29. Unknown member of the Mississippi College Rifles, quoted in Rod Gragg, ed., *The Illustrated Confederate Reader* (New York: Harper and Row, 1989), 22; *Marshall Texas Republican*, December 21, 1861; *Charleston Courier*, June 1, 1861; *New Orleans Crescent*, quoted in Bell Wiley, *The Life of Johnny Reb, the Common Soldier of the Confederacy* (Indianapolis, Ind.: Bobbs-Merrill, 1943), 22.

30. *Mobile Register and Advertiser*, June 25, 1861; *Richmond Whig*, July 9, 1861; *Charleston Courier*, February 26, November 15, 1861.

31. *Franklin (La.) Attakapas Register*, July 25, 1861; B. M. Palmer, "Charge to Washington Artillery," in Thomas Cary Johnson, ed., *The Life and Letters of Benjamin Morgan Palmer* (Richmond, Va.: Presbyterian Committee of Publication, 1906), 238; see also *Natchez Courier*, May 25, 1861; and Ulrich B. Phillips, *The Correspondence of Robert Toombs, Alexander Stephens, and Howell Cobb* (Washington, D.C.: American Historical Association, 1913), 559.

32. *Atlanta Southern Confederacy*, October 4, 1861.

33. George Henry Preble, *The History of the Flag of the United States* (Boston: A. Williams and Co., 1880); Carlton McCarthy, "Origin of the Confederate Battle-Flag," *SHSP* 8 (1880): 497; Alfred Roman, *The Military Operations of General Beauregard in the War between the States, 1861 to 1865* (New York: Harper and Brothers, 1884): 1: 170–73, 480–87; Constance Cary Harrison, "A Virginia Girl in the First Year of the War," *Century* 30 (August 1885): 609–10; Alfred Roman, "Address," *SHSP* 12 (1884): 28–32; General W. L. Cabell, "Vivid History of Our Battle Flag," *Confederate Veteran* 8 (1900): 238–39; Col. Alexander Robert Chisolm, "The Confederate Battle Flag," *Confederate Veteran* 11 (1903): 223; Charles L. Shipley, "Origin of the Confederate Battle Flag," *Confederate Veteran* 15 (1907): 70.

34. *New Orleans Delta*, November 12, 1861; William C. Davis, *Battle at Bull Run: A History of the First Major Campaign of the Civil War* (New York: Doubleday, 1977), 227–28; a slightly different account of battlefield confusion appears in Jubal Early to Jefferson Davis, December 30, 1878 in Dunbar Rowland, ed., *Jefferson Davis, Constitutionalist* (Jackson: Mississippi Department of Archives and History, 1923), 8:303–4.

35. The post-Manassas address can be found in *DeBow's Review* 31 (September 1861), 316. For the bells, see *Savannah Daily Morning News*, March 17, 26, 29, 1862; *Charleston Courier*, March 24, 29, April 3, 1862; and T. Harry Williams, *P. G. T. Beauregard: Napoleon in Gray* (Baton Rouge: Louisiana State University Press, 1955), 123. Final quotation from *Savannah Daily Morning News*, February 18, 1863.

36. *Charleston Mercury*, October 21, 1861, provided a report of this initiative, which was intentionally kept quiet until the display of the flags. On March 12, 1863, the *Southern Illustrated News* explained that these flags had been made by "seventy-five ladies from each one of four or five churches" and that their work was intentionally kept secret "lest the enemy should discover our change of colors and provide themselves with counterfeits to be basely used for our destruction."

37. Mrs. Burton Harrison, *Recollections Gay and Grave* (New York: Charles Scribner, 1911), 56–65; Emily Van Dorn Miller, *A Soldier's Honor: With Reminiscences of Major-General Earl Van Dorn* (New York, 1902), 56; Bell Irvin Wiley, ed., *"Recollections of a Confederate Staff Officer," by G. Moxley Sorrel* (Jackson, Tenn.: McCowat-Mercer Press, 1958), 28–30. The third prototype, made by Hetty Cary, was presented to Joseph Johnston. See Rose, *Colours of the Gray*, 19.

38. Quoted in Roman, *Military Operations* 1: 481, and, via telegraph, in much of the Confederate press on December 4, 1861; *Charleston Mercury*, December 10, 1861.

39. *Charleston Mercury*, December 10, 1861; *Savannah Daily Republican*, December 13, 1861. This ceremony was not the first time the troops had seen the flag; more than a week earlier, Beauregard had requested that "regimental commanders will accustom their men to the flag, so that they may become thoroughly acquainted with it." See O.R., ser. 1, 5:969. For military reviews during this same period in France, see Matthew Truesdell, *Spectacular Politics: Louis Napoleon Bonaparte and the Fete Imperiale, 1849–1870* (New York: Oxford University Press, 1997), 136–55.

40. Julian Bayol to "Dear Parents," December 3, 1861, in Bayol Family Papers, VHS.

41. Roman, *Military Operations*, 1:164; Williams, *P. G. T. Beauregard*; and T. Michael Parrish, "Jefferson Davis Rules," in Gabor Borrit, ed., *Jefferson Davis and His Generals* (New York: Oxford University Press, 1999).

42. *Charleston Mercury*, May 25, 1861; Col. Edward McCrady, Jr., "Reunion of Virginia Division, ANV Association," *SHSP* 14 (1886): 203.

43. *Charleston Courier*, April 9, 1862. For women who hid their sex in order to fight, see Elizabeth D. Leonard, *All the Daring of the Soldier: Women of the Civil War Armies* (New York: W. W. Norton, 1999).

44. *Austin Gazette* quoted in *Richmond Enquirer*, December 17, 1861; *Confederate Veteran* 2 (1894): 118. My reading of the move from local to national orientation departs from Stuart McConnell, "Reading the Flag: Reconsidering the Patriotic Cults of the 1890s," in John Bodnar, ed., *Bonds of Affection: Americans Define Their Patriotism* (Princeton: Princeton University Press, 1996), 102–9, which argues the preeminently localist orientation of flags until the late-nineteenth century.

45. Joseph Allan Frank and George A. Reaves, *"Seeing the Elephant": Raw Recruits at the Battle of Shiloh* (New York: Greenwood Press, 1989); Mitchell, *Civil War Soldiers*; Gerald F. Linderman, *Embattled Courage: The Experience of Combat in the American Civil War* (New York: Free Press, 1987).

46. C. G. Cruikshank, *Elizabeth's Army*, 2nd ed. (Oxford: Oxford University Press, 1966), 57; John P. Curry, *Volunteers' Camp and Field Book* (Richmond, Va.: West and Johnson, 1862), 88. The risks and rewards that marked the life of flag-bearers is discussed in Wiley, *The Life of Johnny Reb*, 81–83; and Michael Howard Madaus, *The Battle-Flags of the Army of Tennessee* (Milwaukee: Historical Society of Wisconsin, 1976), 11–15.

47. Daniel E. Sutherland, ed., *Reminiscences of a Private: William E. Bevens of the First Arkansas Infantry, C.S.A.* (Fayetteville: University of Arkansas Press, 1992); 31; Rev. Wayland Fuller Dunaway, *Reminiscences of a Rebel* (New York: Neale Publishing Co., 1913), 98.

48. John Keegan, *The Face of Battle* (New York: Viking Press, 1976), 184–87.

49. *London Illustrated News*, June 6, 1863. For more on capturing enemy flags, see chapter 7, below.

50. *The Standard Bearer. Words by Major TNP, CSA Music by NS Coleman* (Richmond, Va.: George Dunn and Co., 1864).

51. "Eustanzia," *The Banner of the Starry Cross* (New Orleans, 1863); Henry Tucker, "Our Color Guard," quoted in Willard A. Heaps and Porter W. Heaps, *The Singing Sixties: The Spirit of Civil War Days Drawn from the Music of the Times* (Norman: University of Oklahoma Press, 1960), 170; Margaret Junkin Preston, "The Color Bearer," in W. Gordon McCabe, *Ballads of Battle and Bravery* (New York: Harper, 1879), 143–46.

52. Col. Edward McCrady, "Boy Heroes of Cold Harbor" *SHSP* 25 (1897): 234–37; Ed Porter Thompson, *History of the Orphan Brigade* (Louisville, Ky.: L. N. Thompson, 1898), 200; Richard Lowe, ed., *A Texas Cavalry Officer's Civil War: The Diary and Letters of James C. Bates* (Baton Rouge: Louisiana State University Press, 1999), 190. Two episodes that ended in the loss of the colors-bearer's hand, rather than his life, are related in *Richmond Daily Dispatch*, May 7, 1862; and John H. Worsham, *One of Jackson's Foot Cavalry* (Jackson, Tenn.: McCowat-Mercer Press, 1964), 110–13.

53. Drew Gilpin Faust, "The Civil War Soldier and the Art of Dying," *Journal of Southern History* 67 (February 2001): 3–38; Peter Stearns, *American Cool: Constructing a Twentieth-Century Emotional Style* (New York: New York University Press, 1994), 22–24, 75–76; P. N. Stearns and P. Knapp, "Historical Perspectives on Grief," in R. Harre and W. G. Parrott, eds., *The Emotions* (London: Sage, 1996), 132–50; Lewis O. Saum, "Death in the Popular Mind of Pre–Civil War America," in David E. Stannard, ed., *Death in America* (Philadelphia: University of Pennsylvania Press, 1975), 30–48; Patricia Jalland, *Death in the Victorian Family* (New York: Oxford University Press, 1996); Emma Scarr Ledsham, "The Dying Flag Bearer," quoted in Heaps and Heaps, *The Singing Sixties*, 171.

54. Alice Fahs, "The Sentimental Soldier in Popular Civil War Literature, 1861–1865," *Civil War History* 46 (June 2000): 107–31; John Hill Hewitt, *Give Our Flag to the Breeze: A New National Song* [Richmond, Va.: 1861]; John Hill Hewitt, *Flag of the Sunny South* (Augusta, Ga.: J. H. Hewitt, 1864).

55. John A. Lynn, *The Bayonets of the Republic: Motivation and Tactics in the Army of Revolutionary France, 1791–1794* (Urbana: University of Illinois Press, 1984); John Tone, "The Machete and the Liberation of Cuba," *Journal of Military History* 62 (January 1998): 7–28; Fussell, *The Great War and Modern Memory*.

56. "To the Southern Flag," *Savannah Morning News*, August 15, 1861; "A Baltimore Rebel," *Our Southern Flag* (undated broadside at HEH). For other verse that presents the martial aspect of the Stars and Bars, see "The Soldier's Banner" in *Richmond Enquirer*, October 18, 1861; Robert Lamb, *"Rally around the Stars and Bars"* (undated broadside at HEH); Anna K. Hearn, *The Flag of the South: A Voice from the Old Academy* (Nashville: C.D. Benson, 1861).

57. R. H. G., "Our Battle Flag," in *Charleston Courier*, February 8, 1962; later set to music in *Our Battle Flag! Words by RHG. Composed by James Pierpont* (New Orleans:

P. Werlein and Halsey, 1862); "The Southern Cross," in Moore, *Rebel Rhymes*, 106. The first song circulated quickly, as can be seen by its recitation at a flag presentation in Georgia, as reported in the *Savannah Morning News*, February 25, 1862; its refrain was echoed in Sam Houston, Jr., "The Southern Flag," *Houston Daily Telegraph*, March 9, 1864.

58. *Richmond Enquirer*, May 8, 1863; Edward Porter Alexander, *Military Memoirs of a Confederate*, ed. T. Harry Williams (Bloomington: Indiana University Press, 1962), 493; Gary Gallagher, *The Confederate War: How Nationalism, Will, and Strategy Could Not Stave off Defeat* (Cambridge: Harvard University Press, 1997).

59. John Esten Cooke, "Stonewall Jackson and the Old Stonewall Brigade," *Southern Illustrated News*, February 7, 1863.

60. *Charleston Courier,* May 16, 1863.

61. Sporadic attention to James Jackson can be seen in the *Richmond Enquirer*, August 10, 1861; and the *Savannah Morning News*, March 19, 1862. But an article in the *Richmond Sentinel*, May 25, 1864, indicates that he had all but been forgotten by the third anniversary of his death.

Chapter Five
THE SOUTHERN CROSS AND CONFEDERATE CONSOLIDATION

1. The centrality of army leaders to national purpose is a major theme in Gary Gallagher, *The Confederate War: How Nationalism, Will, and Strategy Could Not Stave off Defeat* (Cambridge: Harvard University Press, 1997).

2. See table 3.2 above for these figures. George Henry Preble traces the Confederate interest in a cross flag to the South Carolina convention, though the topic was more broadly discussed than his account suggests. See *The History of the Flag of the United States* (Boston: A. Williams and Co., 1880), 498.

3. No. 74 in NA-CFD; Gilchrist, no. 16 in NA-CFD; *Charleston Courier*, February 5, 1861.

4. Slightly different versions of Memminger's speech appear in Preble, *History of the Flag*, 502; *Savannah Daily Morning News*, February 11, 1861; and *New Orleans Daily Picayune*, February 13, 1861. Later references to this legend appeared in St. George Tucker, "The Southern Cross," *Southern Literary Messenger* 32 (March, 1861): 189; and A. B. Meek, "The Blue Cross," in *The Southern Soldier's Prize Songster* (Mobile, Ala.: W. F. Wisely, 1864), 25–26. For the historical context of the Constantine legend, see Timothy Harris, "Christianity in the Late Roman Army," in Samuel N. C. Lieu and Dominic Montserrat, *Constantine: History, Historiography, and Legend* (London: Routledge, 1998), 21–51.

5. [George William Bagby], "Editor's Table," *Southern Literary Messenger* 32 (January 1861): 75–76. An apparent reference to this article appears in the *Charleston Courier*, January 11, 1861, quoting the *Memphis Enquirer*.

6. Mark Noll, "The Bible and Slavery," and Eugene Genovese, "Religion in the Collapse of the American Union," both in Randall M. Miller, Harry S. Stout, and Charles Wilson Reagan, eds., *Religion and the American Civil War* (New York: Oxford University Press, 1997), 43–88.

7. Jon Butler, *Awash in a Sea of Faith: Christianizing the American People* (Cambridge: Harvard University Press, 1990), 257–88; Drew Gilpin Faust, *The Creation of Confederate Nationalism: Ideology and Identity in the Slaveholding South* (Baton Rouge: Louisiana State University Press, 1988), 22; Mitchell Snay, *Gospel of Disunion: Religion and Separatism in the Antebellum South* (New York: Cambridge University Press, 1993), 181–209.

8. Tucker, "The Southern Cross."

9. Ibid. For anti-Puritan themes in his novel, see the review of "Hansford; A Tale of Bacon's Rebellion, by St. George Tucker," *Southern Literary Messenger* 24 (April, 1857): 260–72.

10. McMaster, no. 104; DeBow, no. 72; no. 117, all in NA-CFD; *Charleston Courier,* February 14, 1861.

11. Moise no. 137 in NA-CFD.

12. James William Hagy, *This Happy Land: The Jews of Colonial and Antebellum Charleston.* (University: University of Alabama Press, 1993), 55; Robert Rosen, *The Jewish Confederates* (Columbia: University of South Carolina Press, 2000), 15–16.

13. Julia Boutheneau in no. 98, NA-CFD; "A Citizen and Nullifier," no. 115, NA-CFD; Miles in "Debates of the Confederate Congress," *SHSP* 49 (1943): 272; Rosen, *The Jewish Confederates,* 32.

14. Miles to Beauregard, August 27, 1861, and Miles, "Report of the Committee," both quoted in Preble, *History of the Flag of the United States,* 505–14.

15. Miles to Beauregard, August 27, 1861, in Preble, *History of the Flag,* 514; Beauregard to J. E. Johnson, September 5, 1861, in Alfred Roman, *The Military Operations of General Beauregard in the War between the States 1861 to 1865* (New York: Harper and Brothers, 1884) 1:482. While the link with Scotland was not part of the wartime discussion, it has since become part of neo-Confederate lore, as explained in Celeste Ray, *Highland Heritage: Scottish Americans in the American South* (Chapel Hill: University of North Carolina Press, 2001), 194–96.

16. The use of crosses on battle flags outside of Virginia is surveyed in Howard Michael Madaus, *The Battle Flags of the Confederate Army of Tennessee* (Milwaukee: Milwaukee Public Museum, 1976); Michael Madaus and Robert D. Needham, "Unit Colors of the Trans-Mississippi Confederacy," *Military Historian and Collector* (1989): 123–39, 172–83; (1990): 16–21; and Rebecca Ansell Rose, *Colours of the Gray: An Illustrated Index of Wartime Flags from the Museum of the Confederacy's Collection* (Richmond, Va.: Museum of the Confederacy, 1998).

17. *Charleston Mercury,* July 20, 1861; *New Orleans Delta,* December 21, 1861; Bagby, "Editor's Table," *Southern Literary Messenger* 34 (January 1862): 67. See also *Memphis Avalanche,* August 28, 1861; *Richmond Enquirer,* September 26, 1861; *Richmond Examiner,* December 13, 1861. The *Richmond Whig* offered one of the few defenses of the Stars and Bars on August 28, 1861, after printing the petitions of Fredericksburg women for the Southern Cross on August 24, 1861. The other petition campaign was noted in the *Nashville Union and American,* December 21, 1861.

18. *Richmond Examiner,* December 13, 1861; L. Virginia French in *Georgia Crusader,* October 17, 1861; R. S. Trapier to Miles, August 2, 1861, William Porcher Miles Papers, Southern Historical Collection, University of North Carolina, Chapel Hill; Joseph Myers, no. 77; and T. M. Lyle, no. 132, both in NA-CFD.

19. Bagby in *Charleston Mercury*, December 14, 1861, and *Southern Literary Messenger* 34 (January 1862): 67; Joseph Addison Turner, "Our New Flag," *Countryman* (March 4, 1862).

20. *Richmond Dispatch*, December 7, 9, 10, 1861, January 2, 1862. The first letter from the Georgian can also be found in Preble, *History of the Flag*. The debate over the French tricolor in 1848 is explained in Maurice Agulhon, *Marianne into Battle: Republican Imagery and Symbolism in France, 1789–1880*, trans. Janet Lloyd (New York: Cambridge University Press, 1981); and Mona Ozouf, "Liberty, Equality, Fraternity," in Pierre Nora, *Realms of Memory: The Construction of the French Past,* vol. 3; *Symbols* (New York: Columbia University Press, 1996), 97–98,

21. *Charleston Mercury*, December 14, 1861, January 4, March 6, 1862; *Richmond Enquirer*, January 7, 1862. George Henry Preble identified the later *Mercury* writer as Robert Trapier, in *History of the Flag*, 523. This may be true, but Trapier advocated two designs that had nothing to do with slavery in letters to William Porcher Miles of August 2, 1861, and April 22, 1862, both in the Miles Papers. John Daniel made the case for black and white as national colors, to be blended into gray for uniforms, though he saw the pattern as elegant, simple, and dignified, rather than as explicitly invoking slavery. See *Richmond Examiner*, March 28, 29, April 19, 1862. See also the suggestion of the H. D. Starr, in Raphael Thian, *Documentary History of the Flag and Seal of the Confederate States* (Washington, D.C., 1880), 54, one of the few sources in this collection not taken from NA-CFD.

22. *Charleston Mercury*, February 18, March 6, 1862; *Countryman*, March 4, 1862. A great deal of editorial comment is conveniently reprinted in the second part of Thian, *Documentary History of the Flag and Seal.*

23. *Richmond Whig*, April 21, 1862; *Charleston Mercury*, April 22, 1862. The *Richmond Christian Advocate* of May 15, 1862, liked the design, primarily because of the cross included in the background.

24. *Savannah Morning News*, October 10, 1862; *Savannah Republican*, October 12, 1862; *Richmond Whig*, October 14, 1862.

25. Brown in "Debates of the Confederate Congress," *SHSP* 46 (1928): 227; *Richmond Dispatch*, January 20, 1862. Comments on flags at press offices, first in Richmond, then at the two Charleston papers, can be see in *Richmond Dispatch*, January 7, 1862; *Charleston Mercury*, January 4, 17, 27, February 21, March 7, 1862; and *Charleston Courier*, January 9, February 27, October 1, 1862. For more on the Richmond press, see Harry Stout and Christopher Grasso, "Civil War, Religion, and Communications: The Case of Richmond," in Randall M. Miller, Harry S. Stout, and Charles Wilson Reagan, eds., *Religion and the American Civil War* (New York: Oxford University Press, 1997), 360–384.

26. *Richmond Examiner*, March 29, 1862; *Charleston Mercury*, April 22, 1862; *Richmond Dispatch*, March 8, 1862; *Savannah Morning News*, October 10, 1862, *Richmond Enquirer*, March 4, 1863. For other notices critical of Congress, see *Richmond Examiner*, December 3, 1861, March 28, 1862; *Richmond Whig*, April 1, April 19, 1862.

27. *Southern Illustrated News*, September 27, 1862; the ability of the Stars and Stripes to evoke both government and people was made explicit by Francis Lieber, in his letter to Henry Drisler, October 8, 1865, Francis Lieber Papers, HEH.

28. *Richmond Whig*, February 13, 1865; *Richmond Enquirer*, quoted in *Charleston Mercury*, March 13, 1863; *Southern Illustrated News*, March 12, 1863; *Richmond Enquirer*, April 24, 1863.

29. Beauregard in *Charleston Mercury*, May 5, 1863. A growing body of flag scholarship has emphasized flag diversity in the Confederacy, though it has overlooked the changes over time that led to the convergence of symbols. In addition to the important contributions of Howard Michael Madaus (see n. 16), see Devereaux D. Cannon, Jr., *The Flags of the Confederacy: An Illustrated History* (Memphis, Tenn.: St. Luke's Press, 1988); Joseph H. Crute, *Emblems of Southern Valor: The Battle Flags of the Confederacy* (Louisville, Ky.: Harmony House, 1990); Glenn Dedmondt, *Flags of Civil War South Carolina* (Gretna, La.: Pelican Publishing Co., 2000); *Echoes of Glory: Arms and Equipment of the Confederacy* (Alexandria, Va.: Time-Life Books, 1991); Richard Rollins, ed., *The Returned Battle Flags* (Redondo Beach, Calif.: Rank and File Publications, 1995); Richard Rollins, *The Damned Rebel Flags of the Rebellion: The Confederate Battle-Flag at Gettysburg* (Redondo Beach, Calif.: Rank and File Publications, 1997); and Allan K. Sumrall, *Battle-Flags of Texans in the Confederacy* (Austin, Tex.: Eakin Press, 1995). For details on Union colors, see Devereaux D. Cannon, Jr., *The Flags of the Union: An Illustrated History* (Gretna, La.: Pelican Publishing Co., 1994); and Cannon, *Civil War Battle Flags of the Union Army and Order of Battle* (New York: Knickerbocker Press, 1997).

30. *Richmond Examiner* April 24, 1863.

31. Hotze to J. P Benjamin, June 6, 1863, in O.R. Navy, ser. 2, 3:785.

32. *London Index*, May 1, February 26, 1863.

33. *Charleston Mercury*, October 7, 1862.

34. *Richmond Examiner*, February 22, 1862, March 29, 1862, April 24, 1863; "The Great Seal of the United States," *Prologue* 1984 16, no. 3: 184–89.

35. "Debates of the Confederate Congress," in *SHSP* 46 (1928): 226–29; and 47 (1930): 105–6.

36. *Charleston Mercury*, October 7, 1862; *Richmond Examiner* September 25, 1862; *Charleston Mercury*, October 15, 1862; *Charleston Courier*, October 17, 1862.

37. *Richmond Examiner*, February 22, March 29, September 25, October 1, 1862; *Charleston Courier*, October 6, 1861; *Charleston Mercury*, October 7, 15, 1862.

38. "Debates of the Confederate Congress," *SHSP* 48 (1932), 102; *Southern Illustrated News,* March 12, 1863; *Richmond Enquirer*, April 24, 1863. For more on the controversy over the cavalier on the seal, see Robert Bonner "Roundheaded Cavaliers? The Context and Limits of a Confederate Racial Project," *Civil War History* 48 (March 2002): 34–59.

39. George Rable, *The Confederate Republic: A Revolution against Politics* (Chapel Hill: University of North Carolina Press, 1994), 121–23.

40. *Richmond Examiner*, April 24, 1863; "Debates of the Confederate Congress," in *SHSP* 47 (1932): 166, 222–27. John Coski provided me this specific translation of "Deo Vindice," having established in his own research that this was the most widely understood meaning of these Latin words during the war.

41. Sam Barrett to Howell Cobb, May 24, 1861, in Miles Papers. See also no. 100 and no. 133, both in NA-CFD.

42. Charles Grayson Summersell, "Adventures with the Great Seal of the Confederacy," *Alabama Heritage* 47 (1998): 24–31; O.R. Navy, ser. 2, 3:688, 774, 1163–65, 1266. *Richmond Enquirer*, April 24, May 16, 1863. Howard Jones gives a helpful over-

view of the links between slavery and diplomacy in *Abraham Lincoln and a New Birth of Freedom: The Union and Slavery in the Diplomacy of the Civil War* (Lincoln: University of Nebraska Press, 1999).

43. *Savannah Morning News*, April 23–28, 1863. Considerable attention has been given in recent years to the importance of "whiteness" in American culture; in this regard, see the influential works of Alexander Saxton, *The Rise and Fall of the White Republic: Class Politics and Mass Culture in Nineteenth-Century America* (London: Verso, 1990); and David Roediger, *The Wages of Whiteness: Race and the Making of the American Working Class* (London: Verso, 1991).

44. "Our Ensign," in *The Southern Soldiers' Prize Songster*, 50–51; "Subaltern," *The Star-Spangled Cross on the Pure Field of White* (Richmond, Va.: Geo. Dunn and Co., 1864). A direct reference to "Deo Vindice" appeared in Dr. William B. Harrell, *Up with the Flag. Composed and Respectfully Dedicated to the Fourth N.C. Troops* (Richmond, Va.: Geo. Dunn and Co., 1863). Other poems that suggest that the white banner was a sign of purity and holiness include T. V. Russell, *Harrah for the Flag* (Macon, Ga.: J. W. Burke, 1864); "The Flag of the Free Eleven" in *Songs of the South* (Richmond, Va.: Geo. P. Edwards, 1863).

45. Margaret Junkin Preston, "Hymn to the National Flag," in *Richmond Sentinel*, January 17, 1865; Mary Price Coulling, *Margaret Junkin Preston: A Biography* (Winston-Salem, N.C.: John F. Blair, 1993), 113–27.

46. "Eustanzia," *The Banner of the Starry Cross* (New Orleans, 1863); J. P. T., "The Confederate Flag and the Southern Cross," *Richmond Daily Dispatch*, January 23, 1862; Henry C. Alexander, "To the Southern Cross," *Southern Literary Messenger* 37 (August 1863); "The Flag," *Montgomery Weekly Advertiser*, February 10, 1864.

47. The insights of René Girard, *Violence and the Sacred* (Baltimore: Johns Hopkins University Press, 1990), have been applied to modern war by both Barbara Ehrenreich, *Blood Rites: The Origins and History of the Passions of War* (New York: Metropolitan Books, 1997), 29–33; and Carolyn Marvin and David W. Ingle, *Blood Sacrifice and the Nation: Totem Rituals and the American Flag* (New York: Cambridge University Press, 1999), 73–77. For the combination of flags and crosses in military cemeteries, see George Mosse, *Fallen Soldiers: Reshaping the Memory of the World Wars* (New York: Oxford University Press, 1990).

48. A. B. Meek, "Land of My Fathers," "The Blue Cross," and "The Lifting of the Banner," all in *The Southern Soldier's Prize Songster,* 56–57, 25–26, 35–37.

49. Gallagher, *The Confederate War*; Mark E. Neely, Jr., Harold Holzer, and Gabor S. Boritt, *The Confederate Image: Prints of the Lost Cause* (Chapel Hill: University of North Carolina Press, 1987), 55.

50. Wigfall quoted in *SHSP* 48 (1941), 245; *Richmond Enquirer*, June 10, 1863.

51. O.R. ser. 1, 28:2, 93; "History of the Confederate Flag," *SHSP* 28 (1901) 89–90; *Richmond Sentinel*, December 14, 1864, *Richmond Whig*, February 13, 1865.

52. *Southern Punch*, February 20, 1864; *Richmond Whig*, February 14, 1865.

53. *Richmond Dispatch*, August 1, 1862; Grover Criswell and Herb Romer, *The Official Guide to Confederate Money and Civil War Tokens* (New York: HC Publishers, 1971); Alphaeus Homer Albert, *Buttons of the Confederacy* (Hightstown, N.J.: n.p., 1952), 12, 15. John Coski and John A. Ahladas brought the *Dispatch* advertisement for the badge to my attention.

54. John Higham, *From Boundlessness to Consolidation: The Transformation of American Culture, 1848–1860* (Ann Arbor, Mich.: William L. Clements Library, 1969); Iver Bernstein, *The New York City Draft Riots: Their Significance for American Society and Politics in the Age of the Civil War* (New York: Oxford University Press, 1990); Wilfred McClay, *The Masterless: Self and Society in Modern America* (Chapel Hill: University of North Carolina Press, 1994).

55. Don E. Fehrenbacher, *The Slaveholding Republic: An Account of the United States Government's Relations to Slavery* (New York: Oxford University Press, 2001); Arthur Bestor, "State Sovereignty and Slavery: A Reinterpretation of Proslavery Constitutional Doctrine, 1846–1860," *Journal of the Illinois State Historical Society* 54 (1961): 117–80; Richard Franklin Bensel, *Yankee Leviathan: The Origin of Central State Authority in America* (New York: Cambridge University Press, 1990).

56. Drew Gilpin Faust, ed., *The Ideology of Slavery: Proslavery Thought in the Antebellum South, 1839–1860* (Baton Rouge: Louisiana State University Press, 1981); Eugene Genovese, *The Slaveholder's Dilemma: Freedom and Progress in Southern Conservative Thought, 1820–1860* (Columbia: University of South Carolina Press, 1992); Faust, *The Creation of Confederate Nationalism.*

57. Richard E. Beringer, Herman Hattaway, Archer Jones, and William N. Still, Jr., *Why the South Lost the Civil War* (Athens: University of Georgia Press, 1985), 64.

58. "Richmond County," no. 80 and C.E. Brame, no. 120, both in NA-CFD. Jane Cross hit the most recognizable note of fatalism in "The Confederacy," writing that the South "with her starry cross, her flag unfurled . . . kneels to Thee, O God, she claims her birth. . . . She asks of Thee her place upon the earth / For it is Thine to give or to deny," in William Gilmore Simms, ed., *War Poems of the South* (New York: Richardson and Company, 1867), 128–29.

59. Robert H. Kellogg, *Life and Death in Rebel Prisons* (Hartford, Conn.: L. Stebbins, 1865), 200–203.

60. Bagby writing as "Gamma" in *Knoxville and Atlanta Register*, December 10, 1863; Daniel in *Richmond Examiner*, May 8, 1863.

61. Kellogg, *Life and Death*, 200–203; for a rare use of a Confederate flag in a southern church, see Daniel E. Sutherland, ed., *A Very Violent Rebel: The Civil War Diary of Ellen Renshaw House* (Knoxville: University of Tennessee Press, 1996), 116.

62. Winthrop quoted in Preble, *History of the Flag*, 394; Samuel Osgood offered a particularly effective link between the American flag and northern private life in "The Home and the Flag," *Harper's New Monthly Magazine* 26 (April 1863), 664–70.

Chapter Six
TREASON'S BANNER AND THE COLORS OF LOYALTY

1. Francis Lieber to Henry Drisler, October 8, 1865, Francis Lieber Papers, HEH.

2. Sasha Weitman, "National Flags: A Sociological Overview," *Semiotica* 8 (1977): 328–67. William Gilmore Simms to William Porcher Miles in *The Letters of William Gilmore Simms* (Columbia: University of South Carolina Press, 1955) 4:363–66. The rebel yell is discussed in Grady McWhiney and Perry D. Jamieson, *Attack and Die: Civil War Military Tactics and the Southern Heritage* (University: University of Alabama Press, 1982), 190–91; while Michael C. C. Adams suggests that Confederate intimidation was

successful in *Our Masters the Rebels: A Speculation on Union Military Failure in the East, 1861–1865* (Cambridge: Harvard University Press, 1978).

3. Lester C. Olson, *Emblems of American Community in the Revolutionary Era: A Study in Rhetorical Iconography* (Washington, D.C.: Smithsonian Institution, 1991), 21–74; George Henry Preble, *The History of the Flag of the United States* (Boston: A. Williams and Co., 1880), 213–16; no. 56 and no. 57 both in NA-CFD. For a secession-era rattlesnake with its fangs exposed, see the illustrated cover of *Secession Quickstep: The South, the Whole South, and Nothing but the South* (Macon, Ga.: John C. Schreiner and Sons, n.d.).

4. *Proceedings of the Mississippi State Convention* (Jackson, Miss.: Power and Cadwallader, 1861), 42; song lyrics quoted in Willard A. Heaps and Porter W. Heaps, *The Singing Sixties: The Spirit of Civil War Days Drawn from the Music of the Times* (Norman: University of Oklahoma Press, 1960), 56. A similar debate about the Judeo-Christian symbolism of the snake occurred during the Revolution, as explained in Olsen, *Emblems of American Community*, 34–41.

5. *Frank Leslie's Illustrated Weekly*, March 11, 1861; *New York Herald*, March 7, 1861; Preble, *History of the Flag*, 402–4; Everett quoted in *Christian Recorder* June 15, 1861.

6. Philip J. Reyburn and Terry L. Wilson, eds., *Jottings from Dixie: The Civil War Dispatches of Sergeant Major Stephen F. Fleharty, U.S.A.* (Baton Rouge: Louisiana State University Press, 1999), 57; Charles D. Drake, *Union and Antislavery Speeches, Delivered during the Rebellion* (New York, 1864), 78–79; Heaps and Heaps, *The Singing Sixties*, 61.

7. Mark E. Neely, Jr. and Harold Holzer, *The Union Image: Popular Prints of the Civil War North* (Chapel Hill: University of North Carolina Press, 2000), 13–14. Major collections of patriotic envelopes from the 1860s are held by the American Antiquarian Society and the Southern Historical Collection of the University of North Carolina. The latter collection forms the basis of Stephen W. Berry, "When Mail Was Armor: Envelopes of the Great Rebellion, 1861–1865," *Southern Cultures* 4 (Fall, 1998): 63–83.

8. W. W. Broom, *An Englishman's Thoughts on the Crimes of the South, and the Recompense of the North* (New York, 1865).

9. "The Southern Cross," *Atlantic Monthly* 9 (March, 1862): 337–38.

10. Heaps and Heaps, *The Singing Sixties*, 169, 329, 70–72, 335.

11. *Louisville (Ky.) Journal* quoted in *Memphis Avalanche*, July 10, 1861; John David Smith and William Cooper, Jr., eds., *A Union Woman in Civil War Kentucky: The Diary of Frances Peter* (Lexington: University of Kentucky Press, 2000) 8, 30–33, 62.

12. Pickens quoted in *Wilmington (N.C.) Daily Observer*, May 6, 1861.

13. *Memphis Avalanche*, March 23, 1861; J. Matthew Gallman, *Mastering Wartime: A Social History of Philadelphia during the Civil War* (New York: Cambridge University Press, 1990), 170–72; Clifford Merrill Drury, *William Anderson Scott: "No Ordinary Man"* (Glendale, Calif.: H. Clark Co., 1967), 240, 258–67.

14. O.R. ser. 1, 41:2, 274–75; this order is put in context by Michael Fellman, *Inside War: The Guerilla Conflict in Missouri during the American Civil War* (New York: Oxford University Press, 1989), 92–93.

15. O.R., ser. 1, 2:31; Morgan Dix, *Memoirs of John Adams Dix* (New York, 1883), 2:26–27; for efforts to carry out these policies, see O.R. ser. 3, 1:591–92, 2: 152; *New York Herald*, September 9, 1861; Sidney T. Matthews, "Control of the Baltimore Press

during the Civil War," *Maryland Historical Magazine* 36 (1941): 150–70. Mark E. Neely, Jr., *The Fate of Liberty: Abraham Lincoln and Civil Liberties* (New York: Oxford University Press, 1991), surveys Union policy toward civilians elsewhere, as do Stephen V. Ash, *When the Yankees Came: Conflict and Chaos in the Occupied South, 1861–1865* (Chapel Hill: University of North Carolina Press, 1995); and Mark Grimsley, *The Hard Hand of War: Union Military Policy Toward Southern Civilians, 1861–1865* (New York: Cambridge University Press, 1995).

16. Dix, *Memoirs*, 104–5; Chester G. Hearn, *When the Devil Came Down to Dixie: Ben Butler in New Orleans* (Baton Rouge: Louisiana State University Press, 1997), 68–73.

17. Hearn, *When the Devil Came Down*; O.R., ser. 1, 15:906–8; Robert Justin Goldstein, *Desecrating the American Flag: Key Documents of the Controversy from the Civil War to 1995* (Syracuse, N.Y.: Syracuse University Press, 1996), 1–4; *Charleston Mercury*, December 29, 1862; *Savannah Morning News*, November 13, 1862, May 30, June 8, December 8, 1863; *Atlanta Southern Confederacy*, December 29, 1861.

18. *Charleston Courier*, March 27, 1862; *Mobile Register*, May 21, 1862; *Richmond Daily Dispatch*, May 28, 1862; Benjamin F. Butler, *Butler's Book: Autobiography and Personal Reminiscences* (Boston: A. M. Thayer, 1882), 450–52. Michael Fellman documents the arrest of a St. Louis woman for sewing flags in *Inside War*, 43; while the arrest of two young girls in Huntsville for wearing flags on their skirts is recorded in a contemporary diary reproduced in Malcolm McMillan, *The Alabama Confederate Reader* (University: University of Alabama Press, 1952), 162.

19. Charles East, ed., *The Civil War Diary of Sarah Morgan* (Athens, Ga.: University of Georgia Press, 1991), 67–71; Drew Gilpin Faust explores Morgan's relationship to clothing in *Mothers of Invention: Women of the Slaveholding South in the American Civil War* (Chapel Hill: University of North Carolina Press, 1996), 220–23.

20. *Richmond Dispatch*, February 4, 1862; *Savannah Morning News*, April 19, 1862, May 27, 1863. Punishment of children with rebel flags is addressed in "South Carolina," *The Confederate* (Mobile: n.p., 1863), 82–83.

21. *Mobile Advertiser and Register*, June 16, 1861; H. W. R. Jackson, *The Southern Women of the Second American Revolution* (Atlanta: Intelligencer Steam Press, 1863), 12, 14–15; *Savannah Morning News*, June 8, 1863; Fellman, *Inside War*, 46; Austin C. Stearns, ed., *Three Years with Company K* (Rutherford, N.J.: Fairleigh Dickinson University Press, 1976), 58–59, 208–9.

22. Civilian use of flags to gain the favor of enemy armies is seen in Kathleen A. Ernst, *Too Afraid to Cry: Maryland Civilians in the Antietam Campaign* (Mechanicsburg, Pa.: Stackpole Books, 1999), 112; and in J. G. de Routhac Hamilton, *The Papers of Randolph Abbott Shotwell* (Raleigh: North Carolina Historical Commission, 1929–36), 1:101. The quoted verse is from "The Flag of the South," *Charleston Mercury*, April 7, 1862.

23. John Greenleaf Whittier, "Barbara Frietchie," *Atlantic Monthly* 12 (September 1863): 495–97; for more on these circumstances, and the subsequent dispute about the facts, see Preble, *History of the Flag*, 482–91. Mark E. Neely, Jr., makes an important point that as a matter of policy, combatant and civilian distinctions remained crucial to how this war was fought, a theme that will be taken up in more depth below. See Neely's "Was the Civil War a Total War?" *Civil War History* 37 (March 1991).

24. *New Orleans Daily Crescent*, March 19, 1862; O.R., ser. 2, 1:863, 906. See also *Charleston Courier*, June 13, 1861; Mark E. Neely Jr., *Southern Rights: Political Prisoners*

and the Myth of Confederate Constitutionalism (Charlottesville: University Press of Virginia, 1999).

25. Thomas G. Dyer, *Secret Yankees: The Union Circle in Confederate Atlanta* (Baltimore: Johns Hopkins University Press, 1999), 160–61, 193–94, 288, 308.

26. *New York Herald*, March 9, 1862.

27. Suzanne L. Bunkers, ed., *The Diary of Caroline Seabury, 1854–1863* (Madison: University of Wisconsin Press, 1991), 107–9.

28. William Freehling, *The South versus the South: How Anti-Confederate Southerners Shaped the Course of the Civil War* (New York: Oxford University Press, 2001).

29. Frederick Douglass to Samuel J. May, August 30, 1861, quoted in Louis Masur, *". . . The Real War Will Never Get in the Books"* (New York: Oxford University Press, 1993), 105–6.

30. David Brion Davis, *The Problem of Slavery in Western Culture* (New York: Oxford University Press, 1966), 125–64; Thomas Jefferson, *Notes on the State of Virginia* (1787; reprint, Chapel Hill: University of North Carolina Press, 1954), 162–63; Robin Blackburn, *The Overthrow of Colonial Slavery, 1776–1848* (London: Verso, 1988), 265–92.

31. William Beattie, ed., *Life and Letters of Thomas Campbell* (London: Edward Moxon, 1849), 3:264. Abolitionists echoed this association as can be seen, for instance, in those remarks of Harriet Jacobs that appear in C. Peter Ripley et al., *The Black Abolitionist Papers* (Chapel Hill: University of North Carolina Press, 1992), 5:168–69.

32. *Weekly Anglo African*, April 27, 1861. The despair of the 1850s is explored in James Oliver Horton, "Defending the Manhood of the Race: The Crisis of Citizenship in Black Boston at Midcentury," in Martin H. Blatt, Thomas J. Brown, and Donald Yacovone, eds., *Hope and Glory: Essays on the Fifty-fourth Massachusetts Regiment* (Amherst: University of Massachusetts Press, 2001), 7–20.

33. *Charleston Mercury*, February 2, 1861. Among other examples, see *Charleston Mercury*, April 26, 1861; *Savannah Daily Morning News*, June 2, 1863; *Savannah Daily Republican*, May 30, 1863.

34. White Confederates' frustration in calculating their slaves' loyalties is explored in Leon Litwack, *Been in the Storm So Long: The Aftermath of Slavery* (New York: Knopf, 1979), 3–63; Michael Burlingame, ed., *Lincoln's Journalist: John Hay's Anonymous Writings for the Press, 1860–1864* (Carbondale: Southern Illinois University Press, 1998), 138–39.

35. *Weekly Anglo-African*, May 4, 1861; *Liberator*, October 18, December 27, 1861.

36. John Hope Franklin, *The Emancipation Proclamation* (New York: Doubleday, 1963), 89–128; *New York Times*, January 4, 1863; *Liberator*, January 16, 1863.

37. Willie Lee Rose provides an overview of this celebration in *Rehearsal for Reconstruction: The Port Royal Experiment* (Oxford: Oxford University Press, 1964), 195–98; while Eugene Genovese makes it the concluding scene of his aptly titled chapter "The Flag of Our Country," in *From Rebellion to Revolution: Afro-American Slave Revolts in the Making of the Modern World* (Baton Rouge: Louisiana State University Press, 1979). Of contemporary accounts, the most famous is that of Thomas Wentworth Higginson's journal, originally published in "Leaves from an Officer's Journal," *Atlantic Monthly* 14 (November–December 1864): 521–29, 740–48 and which later appeared as part of *Army Life in a Black Regiment* (Boston: Fields, Osgood and Co., 1870). More details of the day, especially of the multiple black responses, can be seen in Elizabeth Ware Pearson, ed., *Letters from Port Royal, Written at the Time of the Civil War* (Boston: W. B.

Clarke Co., 1906); Ray Allen Billington, ed., *The Journals of Charlotte Forten* (New York: Oxford University Press, 1988); *New York Herald,* January 7, 1863. This and the following paragraphs draw from all of these sources.

38. Higginson, "Leaves from an Officer's Journal," 529.

39. *Frank Leslie's Illustrated Weekly,* January 24, 1863. For the transformation of "God Save the King" in England, see Linda Colley, *Britons: The Forging of the Nation* (New Haven: Yale University Press, 1992), 43–44.

40. *New York Herald,* January 7, 1863; Ella Forbes, *African-American Women during the Civil War* (New York: Garland, 1998), 104–9; William Wells Brown, *The Negro in the American Rebellion, His Heroism and His Fidelity* (Boston: A. G. Brown and Co., 1880), 148–58; Edwin S. Redkey, ed., *A Grand Army of Black Men: Letters from African-American Soldiers in the Union Army, 1861–1865* (New York: Cambridge University Press, 1992), 90–91.

41. Ira Berlin et al., *The Black Military Experience* (New York: Cambridge University Press, 1982), 523–27 (carrying flag in to Georgia), 549 (capture of rebel colors), 416 ("petticoat" flag); Noah Andrew Trudeau, *Like Men of War: Black Troops in the Civil War, 1862–1865* (Boston: Little, Brown, 1998), 290–94.

42. Laurent Dubois, "'The Price of Liberty': Victor Hughes and the Administration of Freedom in Guadeloupe, 1794–1798," *William and Mary Quarterly* 56 (1999): 363–93; Peter M. Beattie, "Conscription versus Penal Servitude: Army Reform's Influence on the Brazilian State's Management of Social Control, 1870–1930," *Journal of Social History* 32 (1999): 847–59. Patriotism was probably not the primary motivation of those slaves who, late in the war, entered the Confederate army to escape from Virginia jails, an incident mentioned in Ervin Jordan, *Black Confederates and Afro-Yankees in Civil War Virginia* (Charlottesville: University Press of Virginia, 1995), 248.

43. Brown, *The Negro in the American Rebellion,* 157–58; G. E. Stephens in Ripley, *The Black Abolitionist Papers* 5:242–43; Dudley Taylor Cornish, *The Sable Arm: Black Troops in the Union Army* (New York, Longmans, Green, 1956).

44. *Weekly Anglo-African,* April 18, 1863, reprinted in Ripley, *Black Abolitionist Papers* 5:187–91.

45. Ira Berlin et al., *Slaves No More: Three Essays on Emancipation and the Civil War* (New York: Cambridge University Press, 1992), 203.

46. Hayne, "The Black Flag," in *Allan's Lone Star Ballads* (Galveston, Tex., 1874); for a more graphic verse portrayal of retaliatory war see S. Tackle Wallis, *The Guerillas: A Southern War Song* (Richmond, Va., 1862). *Charleston Mercury,* November 18, 22, 1861, August 2, 7, 1862, January 21, August 25, 1863, February 18, May 3, 1864; *Atlanta Southern Confederacy,* November 24, 1861.

47. O.R., ser. 1, 24:1, 2; ser. 1, 43:1, 480; ser. 1, 15:550; *Atlanta Southern Confederacy,* December 1, 1861.

48. J. G. Randall, *Constitutional Problems under Lincoln,* rev. ed. (Urbana: University of Illinois Press, 1963), 84–92. Neither Lincoln's dilemma nor his solution of unofficially treating rebels as legitimate enemies was unique, as Barbara Donagan has shown in "Atrocity, War Crime, and Treason in the English Civil War," *American Historical Review* 99 (October 1994): 1137–66.

49. *Savannah Morning News,* October 6, September 4, 1862, May 25, June 13, 1863.

50. Richard Shelly Hartigan, *Lieber's Code and the Law of War* (Chicago: Precedent Press, 1983), 38–41.

51. Ibid., 57, 64–65; an earlier Union order that promised "no quarter" to "savage-like" Confederates carrying Union flags or wearing Union uniforms appears in O.R., ser. 1, 23:2, 53–54. The controlled nature of the Civil War was seen both in the detailed regulation of battlefield protocol and in the commitment to distinguishing between soldiers and civilians, a theme that Mark E. Neely, Jr., presents in "Was the Civil War a Total War?"

52. Albert North Whitehead, *Symbolism: Its Meaning and Effect* (New York: Macmillan, 1927), 74–77; Richard Rollins, *The Damned Rebel Flags of the Rebellion* (Redondo Beach, Calif.: Rank and File Publications, 1997).

53. *Charleston Courier*, March 22, 1862; *Savannah Republican*, August 13, 1862; *Savannah Morning News*, May 10, July 14, 21, 1863; O.R., ser. 2, 1:161. For an especially well publicized case of misuse of a truce flag, which caused Union officials to hold Confederate civilians as hostages in response, see Neely, *The Fate of Liberty*, 152–55.

54. Barbara Ehrenreich, *Blood Rites: The Origins and History of the Passions of War* (New York: Metropolitan Books, 1997), 127.

55. Compare Robert Kerby, "Why the Confederacy Lost," *Review of Politics* 35 (July, 1973): 326–45, and Beringer et al., *Why the South Lost*, to Gallagher, *The Confederate War*.

56. John Rhodehamel and Louise Taper, eds., *"Right or Wrong, God Judge Me": The Writings of John Wilkes Booth* (Urbana: University of Illinois Press, 1997), 124–130.

Chapter Seven
CONQUERED BANNERS, FURLED AND UNFURLED

1. *Southern Illustrated News*, October 4, 1862.

2. O.R., ser. 1, 1:478–80; David Detzer, *Allegiance: Fort Sumter, Charleston, and the Beginning of the Civil War* (New York: Harcourt, 2001), 285–310. For a later instance of respect shown a Union flag during surrender, see Edward D. Jervey, ed., *Prison Life among the Rebels: Recollections of a Union Chaplain* (Kent, Ohio: Kent State University Press, 1990), 12–13.

3. Richard Barksdale Harwell, ed., *Kate: The Journal of a Confederate Nurse* (Baton Rouge: Louisiana State University Press, 1959), 199; *Savannah Morning News*, October 8, 1863; A. O. Abbott, *Prison Life in the South . . . during the Years 1864 and 1865* (New York, 1865), 22–23; William H. Runge, ed., *Four Years in the Confederate Artillery: The Diary of Private Henry Robinson Berkeley* (Chapel Hill: University of North Carolina Press, 1961), 76.

4. Les Jensen, "Medals and Decorations," in Paul Escott, ed., *The Encyclopedia of the Confederacy* (New York: Simon and Schuster, 1993), 1021–22; *Camden (S.C.) Confederate*, November 28, 1861; *Savannah Republican* July 3, 1862; O.R., ser. 1, 40:3, 759–60; ser. 1, 20:1, 673; ser. 1, 51:2 (suppl.), 756, 785; ser. 4, 3:571. Captured flags were also sent to state governors, as seen in Allen D. Candler, ed., *The Confederate Records of the State of Georgia* (Atlanta: C. P. Byrd, 1909–11), 2:550–551.

5. O.R., ser. 1, 1:566–67; 45:1, 260–61; Noah Andre Trudeau, *Like Men of War: Black Troops in the Civil War, 1862–1865* (Boston: Little, Brown, 1998), 82–85; O.R., ser. 1, 38:3, 557. After ripping the Confederate flag, Stevenson was briefly "knocked senseless by a piece of shell" and then "resumed his musket, though suffering severely, and fought with the utmost gallantry the remainder of the day."

6. O.R., ser. 1, 45:1, 410, 690. The details of capturing regimental flags is memorably described throughout Richard Rollins, *The Damned Red Flags of the Rebellion: The Confederate Battle Flag at Gettysburg* (Redondo Beach, Calif.: Rank and File Publications, 1997).

7. Rebecca Ansell Rose, *Colours of the Gray: An Illustrated Index of Wartime Flags from the Museum of the Confederacy's Collection* (Richmond, Va.: Museum of the Confederacy, 1998), 42; medals awarded for these appear in O.R., ser. 1, 46:1, 509.

8. O.R., ser. 3, 1:898; 42:2, 922.

9. O.R., ser. 1, 42:2, 954, 968; ser. 1, 46:2, 865.

10. John Kent Folmar, ed., *From that Terrible Field: Civil War Letters of James M. Williams, Twenty-first Alabama Infantry Volunteers* (University: University of Alabama Press, 1981), 50; George D. Harmon, "Letters of Luther Rice Mills—A Confederate Soldier," *North Carolina Historical Review* 4 (July 1927), 303–8; Charles Nordhoff, "Two Weeks at Port Royal," *Harper's New Monthly Magazine* 27 (June 1863): 118.

11. John Esten Cooke, *Mohun; or, The Last Days of Lee and His Paladins* (Richmond, Va., 1867), 140–45; John Esten Cooke, *Wearing of the Gray* (1867; reprint, Bloomington: Indiana University Press, 1959), 375.

12. *Richmond Examiner* quoted in *Charleston Mercury*, January 12, 1864.

13. "The Confederate Flag," in *Montgomery Weekly Advertiser*, February 10, 1864; "The Rally," in *Richmond Sentinel*, March 4, 1865; John Hill Hewitt, "The Confederate Flag," in *Richmond Evening Courier*, March 29, 1865.

14. James I. Robertson, Jr., ed., *One of Jackson's Foot Calvary* (Jackson, Tenn.: McCowat-Mercer Press, 1964), 182; *The Flag of the First Regiment, South Carolina Regular Artillery* (Charleston, S.C., 1893), 8.

15. John N. Edwards, *Shelby and His Men; Or, the War in the West* (Cincinnati, Ohio: Miami Printing, 1867), 546–51. For a flag buried in the waters of the Appomattox River see "Historical Sketch of the Forty-fourth N.C. Infantry" *SHSP* 25 (1897): 344–45.

16. Gaines Foster discusses the context and impact of Ryan's poem in *Ghosts of the Confederacy: Defeat, the Lost Cause and the Emergence of the New South* (New York: Oxford University Press, 1987), 36; a more sensational account can be found in "Origin of the Conquered Banner" *Confederate Veteran* 5 (1897): 436–37. The poem, widely reprinted, can be found in Abraham Joseph Ryan, *Poems: Patriotic, Religious, Miscellaneous* (Baltimore: John B. Piet, 1880).

17. Ryan, "The City of the Dead," in *Poems*, 83; Foster, *Ghosts of the Confederacy*, 36–46; David Blight, *Race and Reunion: The Civil War in American Memory* (Cambridge: Harvard University Press, 2001), 64–97.

18. A. J. Requier, "Ashes of Glory," in William Gilmore Simms, ed., *War Poems of the South* (New York: Richardson and Company, 1867), 480–82; Col. A. M. Hobby, "Our Dead," in Emily V. Mason, ed., *The Southern Poems of the War* (Baltimore: John Murphy and Company, 1867), 440–42; J. C. M., "Cruci Dum Spiro, Fido," in Mason, *Southern Poems*, 384. For more on the religious nature of the Lost Cause, see Lloyd A. Hunter, "The Immortal Confederacy: Another Look at Lost Cause Religion," in Gary Gallagher and Alan T. Nolan, eds., *The Lost Cause and Civil War History* (Bloomington: Indiana University Press, 2000), 185–218; and Charles Reagan Wilson, *Baptized in Blood: The Religion of the Lost Cause, 1865–1920* (Athens: University of Georgia Press, 1980).

19. H. L Flash, "The Confederate Flag," *Crescent Monthly* 1 (May 1866): 176. John Coski makes this connection between flags and mourning in his very helpful "Confederate Battle Flag in Historical Perspective," in J. Michael Martinez, William D. Richardson, and Ron McNinch-Su, eds. *Confederate Symbols in the Contemporary South* (Gainesville: University of Florida Press, 2000), 89–129.

20. Julia Ward Howe, "The Flag," *Atlantic Monthly* 11 (April 1863): 443–44; Mary Elizabeth Massey, *Bonnet Brigades* (New York, Knopf, 1966), 177; *Richmond New Nation,* August 16, 1866.

21. George Henry Preble, *The History of the Flag of the United States* (Boston: A. Williams and Co., 1880), 480; Nina Silber, *The Romance of Reunion: Northerners and the South, 1865–1900* (Chapel Hill: University of North Carolina Press, 1993), 26–28, 111–12, 165–66; George C. Rable, *Civil Wars: Women and the Crisis of Southern Nationalism* (Urbana: University of Illinois Press, 1989), 226–30, 360–61; Katharine M. Jones, *When Sherman Came: Southern Women and the "Great March"* (Indianapolis, Ind.: Bobbs-Merrill, 1964), 91, 101; Edward L. Ayers, *The Promise of the New South: Life after Reconstruction* (New York: Oxford University Press), 332.

22. Preble, *History of the Flag*, 531; Louisa Wigfall Wright, *A Southern Girl in '61* (New York: Doubleday, Page, 1905), 249–50; "The Flag of Tears," *Confederate Veteran* 6 (1903): 249–50; Alice Fahs, "The Feminized Civil War: Gender, Northern Popular Literature, and the Memory of the War, 1861–1900" *Journal of American History* 84 (March 1999): 1461–94; Foster, *Ghosts of the Confederacy*, 116–17, 172–79; Blight, *Race and Reunion*, 272–84.

23. Carlton McCarthy, "Origin of the Confederate Battle-Flag," *SHSP* 8 (1880): 497; McCarthy's article was originally given as a speech in December 1878.

24. Pollard quoted in *Richmond Southern Opinion*, February 22, 1868.

25. *The Easter Fair of the Washington Light Infantry* (Charleston, S.C.: News and Courier Press, 1875), 9; Benjamin H. Hill, "The Stars and Stripes," in *Senator Benjamin H. Hill of Georgia: His Life, Speeches, and Writings* (Atlanta: T. H. P. Bloodworth, 1891), 461–72.

26. Foster, *Ghosts of the Confederacy,* 146–48; Silber, *Romance of Reunion,* 178–85.

27. On veterans, see R. B. Rosenburg, *Living Monuments: Confederate Soldiers' Homes in the New South* (Chapel Hill: University of North Carolina Press, 1993); Emma Eve Gardner, "To the Stars and Bars," *Confederate Veteran* 22 (1915): 248.

28. Sarah A. Tillinghast, "Answer to the Conquered Banner," in *War Days in Fayetteville, North Carolina* (Fayetteville, N.C.: Fayetteville Printing Company, 1910), 59. For efforts to make the flag story a part of Confederate civics, see M. Jemison Chestney, *The Service of the Confederate Flags* (Macon, Ga., 1926); and Tony Horwitz, *Confederates in the Attic: Dispatches from the Unfinished Civil War* (New York: Pantheon, 1998), 23–24. See also Eron Opha Gregory, "The Returned Battle Flags," in *The Returned Battle Flags*; Grace Emma Gish, "Flag of Their Glory," *Confederate Veteran* 24 (1917): 64; Miss Katherine Davis, "The Confederate Flag," *Confederate Veteran* 29 (1921): 82.

29. Blight, *Race and Reunion*, 140–210.

30. *New York Tribune*, May 26, 27, 1861; *Congressional Globe*, 37th Cong., 2nd sess. 912; *Christian Recorder*, March 1, 1862, 89; Preble, *History of the Flag*, 582–88; Nannie M. Tilley, *Federals on the Frontier: The Diary of Benjamin F. McIntyre* (Austin: University of Texas Press, 1963), 89.

31. Joshua Chamberlain, *The Passing of the Armies*, ed. Brooks Simpson (Lincoln: University of Nebraska Press 1998), 260–62.

32. Chris M. Calkins, *The Final Bivouac: The Surrender Parade at Appomattox and the Disbanding of the Armies* (Lynchburg, Va.: H. E. Howard, 1988); Cooke, *Wearing of the Gray*, 563. See also J. Tracy Power, *Lee's Miserables: Life in the Army of Northern Virginia from the Wilderness to Appomattox* (Chapel Hill: University of North Carolina Press, 1988), 283–85; and William Marvel, *A Place Called Appomattox,* (Chapel Hill: University of North Carolina Press, 2000), 259–66, 358–59.

33. In addition to the celebrated appearance of Chamberlain's account in Ken Burns's Civil War PBS television series it also appears in Wiley Sword, *Southern Invincibility: A History of the Confederate Heart* (New York: St. Martin's Press, 1999), 335–36; Bertram Wyatt-Brown, *The Shaping of Southern Culture: Honor, Grace, and War, 1760s–1890s* (Chapel Hill: University of North Carolina Press, 2001), ix–xi; and Jay Winik, *April 1865: The Month that Saved America* (HarperCollins, 2001), 196–98.

34. Herman Melville, *Battle-Pieces and Other Aspects of the War* (New York, 1866), 144–45; a similar appeal can be seen in Cooke, *Wearing of the Grey*, 375.

35. Silber, *Romance of Reunion*, 13–38; *Harper's Weekly*, May 20, 1865; Mark E. Neely, Jr., Harold Holzer, and Gabor S. Boritt, *The Confederate Image: Prints of the Lost Cause* (Chapel Hill: University of North Carolina Press, 1987), 68–72.

36. For the theme of buttons and uniforms, see R. J. M. Blackett, ed., *Thomas Morris Chester, Black Civil War Correspondent: His Dispatches from the Virginia Front* (Baton Rouge: Louisiana State University Press, 1989), 364; Myrta Lockett Avary, *Dixie After the War* (Boston: Houghton Mifflin Company, 1937), 123–24; and the series of poems in Mason, *The Southern Poems of the War*, 387–405.

37. [Charles Henry Smith], *Bill Arp's Peace Papers* (New York: Carleton, 1873); Raymond Firth, *Symbols, Public and Private* (Ithaca: Cornell University Press, 1974), 354. John Coski's extensive research on this issue has established few instances of federal suppression of Confederate emblems. See "The Confederate Battle Flag in Historical Perspective," 100–101.

38. Blight, *Race and Reunion*, 81–82; Jeffrey D. Mason, *Melodrama and the Myth of America* (Bloomington: Indiana University Press, 1993), 155–87. GAR information from Wallace Evans Davis, *Patriotism on Parade: The Story of Veterans' and Hereditary Organizations in America, 1783–1900* (Cambridge: Harvard University Press 1955), 257–60, 265. For a similarly negative response by Northern newspapers to the display of flags in 1890, see Blight, *Race and Reunion*, 296.

39. H. M. Clarkson, "The Southern Flags," newspaper clipping dated 1887 in United Daughters of the Confederacy scrapbook, MOC; A. H. Markland to Jefferson Davis in Dunbar Rowland, ed., *Jefferson Davis, Constitutionalist* (Jackson: Mississippi Department of Archives and History, 1923), 9:571–72; H. L. Blanchard, "Our Battle Flag," *Confederate Veteran* 1 (1893); Other descriptions of the battle flag issue appear in Stuart McConnell, *Glorious Contentment: The Grand Army of the Republic, 1865–1900* (Chapel Hill: University of North Carolina Press, 1992); Silber, *Romance of Reunion*, 98; and Carol Reardon, *Pickett's Charge in History and Memory* (Chapel Hill: University of North Carolina Press, 1997), 96–98.

40. "The Confederate Flag," *Confederate Veteran* 3 (1895): 353–54; John Manly Richardson, "Exaltation of the Confederate Banner," *Confederate Veteran* 1 (1893): 48; Ransom W. Davenport, "Patriotism of the South," *Confederate Veteran* 18 (1910): 121.

41. John Howard Jewett, "Those Rebel Flags," in Lois Hill, *Poems and Songs of the Civil War* (New York: Gramercy Press, 1990), 187–88; Richard Rollins, ed., *The Returned Battle Flags* (Redondo Beach, Calif.: Rank and File Publications, 1995), i–iv; Fred. A. Cambell, "Let It Wave!" broadside dated 1907 in United Daughters of the Confederacy scrapbook, MOC.

42. "The Story of a Star," *Confederate Veteran* 23 (1916): 499; similar imagery appears at the end of Albert Sidney Morton, "To a Confederate Battle Flag," *Confederate Veteran* 1 (1893): 175.

43. Stephen Crane, *The Red Badge of Courage* (1895: reprint, New York: Dover Thrift, 1990), 24; last quote from Susan Williams Benson, ed., *Berry Benson's Civil War Book: Memoirs of a Confederate Scout and Sharpshooter* (Athens: University of Georgia Press, 1992), 28; Cecilia O'Leary, *To Die For: The Paradox of American Patriotism* (Princeton: Princeton University Press, 1999), 129–49.

44. Rollins, *The Damned Red Flags of the Rebellion,* 106. For more on the Gettysburg reunion see Blight, *Race and Reunion*, 383–90; and O'Leary, *To Die For*, 194–205.

45. Blight, *Race and Reunion*, 3, 57.

46. Ibid., 132; Hill, "The Stars and Stripes," 470; quotation from E. L. Godkin, cited in Blight, *Race and Reunion*, 138.

47. Ulrich B. Phillips, "The Central Theme of Southern History," *American Historical Review* 34 (October 1923): 30–43. The monuments that also date from this period are superbly analyzed by Kirk Savage, *Standing Soldiers, Kneeling Slaves: Race, War, and Monument in Nineteenth-Century America* (Princeton: Princeton University Press, 1997), 129–61.

48. "Blood brotherhood" is coined in O'Leary, *To Die For*, 129–49; Douglass quoted in Philip S. Foner and Robert James Branham, *Lift Every Voice: African-American Oratory, 1787–1900* (Tuscaloosa: University of Alabama Press, 1998), 413; "Novice," *Taking the Oath, a Poem* (Augusta, Ga.: Constitutionalist Office, 1865); Semmes quoted in Preble, *History of the Flag*, 509–10.

49. James Mc.C. Simpson, "Let the Banner Proudly Wave," in *The Emancipation Car, Being an Original Composition of Anti-Slavery Ballads* (1874; reprint, Miami, Fla.: Mnemosyne Publishing, 1974), 144; Adams quoted in Foner and Branham, *Lift Every Voice*, 461. For more on black patriotism in the immediate postbellum period, see Blight, *Race and Reunion*, 65–77; and Kathleen Clark, "Celebrating Freedom: Emancipation Day Celebrations and African American Memory in the Early Reconstruction South," in Fitzhugh Brundage, *Where These Memories Grow: History, Memory and Southern Identity* (Chapel Hill: University of North Carolina Press, 2000), 107–32.

50. Quotations from Edwin S. Redkey, ed., *Respect Black: The Writings and Speeches of Henry McNeal Turner* (New York: Arno Press, 1971), 11, 60.

51. Booker T. Washington, *Up from Slavery* (New York: Doubleday, 1901), 252–53; Du Bois quotation from William H. Wiggins, Jr., *O Freedom! Afro-American Emancipation Celebrations* (Knoxville: University of Tennessee Press, 1987), 59; Wiggins's book provides a good overview of recent African American celebrations and the centrality of American flags at such events. Tony Horwitz develops the notion of the twin heroic periods of the Civil War and the Civil Rights movement in *Confederates in the Attic*, 359–78.

52. Coski, "The Confederate Battle Flag," 109–12; J. Michael Martinez, "Traditionalist Perspectives on the Confederate Flag," in Martinez, Richardson, and McNinch-Su,

Confederate Symbols in the Contemporary South, 243–80. Current disputes are thoughtfully explored in Sanford Levinson, *Written in Stone: Public Monuments in Changing Societies* (Raleigh, N.C.: Duke University Press, 1998); and Ernest B. Furgurson, "Recalling History," *Preservation* 49 (1997): 62–67. A narrower and less persuasive approach is presented in George Schedler, *Racist Symbols and Reparations: Philosophical Reflections on Vestiges of the American Civil War* (Lanham, Md.: Rowman and Littlefield, 1998).

53. Charles Reagan Wilson, "Uniting the Symbols of Southern Culture," in *Judgment and Grace in Dixie* (Athens: University of Georgia Press, 1995), 159–63; and James C. Cobb, "Searching for Southerness: Identity and Community in the Contemporary South, in *Redefining Southern Culture* (Athens: University of Georgia Press, 1999), 125–49; Elasar Barkhan, *The Guilt of Nations: Restitution and Negotiating Historical Injustices* (New York: W. W. Norton, 2000), 248–51.

54. Jack Hitt, "Confederate Chic," *Gentleman's Quarterly* 67 (November 1997): 261–70; Robert Bonner, "Transforming a Flag—And Its Meaning," *Los Angeles Times*, January 20, 2000. In several respects, the NuSouth initiative recalls the countermonuments of Holocaust concentration camps, which are discussed in Claudia Koonz, "Between Memory and Oblivion: Concentration Camps in German Memory," in John R. Gillis, ed., *Commemorations: The Politics of National Identity* (Princeton: Princeton University Press), 258–80.

INDEX

Page references in italics indicate an illustration.

Adams, Rev. E. J., 175
African Americans: attachment to U.S. and regiment flags by, 145, *146*, 147–48; celebrating Emancipation Proclamation (1863), *142*, 143; distrust of U.S. flag by, 140–41; emotional response to rebel flag by, 1–2; fight for Stars and Stripes/freedom by, 7; Fort Pillow incident and, 150; gradual embrace of Union patriotism by, 141–48; issues of patriotic allegiances of, 139–40; Ku Klux Klan campaign against, 170; NuSouth clothing aimed at, 177–78, 212n.54; patriotic conventions linking Union/black freedom by, 175–77; singing of patriotic hymns by, 144–45; white reconciliation (late-19th century) and, 174–75. *See also* slavery
Alexander, Henry C., 117
"all-seeing eye" symbolism, 25, 29
American Revolution, 25–26, 27
Anderson, Rev. William J., 131
Anderson, Robert, 13, 154
Andrew, John A., 145
Appomattox surrender, 168, 169–70, 171

Bagby, George, 98, 100, 103, 104, 106, 123
Baltimore flag disputes, 132, 133
"Barbara Frietchie" lyric (Whittier), 136–37
Bartow, Francis, 79
Bates, Gilbert H., 165
battle of Buena Vista (1847), 11, *12*, 18
"Battle Cry of Freedom" (Root), 130, 131
battlefield poetry. *See* poetry
battle of First Bull Run, 87, 94
battle flags: African American attachment to U.S./regiment, 145, *146*, 147–48;

Appomattox surrender and captured, 168–70, *169*, 171; with battle scars, 158–59; and Confederate consolidation, 122–23; constructed by female patriots, 86–87; controversy over returning southern, 171–74, *173*; display of captured, 156; engagements listed directly on, *157*, 158; illustration of women presenting, *87*; military significance of surrendering, 151, 155–58; newspaper attacks against rebel, 131; passions unleashed by, 67–68; patriotism through civilian use of, 131–35; poetry written about, 93–94, 117, 118, 159–60, 162, 171, *172*; regiment, *76-77*; St. Andrew's cross of Scotland, 103, 108–9; saved from capture during surrenders, 160; standardbearers and, 88, *89*, 90–91; wartime conventions governing capture of, 156–58. *See also* Confederate flags; Stars and Stripes flag
battle of Milvian Bridge (Roman Empire), 98
battle of Shiloh, 87
Bear Flag (California), 21, 35
Beauregard, P.G.T., 15, 82, 83–84, 85, 86, 87, 103, 108, 109, 154–55
Benjamin, Judah, 113
Bible symbolism, 24, 98, 100
black flag controversy, 148–52
Black Flag Riflemen of New Orleans, 149
Blight, David, 174
blood sacrifice/death. *See* martyrdoms
"bloody shirt" metaphors, 170
"Blue and the Gray" cloth metaphors, 170
Blunt, Ellen Key, 63–64
"Bonnie Blue Flag" (song), 30–31, *32*, 33
Booth, John Wilkes, 152

Boutheneau, Julia, 46, 47, 48
Boyce, W. W., 47
Breckinridge, Mrs. John C., 86
Brisbane, David, 143
Brooke, Walker, 41–42, 43, 45, 53
Brown, Albert Gallatin, 107
Brown, Henry Kirke, 48, 49
Brown, John, 69, 140, 165
Buchanan, James, 13
Butler, Benjamin, 132, 133

Campbell, Thomas, 140
captured battle flags: Appomattox surren-
    der and, 168–70, *169*, 171; contro-
    versy over return of southern, 171–74,
    173; military significance of surren-
    dering and, 151, *155*-58; southern col-
    ors saved from being, 160; wartime
    conventions governing, 156–58
Carlyle, Thomas, 67–68
Carney, James, 156, 176
Carpenter, Mary, 50
Cary, Constance, 83–84
Cary, Hetty, 83–84
Cary, Jenny, 83–84
Chamberlain, Joshua, 168, 169
Charleston Harbor battle (1776), 25
Charleston Harbor stand-off (1861), 13,
    34–35, 59
Chesnut, Mary, 55
Christianity: Confederacy associated
    with, 118; Jewish concerns on state
    linked to, 101–2, 104. *See also* cross
    symbolism; religious symbolism
Christy's Minstrels (blackface entertain-
    ers group), 31
"The City of the Dead" (Ryan), 162
civilians: battle flags constructed by fe-
    male, 86–87; Confederate flag design
    role by, 46–47*t*; flag clashes involving,
    132–33; flag culture role by female,
    77–82, *78*; flag disputes involving
    southern female, 133–37, *134*,
    204n.18; going outside "civilized" war
    code, 152; introduction into flag cul-
    ture of, 87–88; patriotism through flag
    display by, 131–35; Reconstruction Pe-

riod "ceremonial bereavement" by,
    162–64; relationship between Confed-
    erate army and, 118–19. *See also* Mar-
    shall House Affair (1861)
Civil Rights movement: association of
    Stars and Stripes with, 176; mobilized
    by rebel flag, 7; success of, 1
Civil War: community-forming media
    evolution during, 22–24, *23*; conven-
    tions governing capture of flags dur-
    ing, 156–58; firing on Stars and
    Stripes as beginning of, 68; functions
    of Confederate flags during, 153–54;
    Lieber's code of war (1863) during,
    150–51; "melodramatic mode" during,
    6; sentimental culture of, 4–5; war
    flag rules consensus during, 148–52.
    See also Confederacy; flag culture;
    Union states
Clay, C. C., 113
Clay, Henry, Jr., *12*
Cleveland, Grover, 171
color-bearers, 88, *89*, 90–91
Confederacy: army/civilian relationship
    in, 118–19; Christianity linked to,
    118; consolidation of unity in, 120–
    23; flag displays by Unionists in, 136–
    39; impact of new flag on, 55–56, 58;
    latent feelings for American symbols
    in, 41–43; rattlesnake/serpent symbol-
    ism and, 127; response to growing
    Stars and Stripes flag displays by, 59–
    60; Southern Cross flag officially
    adopted (1863) by, 108; special sea
    status of naval forces, 35; state flags
    of, 28–30, 35–36. *See also* Civil War;
    Confederate nationality; Union states
Confederate flag controversies: on being
    returned to south, 171–74, *173*; focus
    of current, 96; during the 1990s, 1;
    significance of, 1–2
Confederate flag culture: and wartime
    consolidation, 120–23; distinct stages/
    emblems of, 5–6; female role in local,
    77–82, *78*; feminine aspects of, 80–81,
    135–37; first manifestations of, 20–21;
    impact of American flag culture on,

17–18; introduction of civilians into, 87–88; Marshall House Affair (1861) and, 68–74, *71*, 131; melodramatic features of, 6; political community involvement in, 15, 17; postwar characterization/rituals of, 4; postwar vision of past and, 154; role of southern newspapers in, 23–24; totem rituals associated with, 75-76, 81–82; values/ code of honor represented by, 6; wartime characterization/rituals of, 3–4; wartime functions of, 153–54. *See also* flag culture; Lost Cause tradition

Confederate flag designs: cross symbolism in proposed, 97, *99*; Davis' interest in, 14–15; debate over color scheme/stripes of, 52–53; debate over star metaphor in, 51–52; entries including cross symbolism in, 97; as evidence of fragile nationalism, 53–54; female participation in, 46–47*t*; housed in National Archives, 45–46; identifiable petitioners of, 47*t*-48; international influence on, 109, 111; Lieber's examination/response to, 126–27; newspaper reports on, 54, 189n.15, 199n.21; petitions/actions taken (1861–63) on, 104*t*; religious symbolism of Southern Cross, 96–97; slavery symbolism in, 48–49; submitted to Montgomery Congress, 52*t*; variety of proposed, 48–54

Confederate flags: Appomattox surrender and captured, 168–70, *169*, 171; association between slavery and, 130, 154, 178; controversy during 1990s over, 1; cross symbolism used in, 97-*99*, 100–104, 108–9; display of captured, 156; female-led "ceremonial bereavement" and, 162–64; focus of current controversies over, 96; illustration of women presenting, *87*; modern commercialization of, 177–78; saved from capture during surrenders, 160; scholarship on diversity of, 200n.29; significance of controversies over, 1–2. *See also* battle flags; Southern Cross

flag; Stainless Banner flag; Stars and Bars flag

"The Confederate Flag" (Wright), 164

Confederate nationalism: claims of distinctiveness and, 2–3; derivative nature of Confederate flag design and, 53–54; examining emotional dimensions of, 3; musical element of, 61–66. *See also* Confederacy; nationalism

Confederate Provisional Congress (1861): Brooke and Miles exchange during, 41–43; call to create national flag during, 41–42; Confederate seals suggestions during, 111–12; flag designs submitted to, 45–54, 47*t*, *50*, 52*t*, *99*; flag presentations during, 43, *44*, 45; issues facing, 40–41; Jewish concerns related to, 101–2

Confederate seal: casting of, 115; selection of designs for, 109, *110–11*, 112–14; selection of motto/emblems for, 114

Confederate symbolism: cross, 97-*99*, 100–104, 108–9; modern commercialization of, 177–78; pollution and purity, 81; postwar reconciliation by Unionists and, 167–74; proposed flag designs with slavery, 48–49, 98, 100; during Reconstruction Period, 163, 164–65; secession, 24–37, 187n.39. *See also* flag symbolism; symbols/symbolism

"The Conquered Banner" (print), *161*

"Conquered Banner" (Ryan), 160, 162, 167

consolidation of Confederacy, 120–23

Constantine, 98, 100, 117, 145

Cooke, John Esten, 95, 158–59, 168

Crane, Stephen, 172

cross symbolism: association between Christianity and, 97–98; growing prominence of, 119–20; Jewish concerns with, 101–2, 104; in Montgomery Congress flag designs, 97, *99*; patriotic martyrdoms testimony using, 117–18; St. Andrew's cross of Scotland, 103, 108–9; slavery controversy

cross symbolism (*cont'd*)
  and, 98, 100. *See also* Christianity;
  religious symbolism
Curtis, Samuel, 132

Daniel, John, 103, 104, 112, 114, 123
Danton, Georges Jacques, 21
Daughters of the Confederacy, 167
Davis, Jefferson: Beauregard transferred
  by, 85; commitment to Stars and
  Stripes, 11; political consolidation
  condemned by, 120–21; depicted in
  petticoats by Northern illustrators,
  170; as "Jefferson Davis on His Stand"
  (print) subject, *17*; as Mexican War
  hero, 11, *12*; Mississippi legislation
  speeches (1858) by, 11–12; on Mumford execution, 133; presidential inaugural of, 113–14; regarding disposal of
  captured flags, 156; role in selecting
  Confederate flag design, 14–15; satanic depiction by Union, 128; selected as Confederate president, 45;
  Senate speech (1861) by, 12–14, 19;
  on shift of flag allegiances, 15; foray
  into history of U.S. flag by, 8–9; as
  "The Traitor's Dream" (lithography)
  subject, *16*
Davis, Varina, 18
death/blood sacrifice. *See* martyrdoms
DeBow, Frank, 36, 37
DeBow, James B. D., 26, 51, 101
"Deo Vindice" motto (Confederate seal),
  114, 115, 116, 200n.40
Dew, Charles, 49
"Dixie" (song), 30, 31, 61
Dix, James A., 132
Douglass, Frederick, 139, 140, 174, 175
Drake, Charles, 128
Du Bois, W.E.B., 176
Durkheim, Emile, 75–76
Dyer, Thomas, 137

Elder, Susan, 65
Ellsworth, Elmer, 68, 70–74, *71*, 167
Emancipation Proclamation celebration
  (1863), *142, 143*

"Ethnogenesis" (Timrod), 34
Evans, Augusta Jane, 24
Everett, Edward, 58–59

Fahs, Alice, 6
Farragut, David, 133
Fate of the Rebel Flag, 128
Faust, Drew, 3, 92
Fifty-fourth Massachusetts Regiment
  monument (1897), 176
"fight for the flag" mentality, 59
Fitzhugh, George, 121
flag culture: Civil War patriotism expressed through, 125–26; female role
  in local, 77–82, *78*; feminine aspects
  of, 80–81; "fight for the flag" mentality
  and, 59; insights from examining
  Civil War, 7; introduction of civilians
  into, 87–88; hopes for sectional reconciliation through, 163; passions unleashed by battle flags, 67–68; patriotic bloodshed associations of, 67–68,
  79; poetry celebrating, 65, 66, 73, 79,
  81; role of southern newspapers in
  forming Civil War, 23–24; totem
  rituals associated with, 75-76, 81–82;
  white flag of truce element of, 151–
  52. *See also* Confederate flag culture;
  martial flag culture; Stars and Stripes
  flag culture
flag disputes: involving civilians, 132–
  33; involving southern Unionists,
  136–39; involving southern women,
  133–37, *134,* 204n.18; Marshall
  House Affair (1861) as defining moment of, 68–74, *71,* 131
flag emblems: Civil War consensus regarding rules of, 148–52; controversy
  over black flag, 148–52; Marshall
  House Affair (1861) over, 68–74, *71,*
  131; modern commercialization of
  rebel, 177–78; postwar reconciliation
  and Confederate, 167–74; as quasi-religious totems, 72–73; word messages
  included in, 76–77
"The Flag" (Howe), 163
flag poetry. *See* poetry

flag presentation ceremonies: direction reversed in the case of trophy flags, 158; evoked in Beauregard's introduction of Stars and Bars, 83–84; in local communities, 74–82; at military encampments, 86–87; at state secession conventions, 33

"The Flag of the South" (song), *63*

flag symbolism: American use of, 19–20; Civil War consensus regarding rules of, 148–52; as communication medium, 21–22; contributions to patriotism/political conviction by, 60; cross, 97-99, 100–104, 108–9; design impact on emotional appeal of, 30–35; Gettysburg fiftieth anniversary celebration and, 172–74; impact of French Revolution on American, 26–27; Jasper's cult as part of 19th century, 26; newspaper reports on secession, 20, 21–24, *23*, 29; newspaper reports on significance of, 107; pollution and purity, 81; relations between local/national community and, 86–87; representing Ark of the Covenant, 102; during secession period, 9–11, 19–20. *See also* Confederate symbols; symbols/symbolism

Fort Moultrie, 70, 90

Fort Pillow incident, 150

Fort Sumter, 13, 30, 40, 56, 58, 59, 68

Franklin, Benjamin, 127

Freitchie, Barbara, 163

French, L. Virginia, 103

Fussell, Paul, 80

Gallagher, Gary, 3, 118, 120

Gaston, F., 48

German Turner Association (Richmond), 137

Gettysburg fiftieth anniversary celebration, 172–74

Gilchrist, Robert, 45, 46

Girard, René, 118

Grant, U.S., 170

Great Britain: Confederate belligerent status granted by, 35; "fight for the flag" battles fought by, 59

Greeley, Horace, 170

Hamilton, Schuyler, 8, 9, 11, 13

Hammond, James Henry, 36, 37

Hardee, William, 109

Harpers Ferry raid, 140

Hayes, Rutherford B., 35

Hayne, Paul Hamilton, 148

Hearn, Anna K., 63

Hewitt, John H., 31–32, 65, 92

Higginson, Thomas Wentworth, 143, 144

Hill, Benjamin H., 165, 174

"The History of Our Flag" (song), 64

Holcombe, Henry, 73

Holmes, George Frederick, 121

Hood, John Bell, 156–57

Hotze, Henry, 109

Howe, Julia Ward, 163

Hughes, Henry, 121

"Hymn to the National Flag" (Preston), 117

Ingle, James, 72

Jackson, Andrew, 10, 116

Jackson, James William, 68–74, *71*, 95, 131, 133, 168

Jackson, Thomas J. "Stonewall," 94–95, 137, 171

James Gray incident, 34

Jasper, William, 25–26, 27-28, 70, 90

Jewish population: concerns over flag cross symbolism by, 101–2; dismissal of concerns by, 104

Jim Crow institutions, 174–75

Johnston, Joseph, 82

Junkin, Rev. George, 117

Keegan, John, 90

Keitt, Laurence, 46

Kellogg, Robert, 122, 123

Kemper, James, 171

Key, Francis Scott, 9, 60, 61, 63, 64
Ku Klux Klan, 170

Ladd, Mrs. C., 46, 47
Lanier, Sidney, 5
Lee, Robert E.: headquarters flag designed by, 102; editorial praise of, 94; regarding disposal of captured flags, 156; and state allegiance of, 11; sword offered to Grant by, 170
Libby Prison, 156
Lieber, Francis, 49, 126–27, 150
Lieber's code of war (1863), 150–51
Lincoln, Abraham: announces plans to free slaves under rebel control, 142; assassination of, 152; Confederate flag ceremony and office taking by, 54; inaugural address of, 55; *James Gray* incident following election of, 34–35; reassurances made to loyal southern masters by, 140; reelection of, 159; secession banners following election of, 24; southern concerns regarding election of, 11
Lincoln, Mary Todd, 70
Lone Star flag (Texas), 21, 28
Lost Cause tradition: Carys sisters as heroines of the, 84; Confederate symbolism and, 163, 164–65; female-led "ceremonial bereavement" defining, 162–64; illustrated expression of, *161*; impact of Southern Cross commercialization on, 177; poetry expressing the, 160, 162–63, 164, 167; postwar rehabilitation of Southern Cross and, 164–65; rebel emblems framed within U.S. patriotism, *173*; as Reconstruction flag culture, 7. *See also* Confederate flag culture

Macarthy, Harry, 30, 31, *32*, 64
Macarthy, Lottie Estelle, 31, *32*
McCabe, John, 62–63
McCarthy, Carlton, 164
McKerall, Louisa, 74
McMaster, Francis, 101
Maimi, M. L., 147–48

"Marseillaise" (song), 30, 31
Marshall House Affair (1861), 68–74, *71*, 131
martial flag culture: battlefield inscriptions on flags and, *157-58*; battle flags with scars, 158–59; flag capturing conventions of, 156–58; newspaper article reporting on, 159; poetry on shared, 170; on saving battle flags from capture, 160; warrior class formed through, 154–55. *See also* battle flags; military forces
martyrdoms: cross flag testimonies on, 117–18; flag culture association with, 67–68, 79, 92–93; illustration of color-bearer, *89*; Marshall House Affair (1861), 68–74, *71*, 131; soldier incentive provided through, 97–98; of standardbearers, 90–92; of William Jasper, 25–26, *27-28*, 70, 90; women's flag-waving compared to soldier, 135–37. *See also* military forces; patriotism
Marvin, Caroline, 72
Meek, A. B., 118
Melville, Herman, 170
Memminger, Christopher, 98, 100
Mexican War, 10–11
Miles, William Porcher, 15, 41, 42, 43, 45, 49, 82, 102–3, 109
military forces: African Americans in Union, 145, *146*, 147–48; Lieber's code of war (1863) during, 150–51; loyalty to U.S. flag by southern veterans of, 164–66; saving battle flags from capture, 160; significance of battle flag surrender by, 151, *155-58*; standardbearers of, 88, *89*, 90–92; Union prisoners of war, *155*; war flag rules consensus during, 148–52; wartime conventions governing capture of flags by, 156–58. *See also* battle flags; martial flag culture; martyrdoms
Mitchell, Maggie, 31, 37
Moise, Charles, 101–2
"moistening" practice, 30
Montgomery Congress. *See* Confederate Provisional Congress (1861)

Morgan, Sarah, 133–35
Morse, Samuel B., 127–28
Moses, Myer, 102
Moultrie, William, 25
Mumford, William, 133
music: African Americans and patriotic, 144–45; association between Confederate flags/nationalism and, 60–66; association between U.S. flag and, 9, 60; melodramatic scenes expressed through, 92–93; used during "moistening" practice, 30; expressing southern farewells to U.S. flag, 62–63; of secession period, 30–31; standardbearer tribute through, 90–91

nationalism: artificiality/ancient lineage pretenses of, 3; claims of distinctiveness by southern, 2–3; colonial heritage and American, 53–54; Confederate flag design and southern, 53–54; distinction between patriotism and, 180n.5; historical scholarship on deficiency on southern, 3; martial associations with American, 10–11; patriotic celebrations of U.S., 10; postwar southern hopes for renewal of American, 163; recent scholarship on emotional life of, 4–5; shifting flag allegiances and, 15. *See also* Confederate nationality
New Orleans flag disputes, 132–33
newspapers. *See* print media
New York Church of the Puritans, 143
New York City "monster rally" following Fort Sumter 58
NuSouth clothing, 177–78, 212n.54

Old Glory. *See* Stars and Stripes flag
Order of the Star-Spangled Banner (1850s), 9
O'Riley, James, 156

Palmetto Fort, 25, 26
Palmetto Fort flag, 26
palmetto tree symbolism, 24, 25, 26, 27, 28

The Passing of the Armies (Chamberlain), 168
patriotic envelopes, 57, *129, 140, 166,* 203n.7
Patriotic Gore (Wilson), 5
patriotism: African American embrace of Union, 141–48; distinction between nationalism and, 180n.5; dying/victory paradox of Civil War, 94–95; expressed by civilian use of flags, 131–35; "fight for the flag" mentality and, 59; flag culture association with bloodshed and, 67–68, 79, 92–93; flag culture at heart of Civil War, 125–26; issues of African American, 139–40; Lost Cause rebel emblems framed within U.S., *173;* romantic overtones of 19th century, 80; southern female-led "ceremonial bereavement" form of, 162–64; wartime communication facilitating, 88, 90–91. *See also* martyrdoms
Pelican Flag (Louisiana), 28, 36–37, 187n.39
Peter, Frances, 131
Platt, Jacob, 46
poetry: on accepting southern defeat, 171; antislavery, 130; "Barbara Frietchie" lyric, 136–37; on battle flags, 93–94, 117, 118, 159–60, 162; on black flag emblem, 148; on captured battle flags, 171, 172; castigating Southern Cross, 130; celebrating flag culture, 65, 66, 73, 79; on Christian anti-abolitionist flag, 100; to describe 19th century patriotism, 80; dramatic martyrdom subject of, 91–92; history of battlefield, 93; on the last of Civil War veterans, 167; Lost Cause tradition, 161, 162–63, 164, 167; on martial flag culture, 170; using purity symbolism, 81; on Stainless Banner tribute, 116–17; on threat of rebel flags, 130–31
Polk, Bishop Leonidas, 103
Pollard, Edward, 60, 165

Port Royal Emancipation Day celebration, 143, *144*

Potter, David, 42

Powell, William P., 141

Preston, Margaret Junkin, 117

print media: on Appomattox surrender, 169–70; attacks against rebel emblems/flags in, 128–29, 131; use of "Bars" to distinguish Confederacy flag, 45; on black flags, 148, 149; community-forming role of, 22–24; on Confederate army/civilian relationship, 119; on first Confederate flag ceremony, 54–55; on Confederate flag design efforts, 54, 189n.15, 199n.21; coverage of totem flag rituals by, 75, 81–82; on cross symbols, 101; on debate over Southern Cross flag status, 105–9; on Gettysburg fiftieth anniversary celebration, 173; on importance of flag to nation, 163; on influence of female patriots, 86; on Lincoln's inaugural address, 55; Marshall House affair reports by, 70–74, *71*; on martial flag culture, 159; on military leadership of Lee, 94; regarding Charleston Jews, 102; reporting combat heroics, 88, *89*, 90; reports on flags/banners by, 20, *21*–24, *23*, 29; on right of Confederacy to claim U.S. flag, 41; on selection of Confederate seal, 112–13; on significance of Confederate flag, 39–40; on Southern Cross ceremony, 84–85, 195n.36; Stars and Bars news spread by, 56; supporting Southern Cross as official flag, 103; on adoption of southern state flags, 29–30

purity/pollution flag symbolism, 81; and Stainless Banner, 116–17

Purvis, Robert, 142–43

Quitman, John, 10–11

racism: associations of Confederate flag and, 154; white reconciliation (late-19th century) and, 174–75

rattlesnake symbolism, 127

"Rebel Color-Bearers at Shiloh" (Melville), 170

Reconstruction Period: Confederate flag display during, 170–71; Confederate symbolism of, 163, 164–65; controversy over returning battle colors during, 171–74, *173*; female-led "ceremonial bereavement" defining, 162–64; flag culture during, 7; loyalty to U.S. flag by southern veterans during, 164–66; poetry on shared martial flag culture of, 170; postwar reconciliation by Unionists during, 167–74; postwar rehabilitation of Southern Cross during, 164–65

The Red Badge of Courage (Crane), 172

regimental flags. *See* battle flags

religious symbolism: Ark of the Covenant, 102; used to inspire soldiers, 117–18; Jewish concerns with, 101–2, 104; used in secession banners, 24–25; of Stainless Banner, 117. *See also* Christianity; cross symbolism; sacred aura

resistance banners. *See* secession banners

Rhett, Robert Barnwell, 20, 21

Ripley, Eliza, 55

Rivers, Prince, 144

Root, George, 130

Rose, Anne, 5

Ross, Betsy, 26

Royster, Charles, 3

Russell, William Howard, 39, 40, 56, 59, 65, 120

Ryan, Father Abraham, 160

sacred aura: of battle flags, 67–8, 72–3, 75–7, 81, *89*, 92–3, 153, 159; of first state flags, 33; of Lost Cause relics, 162; violence as source of 117–18

St. Andrew's cross of Scotland, 103, 108–9

satanic symbolism, *16*, 127, 128, *129*

Savage, Kirk, 48

Seabury, Caroline, 138

secession banners: Confederate flag culture initiated by, 37–38; Jasper's cult association with, 26; newspapers reports on, 20, 21–24, *23*; practice of "moistening," 30; secession messages on, 21. *See also* Confederate flag

secession banner symbolism: "all-seeing eye," 25, 29; birth metaphor of, 33–34; and defiance expressed towards northern enemies, 126; flag design and emotional potential of, 30–35; French Revolution and emerging, 26–27; palmetto tree, 24, 25, 26, 27, 28; pelican, 28, 36–37, 187n.39; single star, 28-*29*

secession period: Davis speeches (1858/1861) by, 11–14; flag symbolism during, 9–11, 19–24, *23*; Jacobin invocations during, 36–37; music of, 30–31; southern state flags during, 28–36. *See also* secession banners

Sell, Ed Emerick, 46

Semmes, Raphael, 175

Semmes, Thomas, 114

sentimental culture, 4–5

serpent symbolism, *57,* 127

Shelby, Joseph, 160

Shellman, Joseph, 46

Sherman, William T., 159

Simms, William Gilmore, 80, 126–27

single star symbolism, 28-*29*

slavery: associations of Confederate flags and, 130, 154, 178; association of U.S. flag/Constitution with, 140; Confederate symbols deflecting attention away from, 49; Emancipation Proclamation celebration (1863) ending, *142, 143;* explicit invocation in Civil War-era flags, 24, 48–49, 98, 100; invoked by earliest advocates of Southern Cross flag, 98. *See also* African Americans

soldierly sacrifice. *See* martyrdoms

Sons of Confederate Veterans, 167

South Carolina: Charleston Harbor battle (1776) of, 25; Charleston Harbor stand-off (1861) in, 13, 34–35, 59; palmetto tree symbolism association with, 24, 25, 26, 27, 28

Southern Cross flag: consolidation through, 121–23; debate over official status selection of, 104–9; emotional power of, 97; geographical connotations of, 105, 118; growing prominence of, 94–95, 119–20; incorporated into the Stainless Banner (1863), 5; introduction of, 68, 82–83; link between women and initiative of, 83–85; media supporting official status of, 103; modern commercialization of, 177–78; newspaper reporting on ceremony of, 84–85, 195n.36; Northern rally against symbol of, 7; poetry castigating the, 130; postwar efforts to rehabilitate, 164–65; promoted by Miles, 102–3; religious message of cross design of, 96–97; representation after 1862, 117. *See also* battle flags; Confederate flags

"The Southern Cross" (Blunt), 64

"Southern Cross" (Tucker), 100, 117, 126

"Southern Marseillaise" (song), 30, 37

southern state flags: emotional appeal and design of, 30–35; message conveyed by, 35; prior to Confederate flag, 28–30; responses to, 35–36; *Sic Semper Tyrannis* motto of Virginia, 58

southern Unionist flag displays, 136–39

South's Ladies' Memorial Association movement, 162

Spanish-American War, 165–67

Stainless Banner flag: association with purity of white race, 115–16; celebration of official status of, 115; combined with British Union Jack image, 109; and elevation of martial sacrifice to national ideal, 94; military criticism of, 119; illustration of, *116;* religious associations of 116–18; Southern Cross incorporated into, 5. *See also* Confederate flags

standardbearers: martyrdom of, *89,* 90–92; public attention focused on, 88

Stars and Bars flag: criticism regarding selection of, 103–4; debate over

Stars and Bars flag (*cont'd*)
Southern Cross replacement of, 104–
9; emotional impact of new, 55–56,
58; first presentation of, 54–55; impact of battle flags prominence on,
93–94; Montgomery Congress
speeches on designs of, 43, 44, 45;
music associated with, 60–62; patriotic envelopes featuring, 57; place in
development of Confederate symbols,
5–6; postwar controversy over its true
designer, 51, 189n.23; prominence of
Southern Cross/Stainless Banner over,
94–95; significance of new, 39–40;
slavery association with, 130; state
flags prior to adoption of, 28–30; submitted designs for new, 45–54, 47t,
50, 52t; symbolic grammar of, 6;
Union response to, 127–29. *See also*
battle flags; Confederate flags
"Star Spangled Banner" (Scott), 9, 60,
61, 100, 122, 138, 142, 145, 163,
191n.41
"The Star Spangled Cross in the Pure
Field of White" (song), *116*
Stars and Stripes flag: African American
attachment to, 145, *146*, 147–48; carried by Davis into Mexico, 18; Civil
War started by firing on, 68; displayed
by southern Unionists, 136–39; displayed in Northern cities, 58–59; efforts to associate black freedom with,
175–77; loyalty pledged by southern
veterans to, 164–66; raised over Fort
Sumter, 13; rebel flags as threatening
the, 130–31; songs on southern dis-
carding of, 62–63; southern claims to,
41–42; southern single star symbolism
replacing, 28-29. *See also* United
States
Stars and Stripes flag culture: cause of
freedom linked to, 7; development
during secession, 9–10; emotional investments in, 9; female role in local,
77–82, *78*; influence on Confederate
flag culture by, 17–18; introduction of
civilians into, 87–88; invoked during

Davis speech (1861), 13–14, 19; martial associations with, 10–11; national
destiny transmitted by, 10; as possible
source of postwar nationalism, 163;
Northern embrace of, 58–60; totem rituals associated with, 75-76, 81–82.
See also Confederate flag culture;
flag culture
Stephens, Alexander, 60
Stevenson, Charles, 156
Stone, Cyrena, 137–38
symbols/symbolism: American use of
flag, 19–20; Civil War consensus regarding rules of flag, 148–52; latent
southern feelings for U.S., 41–43;
used during political changes, 19; rat-
tlesnake/serpent, 127. *See also* Confederate symbolism; flag symbolism

Thian, Raphael, 111
Thornwell, Rev. James Henley,
36, 37
Timrod, Henry, 34
Trent affair (1861), 59
trophy flags. *See* captured battle flags
Tucker, St. George, 100, 117, 126
Turner, Bishop Henry McNeal, 175–76
Turner, Joseph Addison, 104–5
Tyler, John, 54
Tyler, Letitia, 54

Union prisoners of war, *155*
Union states: gradual patriotism of
African Americans to, 141–48;
rattlesnake/serpent symbolism and,
127; response to Stars and Bars by,
127–28; state flags adoption by, 35;
visual depictions against rebel
emblems in, 128–29. *See also* Civil
War; Confederacy
United Daughters of the Confederacy,
163, 164, 167
United States: birth metaphor of state
secession from, 33–34; Cuban cause
fought by, 165–67; flag culture developed during secession from, 9–11,
19–20; patriotic celebrations of nation-

alism in, 10; white reconciliation (late-19th century) in, 174–75. *See also* Stars and Stripes flag

Van Dorn, Earl, 84
Victorian society: anxiety about appetites/drives by, 6; Marshall House Affair and home sanctity value of, 73; understanding sentimental culture of, 4–5
Volck, Adalbert, 135, 136

Waldstreicher, David, 53
Washington, Booker T., 176
Washington, George, 10
Washington Light Infantry of Charleston, 165
Weems, Parson, 25
West Florida rebellion (1810), 28
"What Subjugation Means" (press article, 1864), 159
white flag of truce, 151–52; Stainless Banner mistaken for, 119
Whittier, John Greenleaf, 136, 137

Wigfall, Louis, 118
Wigfall, Mrs. Louis, 86
Wightt, Anne, 51
Wilson, Edmund, 4, 5
Wilson, Woodrow, 173
Winthrop, Robert, 124
Wise, John Sergeant, 33–34
women: battle flags constructed by, 86–87; comparison of soldier martyrdom to flag-waving by, 135–37; Confederate flag design role by, 46–47t; hostility to U.S. flag by southern, 163–64; illustration of flags presented by, 87; link between Southern Cross initiative and, 83–85; local flag culture role by, 77–82, 78; newspapers on military influence of, 86; Reconstruction "ceremonial bereavement" by southern, 162–64; Southern Cross flag supported by Confederate, 103; Yankee authority defiance by southern, 133–37, 134, 204n.18
Wright, Augustus, 50
Wright, Louisa Wigfall, 164